"As a neighbor and friend of Liz Edmunds, The Food Nanny, I can say that she practices what she preaches and cooks! Liz has always had unbounded energy directed daily to her family, attempting to make mealtime—which can be filled with chaos and frenzy—into an enjoyable interlude of fun, conversation, and connection. I endorse Liz and her book because she takes the key ingredients of life—friends and family—and mixes them into a daily tradition of mealtime. These are vital nutrients to keep family and mealtime thriving."

—Debbi Fields, Founder,
Mrs. Fields Cookies, and
mother of five daughters

"For years I watched Liz Edmunds manage her large family from a distance and have especially been interested in the delicious meals she prepares for everyone she knows! I love her easy manage-ment plan for keeping dinnertime at home a huge priority, which in turn helped keep her family close and created wonderful memories.

"In my profession of counseling, I have used Liz's ideas for those that need the extra help in simplifying and encouraging family gatherings around mealtime. Mothers or caregivers who have tried her easy method of planning have experienced immediate results. Dinnertime is fun and doesn't require a lot of thought about what is for dinner. More emphasis is placed on getting everyone together for meals than what the actual dinner is going to be, because those decisions are quickly made with the 'theme' for the night. Liz's meal themes have been a positive strategy that I use to encourage family structure, communication, and a more stress-free home environment. The simplicity of it makes it so valuable to share with meal planners of all ages."

—Shauna Bradley, LCSW, Park City, Utah

"Ther[   ]ng
in a f[   ]
home[   ]
good[   ]
make[   ]
I recommend this book for every family—especially those who think they don't have the time or talent to cook great dishes."

—Dr. Laura Schlessinger, International Radio Talk Host and author, *Stop Whining Start Living* (HarperCollins)

"I met Liz 36 years ago when our sons were six months old. She invited us over for dinner that week. That was the beginning of a very special friendship that always included great meals, lots of laughter, and kids. One of Liz's recipes for leftover chicken and rice became such a staple at our house that the kids just called it 'Liz's Chicken.' She has a great recipe for French bread that got me into bread and roll making.

"Sitting down to good food with your family is a way to celebrate, sort out, talk over, and manage all the good and bad things that happen in normal families."

—Ann Luther, product development manager for a nationally distributed wholesale bakery, Groton, Massachusetts

"When I saw firsthand Liz's passion for eating dinner together as a family, I knew this was what American families could use. Her creativity, her fun recipes, and her easy preparation make any dinnertime a delight. When you use Liz's plan, your family will get good nutrition, enjoy wonderful variety, and increase your quality of dinnertime. Her plan will help you create family memories that will last a lifetime."

—Dian Thomas, Professional Speaker, Author, TV Personality • www.CampingWithDian.com

Liz Edmunds, The Food Nanny, consults with families in their homes about meal planning so the family can eat together at home. Here are notes from her happy clients:

I am so thankful to have had Liz help me get started cooking. I have always wanted to be able to cook good meals for my family, but never knew where to get started. I would try to cook and get overwhelmed and frustrated. Liz made it so easy. She encouraged me and gave me confidence. Her recipes are easy to follow and are so delicious. She has such a cute and energetic personality. Thank you, Liz, for all your help. I can't wait for more recipes.
—**Tamra Heaps**

Thank you so much for all of the helpful information you provided for me and my family. I'm excited about cooking for the first time! Being a mom of an active one-year-old boy and a wife to a hard-working husband, [I think that] time together is valuable. Although all the recipes are wonderful and the food tasted so good, it is the lessons and ideas you gave me that I cherish the most. I never realized how important it is to sit down for a meal and just talk to one another. It is so easy to get caught up in all the activities and responsibilities of everyday life. The tools like the grocery list and the helpful advice on planning your weekly meals have given me a great place to start. Not only did you give me wonderful recipes, but you gave me something more valuable—conversations and quality time spent with my family for years to come that I might not have had. I will forever be thankful for your help and I know you will have continued success for years to come.
—**Jennifer Anderson**

The food all turned out great. Ben loved all of it. The menus are great. I love already knowing what I'm going to do. I think the whole idea is great. It was really good how you would show me how to do something and then have me do it. That is what I really needed—to just do it. I have watched people cook, but I need to do it. Then that shows me that I can at least try. So it was really good for me. Thanks so much for coming and helping. We loved it!

One month later:
I want to let you know that I am still cooking. Really, it has totally changed how we do dinner. Thanks so much for your help. I have tried almost all of the recipes you gave me and they are all great. I can't wait for your book to come out!
—**Lara Harris**

I do not know what I would do without this cookbook. It changed my family's life and love of dinnertime.
—**Dayna Brand**

Not only did you give me amazing recipes and taught me some great cooking skills, you have laid a foundation for my family. I have always believed that sitting down at the table together as a family is so important, but you have given me the kick-start I needed! I can rely on your recipe plan and it takes the stress out of the day-to-day cooking. I can now enjoy cooking without wondering about the next night. Travis has commented constantly on how nice it is to come home to such a great dinner. Some of our favorite recipes are the BBQ pizza, macaroni and cheese, and three-cheese manicotti—yum yum! Now that we have started our family, I feel lucky to have such a great plan for the future when it comes to cooking!
—**Ashley Miller**

I truly appreciate the time you took to come teach me how to cook. I also want to thank you for teaching me how to make a menu for my family. I love it and it saves time and money. I really enjoyed how patient you were with me. I can't wait till your book comes out! Thank you.
—**Claudia Fierro**

You are a talented lady, Liz. You have an air about you that lifts the room. You made me feel excited about going to the grocery store again. I am so excited about the theme nights. What a way to keep dinnertime from getting boring to me or the family. I really liked the different flavors in the foods we chose. I am so excited about the French bread and the sopaipillas. You also gave me a renewed hope for my family. Thank you so much, Liz. I really can't wait till your book comes out.
—**Melissa Merrill**

Not only has The Food Nanny saved dinner, she has saved my family! She taught me that if you wait till 4:30 p.m. to decide what is for dinner, it is too late. Procrastination is one of many reasons my family has lived off of chicken nuggets and macaroni and cheese. We now follow the Food Nanny's dinner schedule and my entire family is so much happier and healthier. They are now excited to see what is for dinner and to spend time together as a family. The recipes are so easy to follow and seriously so good! I have always been too intimidated to make breads, and the Food Nanny's bread recipes are seriously the greatest in the world. They are easy, cheap, healthy, and taste a million times better. Our family will forever be in debt to the Food Nanny!
—**The Kjar Family**

THE FOOD NANNY
RESCUES
DINNER

EASY FAMILY MEALS
FOR EVERY DAY
OF THE WEEK

LIZ EDMUNDS

ANN HESSE GOSCH, EDITOR

A PALMER/PLETSCH
PUBLICATION

Love,
The Food Nanny

This book is dedicated to my husband, Steve,
beloved father of our children, for his dedication to our family;
for his strong values; for his sterling, ever-enduring work ethic;
and for his deep and abiding love and commitment to all of us.

I also dedicate this book to our seven children—
David, Katie, Brent, Emaly, Joey, Aimee, and Lizi—
for their deep commitment in respect, love, and loyalty to their parents.
They are now raising their own wonderful families.

Publisher's Cataloging-In-Publication Data
(Prepared by The Donohue Group, Inc.)

Edmunds, Liz.
   The Food Nanny rescues dinner : easy family meals for every day of the week /
Liz Edmunds ; Ann Hesse Gosch, editor.

   p. : ill. ; cm.

   Includes index.
   ISBN: 978-0-935278-77-4 (perfect bound)
   ISBN: 978-0-935278-78-1 (coil binding)

1. Quick and easy cookery. 2. Entrées (Cookery) 3. Family--Nutrition.
I. Gosch, Ann Hesse. II. Title. III. Title: Easy family meals for every day of the week

TX833.5 .E36 2008
641.555   2008934134

First Edition Copyright © 2008 Liz Edmunds.
Published by Palmer/Pletsch Publishing,
1801 NW Upshur Street, Suite 100, Portland, OR 97209 U.S.A.
www.palmerpletsch.com
Printed in the USA by Quebecor World

Design and production by Linda Wisner; Illustrations by Kate Pryka
Photography by Pati Palmer, Drake Busath, and Linda Wisner
plus p. 104 ©Robyn Mackenzie; p. 177 ©Jacek Chabraszewski; p. 104 ©jean-luc cochonneau; p. 279 ©ivanastar — fotolia.com

The type was set in Avenir with Trajan and Futura headings and subheads and Black Jack decorative font.

TABLE OF CONTENTS

Recipes are listed at the beginning of each chapter.

Each chapter is identified by color for easy reference.

I don't speak at many conferences, but in the spring of 2005 I went to Salt Lake City to speak to the Utah Association of Family and Consumer Sciences. The next day a colleague of mine took me to dinner at the home of Liz and Steve Edmunds outside Park City. It was the first time I'd met Liz, and she told me all about a family cookbook her children wanted her to write. The more I heard, the more intrigued I became. It was so much more than a recipe book. I became entranced with the good that Liz's ideas and strategies for family dinnertime could do for other families and hence society in general. And I found research to back up the importance of time together around the dinner table.

Joseph Califano Jr., chairman and president of the national Center on Addiction and Substance Abuse, says that "the family dinner is more powerful than any law we can pass, any punishment we can level" for protecting children against risky behavior. "Parental engagement is a critical weapon in the fight against substance abuse," he says. "If I could wave a wand, I'd make everyone have family dinners."

When Liz and Steve first came to Oregon to meet with us on this book project, I introduced her to my other business, Mamma Ro—handmade ceramic dinnerware we import from a small family business in Italy. The goal of the Pierallini family, with whom I have been working for 30 years, is *la vita vera*—"the true life." This means having family meals together where everyone talks, bonds, shares, and enjoys good food. Liz and Steve have since met the Pierallinis in Lucca, Italy, and experienced la vita vera personally.

That is the goal of this cookbook—to help you create *la vita vera* in your home. Liz gives you a template to do so. But she is just a facilitator. It is up to you to put it into practice. Use her template as is or add to it with your own favorite recipes or foods that work for your family's individual needs. Liz is passionate about family mealtime, but admits that it takes a lot of effort in the beginning and a commitment. It will get easier after you have made the recipes a few times. Someone in the family has to be the leader and take the responsibility of making family mealtime happen. And that person could be YOU!

As publisher, I dedicate this book to families throughout the world, in their efforts to mold respectful, thinking, caring, loving, nourished human beings, generation after generation . . . one meal at a time.

Pati Palmer
President, Palmer/Pletsch Publishing

www.lavitavera.com

A MESSAGE FROM THE FOOD NANNY

My husband, Steve, is a retired airline pilot, so I have traveled from France to Singapore, from the desert of the Sahara to the bustling modern cities of Hong Kong and Shanghai, from the mountains of Peru to the fjords of Alaska, and from sea to shining sea all over my homeland, America. Everyone across this vast world has one thing in common and that is dinnertime.

*We are all eager for a tasty meal at dinnertime. Trattorias, diners, and restaurants big and small across the world are preparing for those who will come to enjoy the "dinner hour." The dinner hour at home can be even more enjoyable. I want to bring more families **home** for dinner.*

When Steve and I were raising our seven children, our consistent family dinnertime was the glue that kept our family close. We couldn't help but be aware of one another's needs. We knew what was happening every day because we ate dinner together. We all looked forward to dinnertime.

As the Food Nanny, I have been able to help other families find their way to a consistent dinnertime. Everyone loves the two-week menu plan. Most start out with one week and before the week is half over, they are calling me to help them finish another week.

Everyone loves the idea of shopping once every two weeks (except for perishables like milk or produce) and knowing that they have the food in the house ready to go. I also help families with their food budgets, pantry items, and kitchen supplies.

My plan has changed these families' entire outlook toward dinnertime. Everyone loves my theme nights: comfort food,

Italian, fish & meatless, Mexican, pizza, grill, and tradition days. All of this is here in my book to help you and your family, no matter how big or how small.

The aromas of dinner coming from your kitchen can permeate your home every night. This atmosphere cannot happen if you are eating out, where the focus is on the restaurant, not your kitchen or your family.

Nothing was more meaningful to our family each day than the consistency of having dinnertime together. I believe it played the biggest role in keeping the communication between family members wide open. We bonded as a family. We shared in each other's accomplishments and each other's tears. Our loyalty grew toward one another to form a united family.

I wrote this book because I have a passion to help young mothers and families who are struggling to put dinner on the table every night. Even if you're cooking only for yourself, you deserve a meaningful dinnertime. I believe this is the most important thing you can do for yourself and your family each day.

Liz Edmunds

I want to bring families home for dinner.

This book is about getting the family together at mealtime to eat some great-tasting food while sharing ideas and concerns and teaching values—and having a great time in the process. It is about good food that your whole family will eat and that can be made with your family's budget in mind. It is about consistency and simplicity.

This book is a menu-planning tool that you will use for the rest of your life. It is about taking the stress from all you moms and dads who are wondering what to fix for dinner. It's about helping you get organized. It's about helping you and your family to eat more healthfully. It's about helping your family to bond together for a lifetime.

This is more than a cookbook!

This book is about making dinnertime a priority, putting it into your family culture where it belongs.

Food is the heart and soul of our lives. Everyone is hungry at the end of the day and everyone needs to have a place to be at dinnertime. The family dinnertime each night helps everyone to be accountable for their day: what happened, where did you go, what took place? And these family connections provide enormous benefits for children. Just look at these findings:

Two researchers at the University of Minnesota investigated the potential benefits of family mealtimes on children and found that families that dine together tend to have healthier, more well-adjusted children. Their studies indicate that **the more often children and teens eat with their parents—and the happier, more structured these mealtimes are—the more the children gain these benefits:**

- **Better nutrition**
- **Better language and literacy**
- **Fewer eating disorders**
- **Fewer risky behaviors**

The National Center on Addiction and Substance Abuse at Columbia University (Sept. 2005) found that compared with teens who dine frequently with their families (five to seven dinners a week), **teens who have fewer than three family dinners per week are:**

- **Two and a half times likelier to smoke cigarettes.**
- **More than one and a half times likelier to drink alcohol.**
- **Almost three times likelier to try marijuana.**

Says Dr. Harold Koplewicz, director of New York University's Child Study Center: "Mealtime becomes a way for families to bond. It shows children they have access to a caring adult."

I think you can't put a price on the smells and chemistry that permeate the home at the dinner hour. This is what everyone wants in their home. Harmony and peace and love abound in a house where dinner is being cooked and served.

Read on for how to make it work for your family!

MEAL PLANNING AROUND A THEME

The key to consistent dinnertime at home is meal planning. The hardest part of planning any meal is figuring out what to have. If you wait until the end of the day, it is too late. You may be too stressed at that point to even decide, let alone shop for ingredients and prepare the meal. Then it is too easy to just buy processed, packaged foods; stop at the deli; pick up fast food; or go out to dinner. None of these options works as well day after day, week after week, as having the family sit down together over a meal prepared at home. That's where my plan comes in.

What is my plan? I devised "theme nights" as a place to start, and I have been planning meals around these themes for almost 30 years. In my family these are our themes:

MONDAY:	**COMFORT FOOD**
TUESDAY:	**ITALIAN NIGHT**
WEDNESDAY:	**FISH & MEATLESS**
THURSDAY:	**MEXICAN NIGHT**
FRIDAY:	**PIZZA NIGHT**
SATURDAY:	**GRILL NIGHT**
SUNDAY:	**FAMILY TRADITIONS**

These themes are easy to carry out and will keep you consistent in having dinner together as a family. And you know what else? The themes make dinnertime more fun for your children.

I must emphasize that "theme night" does not mean having a "party" every night at dinner. The night's "theme" is merely the starting point for deciding what to have for dinner. Just turn to that chapter and choose a recipe. I rarely carried the theme any further than that. No special centerpiece. No theme music. No party hats.

Still, **my children always looked forward to our theme nights.** The greatest part was that they—and Dad—knew at the end of a hard day that there would be dinner on the table. And they knew it would be something they liked, because all of the recipes are tried and true and delicious.

This plan will get Dad and/or Mom home on time from work, and get kids helping in the kitchen. If parents are working outside the home, then teenagers can get the meal started before they get home. Younger children can help set the table and encourage other family members to be home for dinner. This will bond your family and create the atmosphere that we all want in our homes.

Using theme nights makes menu planning so easy. All you do is go to the chapter for the night you're planning, and choose. There are more than a dozen recipes for each theme, so it's not as if every Tuesday Italian Night is going to be the same lasagna. Plus, there are chapters of salads, breads, side dishes, and desserts, so you can mix and match to your heart's content.

This is a foundation for anyone to put dinner on the table at home at least **five nights a week.** I say five nights a week because I figure you may want to give yourself and your family one or two nights a week "off." After all, we all love to eat out at our favorite fast-food or casual-dining restaurants from time to time. Then again, some weeks we don't feel like going out. No problem. My plan gives you recipes for seven nights a week, and then you choose which nights to take off, if any.

HOW TO MAKE IT HAPPEN

MAP OUT TWO WEEKS AT A TIME

I said earlier that the key to having a consistent dinnertime with a home-cooked meal is meal *planning*.

The key to effective meal planning is mapping out your meal schedule a week or two in advance. (Two is easier.) Here's how:

DINNER MENUS FOR October 6-19

MONDAY COMFORT FOOD	TUESDAY ITALIAN	WEDNESDAY FISH/ MEATLESS	THURSDAY MEXICAN	FRIDAY PIZZA	SATURDAY GRILL NIGHT	SUND TRADIT
Savory Meat Loaf (p. 45) Scalloped Potatoes (p. 43) Baked Buttered Carrots (p. 207) Sour Cream Devil's Food Cake (p. 256)	Red & White Mostaccioli (p. 73) green salad Italian bread (p. 224)	Fish Tacos (p. 95) Santa Fe Lime Rice (p. 123)	Mexican Chicken and Black Bean Soup (p. 121) tortilla chips with fresh salsa (p. 125) melon wedges with lime juice	Pepperoni & Cheese Pizza (p. 138)	Sweet & Sour Baked Chicken (p. 162) On the grill if the weather's nice? white rice steamed broccoli	Tradition Roast Di (p. 170 Butterm Corn B (p. 24
Three-Bean Chili with Sausage (p. 49) carrot sticks Cinnamon Rolls (p. 236)	Baked Chicken and Potatoes Italiano (p. 80) steamed green beans French bread (p. 225)	Mac & Cheese Kids Crave (p. 86) steamed peas	Baja Fajitas (p. 115)	BBQ Chicken Pizza (p. 143)	Sloppy Joes (p. 152) baked beans green salad potato chips	Easy Chic Blew Rice (p ve (

1. **Get out your calendar.**
   Think of when you may eat out. Think of who might be coming for dinner.

2. **Go through my recipes and choose meals**
   or use your own recipes for the different theme nights. Make sure that what you choose will fit within your food budget if you have one. You can see which dishes are inexpensive to prepare; I have plenty of those to choose from. For more on recipe selection, see page 275.

3. **Write down your chosen meals on our form, a sheet of paper, or 5x7-inch card.**

SAMPLE SHOPPING LIST

PRODUCE

2 yams
2 bunches garlic
2 bunches cilantro
5 lbs. potatoes
5 red potatoes
2 yellow onions
3 white onions
1 small red onion
1/2 lb. mushrooms
Broccoli
3 lbs. carrots
1 red bell pepper
1 yellow bell pepper
1 green bell pepper
16 Roma tomatoes
1 lb. green beans
2 green salads
fresh rosemary
1 avocado
1 lemon
2 limes
1 melon
2 serrano chiles
2 jalapeno chiles

CANNED GOODS

Large can baked beans
5 14-oz cans tomatoes
1 small can corn
1 medium can corn
2 cans black beans
1 can pinto beans
2 cans kidney beans
2 cartons chicken broth
1 46-oz can tomato juice
1 small can evaporated milk
8-oz. can pineapple chunks
1 can or carton beef broth
26-ounce jar meatless spaghetti sauce
1 jar salsa

OTHER GROCERIES

White rice
Corn meal
Brown sugar
Devil's food cake mix
Red wine vinegar
1 lb. elbow macaroni
1 lb. mostaccioli pasta
1 lb. fettuccine
12 taco-size flour tortillas
8 corn tortillas
8-pack hamburger buns
Flour
Potato chips
Tortilla chips
Ranch dressing
Walnuts
1 packet fajita seasoning
Sweet BBQ sauce

FISH/MEAT

5 lbs. boneless, skinless chicken
1 lb. maple-flavored sausage
4 slices deli ham
1 lb. thick ham slice
1/4-1/2 lb pepperoni slices
7.5 lbs chicken breasts with ribs
6 chicken thighs
2 lbs. lean ground beef
3 1/2-4 lbs. rump roast
1 lb. tilapia

DAIRY

1/2 pt. buttermilk
1/2 pt. sour cream
1 pt. heavy cream
6 slices (4 oz.) Swiss cheese
4 cups shredded Cheddar cheese
10 cups shredded mozzarella cheese
8 oz. pepper Jack cheese
Small pkg. smoked gouda
8 oz. pkg. cream cheese
Parmesan cheese
Eggs
Milk
Butter

FROZEN

1 16-oz. pkg frozen peas

When we sampled prices here in Salt Lake City, the items on this shopping list for an entire two weeks of dinners for a family of four cost under $150!

4. **Make a grocery list.** Take note of what you need for these meals. What do you have in your freezer? In your pantry? Write down the grocery items you will need to buy, using an 8½" x 11" sheet of paper. Remember to include healthy items for after-school snacks (see p. 269), breakfasts, and lunches on your shopping list.

5. **Go shopping.** By organizing your shopping using the categories on your grocery list, you can be in and out of the store in no time. When you get home, wrap the meats you won't be using right away and put them in the freezer.

Free templates for both the two-week menu plan and the shopping list are available at www.thefoodnanny.com. More sample menu plans are also on the website.

Post each new menu plan on the fridge or on your calendar. Keep a copy in your purse so you can be reminded while you're out and about or at work. This is fun! Your family will love the theme nights.

Before the week (or two-week period) is up, begin planning your next set of menus so you will stay on schedule. Soon you will find that it takes just a short time to choose your meals and write down the ingredients you will need to buy. Go shopping once and then you will have everything for the next meal-planning period except any fresh items you might need mid-week. If you choose to skip a night, then you still have the food for another night. If you miss a couple of nights, just get back on track when you can.

This makes dinnertime so much less stressful for whoever cooks, or for the one who does the meal planning. You'll have regular, consistent meals. If you do this, your family will be happy and healthy, both physically and mentally.

Not "Health" Food—Good Food in Healthful Portions

When I meet my clients as the Food Nanny, people ask how I've kept my weight in check while I've cooked for my family of seven children. Two words: ***portion control.*** You can eat all the foods you love as long as you eat in moderation.

Forget the fad diets and the carb counting! My family and I kept our weight where it should be because I was so consistent. When I made my two-week menu, I was keeping in mind what would be the best *balance* of the foods I was choosing. Fried chicken one night, something lighter the next. Little meat and more vegetables, with just one serving of rice or potatoes. If we were eating a lot of bread one day, the next day I would cut way back on bread. Dessert one night a week is plenty. A cookie here and a small brownie there along the way are not going to make anyone fat!

It's being proven more and more that dieting is not where it's at—diets don't work long-term. It's about eating right (and of course exercising). Cooking and eating at home are healthful from the standpoint of eating a wide variety of freshly prepared foods—as opposed to fast food or packaged prepared foods. If you eat a wide variety of freshly prepared foods and watch your portion sizes (and exercise), you don't have to get caught up in calorie counts, or carb counts, or fat content. You can just enjoy the food—and of course the bonding with your family. All of that great conversation will slow down your eating and help you eat less!

Any one of my meals can be made to fit your family's needs. Your children will learn to eat a variety of foods, which is another key to eating healthy over a lifetime. Teaching by example is your best tool. Let your children see your table manners, the portions you eat, and the vegetables you select. Eating healthy does not cause weight gain. Chew your food slowly, enjoy it, and do not have seconds. You will not gain weight!

Eating dinner on a consistent basis also will help you monitor your kids' eating behaviors. If you see that your child or teen is not eating enough or is eating too much, you can usually correct the problem before it gets out of hand. Don't become a short-order cook, fixing everyone something different. No one should be loading up on his or her favorite food every night of the week. Variety is important for good nutrition and portion control.

My cookbook is not about trendy new or gourmet food ideas. Many of my recipes are not what you might think of as health food. In fact, a few are fairly high in fat. But fat adds flavor and makes food satisfying so you eat less. Higher-fat foods like fried chicken can be served with lower-calorie side dishes—say, one piece of fried chicken, some greens, and a square of corn bread. Or the chicken with steamed broccoli and a steamed or boiled red potato with a dab of butter and parsley flakes on top. Or with brown rice and a green salad. The point is, you can cut way down on fat and calorie intake by what you serve with the main dish. This is my way of cooking. Go ahead and enjoy a high-fat food from time to time. Just limit yourself to one portion and choose side dishes wisely. And eat desserts sparingly.

What Is Proper Portion Size?

With the current trend to super-size meals, it can be difficult to figure out what a recommended portion is. A comprehensive book that can help you do this is the latest edition of the *American Dietetic Association Complete Food and Nutrition Guide*, by Roberta Duyff.

Even handier is the online "calculator" at **www.MyPyramid.gov**. Click on MyPyramid Plan to get a quick estimate of what and how much you need to eat. In an instant, you'll get a listing of the portions of grains, vegetables, fruits, milk,

CHOOSING WHAT TO EAT

Some days you can indulge... but with small portions. The next day pick a lighter recipe to serve for dinner. A balanced diet is not calculated one meal at a time. What is important is that your family is eating good food...together ... day after day.

and lean protein to eat in a day to maintain your weight and health—and then specific tips on how to meet these daily allowances. Enter the age, sex, and activity level of each of your children and note the differences.

Try using smaller plates. They'll look full with less food.

You'll find, for example, that a 9-year-old boy of average height and weight who is moderately active should be consuming about 1,800 calories a day. The ideal 1,800-calorie diet would include the following:

- 6 ounces grains, at least half of which should be whole grain
- 2 1/2 cups vegetables
- 1 1/2 cups fruits
- 3 cups milk (or other dairy products)
- 5 ounces meat and beans (or other lean protein)

Of course as that boy continues to mature, he will need to increase his calorie intake to "feed" his growing body. When my boys were teens and active in sports, it seemed they could never eat enough! But adolescent boys and girls vary so much from one another in growth rates, body type, and activity level that it's impossible to give one calorie count for every age group. Check out the MyPyramid Plan for guidance and then use the following visual cues to guide you and your family on portion size.

PORTION SIZE	VISUAL CUE
1-ounce slice of bread	1 CD
1/2 cup cooked rice, pasta, or cereal (1-ounce serving)	1 small computer mouse
1 cup ready-to-eat cereal (1-ounce serving)	3-inch-diameter baseball
1/2 cup cut-up fresh fruit or cooked vegetables (1 cup =	1 small computer mouse 3-inch-diameter baseball)
1 medium potato or 3-inch-diameter apple (counts as 1-cup serving)	3-inch-diameter baseball
1/2 cup French fries (counts as 1-cup serving)	1 standard deck of cards
1 1/2 ounces cheese (counts as 1-cup serving milk)	2 nine-volt batteries
3 ounces meat, chicken, or fish	1 standard deck of cards
1/4 cup cooked dry beans (1-ounce serving)	1 large egg
1 tablespoon peanut butter (1-ounce serving)	1 nine-volt battery

We need moderation in all things. Our goal is to find a happy medium with food. It can be a struggle for many of us. But it can be done. Consistent dinnertime will do that for your family. Snacking will diminish. When children know that a good dinner will be served, they will want to save their appetite.

Food is a big part of all of our lives. It is the pure satisfaction and enjoyment of life. This book is about good food that your family will eat and that can be made with your family's budget in mind. It is about consistency and simplicity. It's about getting the family together at mealtime for teaching values, sharing concerns, and bonding as a family. **And what's healthier than that?**

Dinnertime is a time to get to know each other.

Having a consistent dinnertime each night ensures good communication and helps maintain positive relationships within the family. Brothers cannot be that angry or upset at their sister (or vice versa) when they are sitting down to dinner together.

Dinner is the most natural meeting place for communicating with our families on a daily basis. It is a comfortable, natural setting. Few families have other opportunities for this kind of interaction, few hours spent just asking questions about one another and getting to know the real Dad, Mom, or kids. Without family dinners, we might not really get to know one another. We will know only what we think we want to know and what we hear from others about our children. The rest will become known only to their friends, teachers, or computer partners.

What to talk about? The list of dinner conversations can go on and on—and the conversations *should* go on and on throughout a child's life. You can almost never start too young with most subjects. Good table manners is one to start with.

Communication is the key to raising children to be responsible adults. Teaching children is the responsibility of the parent(s), not the school or the Sunday school teacher or the coach. If we are to have children who are ready to cope with what is ahead of them, then we must communicate with them on a daily basis. It is our responsibility to keep the door open.

FAMILY TIME AT THE TABLE

Good communication is the most important quality to have between parents and children and among siblings.

Having dinner together at least five nights a week will assure your children of your loyalty to them and their loyalty to one another. Family time is what kids crave (though they don't always realize this). It is what kids need—you and your time, to talk, to laugh, to cry, to share feelings. This is how children learn to trust, to show affection, to communicate, to know what it feels like to be loved.

We grow as a family, together as one in unity and harmony. Good food at the dinner hour will warm our tummies, and at the end of each day we will have succeeded in bonding our relationships. Together, day by day, we will become a true family.

TABLE TALK TOPICS

Conversations don't all have to be serious – they shouldn't be. But here are some serious themes to weave into your dinnertime conversations.

Table Manners

It's easy to think that table manners don't matter that much for a casual meal with the family. But the family dinner table is the best place to teach good habits so they become second nature to your kids when they are at a restaurant, at someone else's home or later, when they're dating. All you have to do is model your own good table manners and then provide reminders as you go along: *David, please wipe your mouth with your napkin, not your sleeve. Katie, please pass the potatoes after you serve yourself. Brent, please chew your food quietly and keep your mouth closed. Emaly, please don't talk with food in your mouth.*

Talking about addiction

Is there a drug problem at your school? If anyone came up to you and offered to sell you drugs, what would you say? Have you made up your mind already not to use drugs?

Be careful with pornography. Friends of yours may want to show you porn photos, videos, and Internet sites, but this is an addiction that you don't want to get started on. Those images never leave your mind.

What do you say to someone who wants you to come over and get drunk with them? Have a cigarette? Let's talk about making up your mind now about what you will do when the situation arises.

Respecting your parents and authority

Define and discuss your family morals and family values. Ask your child how he would respond if a teacher or other authority figure asked him to do something he didn't want to do. Help your child come up with respectful ways to ask clarifying questions when he doesn't understand an instruction. If your child feels that he's being treated unfairly, tell him not to react and talk back—you will discuss the problem with him and then decide what to do.

Forgiveness

Share a story from your past about how forgiving someone helped you grow that relationship. Ask your child what forgiveness means to her. *How do you forgive someone? Why is it important to forgive? How does it help you?*

Budgeting/Debt

How can we as a family live within our budget? Talk about what the budget should include so kids can see there is only so much money to go around.

Gratitude

What are you grateful for? Make a short list of all the things everyone is grateful for around your dinner table some night. (You may be surprised at how grateful they are for the little things in life.)

Accountability

Let's talk about how important it is to be accountable for your actions. Let's talk about how you have to take responsibility for your actions. How did you do today in school? On a test? Were you nice to your friends? Did you clean up your room? Did you use up all the gas in the car? Did you let other kids drive your dad's car? Where are you going after school? What kind of kids are you going to choose to hang out with?

Service to others

We can feel good about ourselves when we give of our time and talents helping others in need. When we spend our days just fulfilling our own needs and worrying about our own problems, we forget that others are even worse off. We forget about how hard it is for the many people in life who are disabled, homeless, lonely, hungry, or just down and out for the time being. Let's look around our family (or neighborhood or community) to see whom you can cheer up or how we can help a friend in need. Sometimes all it takes is a listening ear and a smile!

Dream list of places to visit

Talk with your family about places you could go as a family and vacations that would be within your family budget. Help family members reach a goal to visit a place that is very meaningful to them. Talk about what you have learned about other countries. On Italian Night or Mexican Night, talk about something interesting you have learned about Italy or Mexico.

Kindness

Talk about stories that have happened at school or in the family to illustrate how kindness makes a difference in our lives.

Saying you're sorry

From the time your children are young, talk about how they can say they're sorry on a regular basis. Examples in the home are enough to practice by—if they have hurt another sibling, or said a mean word, or stepped on someone, or spilled milk, or snapped at a parent. (Parents, we need to say we are sorry too, as much as the kids do.)

Dating

Talk openly about what you will expect when your kids are old enough to date. Go over the rules so they are cemented in the kids' minds before they ever start dating. Talk openly about how you feel a boy should treat a girl on a date, and vice versa. Tell them stories of your dating experiences. Keep the communication open at all times about where they will be going and what time they will be coming home. Don't encourage kids to date at an early age. Talk about the pitfalls of birth control and what this practice might lead to. Talk about abstinence in sexual behavior and what the rewards might be because of it. Talk openly together as a family so that each child knows what is expected of him or her.

Honesty

Talk about how the truth will always set you free, that the real truth always comes out even if it takes many years. I always told my kids that as long as we were all telling the truth, there would never be a problem that could not be fixed. Telling the truth and trying to keep those little white lies to a minimum is the best practice. Being true to oneself is most important, and then being true at all times with our siblings, parents, and others.

Work ethic

Talk about what jobs are expected of the children around the house. Talk about keeping your word, being on time, giving your employer a full day's work, and not abusing the system.

Saying "I love you"

We all need to hear loving statements from the people we care about. The way to do this as a family is for the parents to set the example, by getting into the habit of saying "I love you" to each other first, and then to the kids on a daily basis. Your children will not be able to help returning the sentiment of "I love you too."

You'll find conversation starter questions throughout this book.

YES, BUT....

THE 10 MOST COMMON EXCUSES FOR NOT COOKING

Parents, you cannot use your many excuses for not having family dinnertime. I call these the "Yes, buts." You know how great it would be to cook for your family and sit down to dinner together at home . . . But . . . and then come all the excuses. Let's talk about those excuses. Let's talk about the many distractions of real life today. Let's take away all the excuses.

1. I don't know how to cook; I'm not good at it.

Nowadays there are so many ways to learn how to cook. There's always trial and error, but you can reduce the errors significantly by learning a few cooking essentials through cookbooks like this one, videos on Internet websites, and the Food Network on TV. All it takes is desire and the belief that you can cook as well as many of the folks whose food you've been relying on until now.

Does your family eat a lot of hamburgers and frozen dinners? Do they eat mediocre fare at the all-you-can-eat buffet where the food is cheap but the beverage costs add up to a car payment? Trust me, your chicken dinner, home-made biscuits, and a salad you toss yourself will taste better and be better for you than what you can buy at those mediocre fast-casual delis and restaurants. Besides, you'll be filling your home with the irresistible aromas of home cooking and putting the focus on your family rather than on the restaurant.

2. I just don't feel like cooking or eating tonight.

If you don't, who will? This is what you will face:

I don't know how to cook...

"I wonder what we can eat for dinner tonight?" asks a starving 12-year-old as the hunger pangs start to burn.
"What's for dinner?" another child yells out from the TV room. Nobody has a clue.
"Cereal," Mom yells from a nearby room. *"Leftover pot roast from three days ago. Microwave a hot dog."*
"Do we have any buns?" someone yells.
"No, but we have plenty of ketchup and mustard."
"Microwave one of those frozen pizzas," Mom yells.
"Dad, aren't you hungry?"
"No, not really; I had a big lunch out today. I'm still full. Maybe later I'll have a piece of toast or a bowl of cereal."
"Mom, do you want me to throw in a pizza for you?"
"No, thanks, I'm not eating tonight."

What are we teaching our children through this "conversation"? How can we ask them to do well in school if we can't give them proper nutrition? How can we not care enough to have dinner for our family?

3. I'm on a diet and can't be in the kitchen.

Some mothers seem overly concerned about gaining weight if they cook. Food must be out of sight, out of mind. If this is you, you have decided to let your family fend for themselves. But you need to decide instead that your family comes first in your life, not your "diet."

The key to healthful eating is not dieting or fat content or calorie or carb counts. It's been proven over and over that diets don't work long-term. Healthful eating is about eating a variety of freshly prepared foods and paying attention to portion size. A piece of meat the size of your palm is one portion. A serving of vegetables, potatoes, rice, or pasta the size of your fist is one portion. You can cook any nutritious meal and eat one portion of it.

My cry to any mother who wants to keep her feminine form: Don't be afraid to eat! Your job is to teach good nutrition to your family. You cannot teach them to be afraid of eating. For too many girls, putting food into their mouths involves great pain and anxiety, which can lead to eating disorders.

Enjoy sitting down and eating, not until you are full, but until you are satisfied. There lies the difference. Don't think only of yourself when it comes to dinner-time. Your family deserves a well-balanced diet and all the benefits that come from sitting down together for a home-cooked meal.

4. We both work and get home too tired to cook.

Children whose parents are gone all day need consistent dinnertime. It's the bonding as a family that will carry them through each day. Sitting down together at dinner gives everyone time to unwind and to take notice of one another. Mom and Dad have a chance to give a nod of appreciation to each other. My plan will help you do this no matter what your situation.

We're too tired...

Theme nights make meal planning easier. And this cookbook is full of great recipes that you will be excited about cooking and your family will be excited about eating. If you plan menus a week or two in advance, you can have most of the stress out of the way. Come home and unwind in the kitchen with the kids or your partner helping you. Share in the cooking. One can do the chopping and one do the assembly. If your kids are old enough, give them assignments for after-school so you don't always have the sole responsibility.

5. We get home too late to cook.

Little ones cannot wait much past 7 p.m. to eat, and they need to be in bed by 8:00. So hopefully your late work schedule will not have to last forever! School-age children can make a sandwich to tide them over to a late mealtime. As long as they know dinner is coming before they go to bed, they will be fine. They will look forward to it.

Your children can help. Preteens can help in many of the preparations that do not involve the cooktop, such as putting potatoes in the oven to bake, taking something from the fridge directly to the oven, making lemonade, mixing cookie batter, setting the table. Teenagers can definitely be trusted with the burners. If the recipe is laid out and the ingredients are in plain sight, anyone can cook, boys and girls alike. All they have to do is follow the directions.

Many dishes can be put together ahead of time. Get the whole family together on Saturdays or Sundays to put together dishes for the week, or assemble them the night before, or in the morning before heading to work, or just do any chopping or pre-prep and finish them when you get home. Some of my recipes are prepared in the slow cooker that can go all day long. Others are quick to make, and dinner can be prepared start to finish in a short time.

6. My spouse and I just aren't getting along.

You may feel that your own problems are bigger and more important than worrying about getting dinner on the table. So do you let the family fall apart? No. Why make the kids suffer? How about putting the kids first?

Putting dinner on the table will give your mind something positive to zero in on. With my meal plan, dinner will be something you will be proud of at the end of the day, even though your life seems in turmoil. Your spouse may actually come to the table in a better mood. We all love a hot meal. Both of you may decide to be home on time to participate in the family dinner hour. This could be a healing power in your relationship. You both need that interaction with the kids. Bring everyone back to the table and begin again, work out your misunderstandings, and start fresh.

We just aren't getting along.

7. Everyone is going in different directions.

Jobs, extra-curricular activities, the gym—all of these can keep family members away from home at the dinner hour. But if you can get even half of the family home for dinner, you can set the other meals in the fridge (with a plate all ready to heat in the microwave) for when the absentees get home. They'll be famished so they'll be glad to know dinner is waiting for them.

I can remember many, many nights of teenage kids coming in late and popping their plate in the microwave. Oh, how their eyes lit up to see wonderful hot food for them! Nothing fancy has to be waiting for them. Something hot and easy will be the best every time. I visited with my kids as they ate, as did other family members who were still up. The energy from those who had been home for dinner was great, because those who came in late could still benefit from it.

8. Everybody wants something different to eat.

Some families have gotten into the habit of everyone eating their own thing. No wonder mealtime means stress. It's time to change that habit and have everyone sit down to the same meal. Besides easing your workload and giving everyone a chance to bond over dinner, this provides other benefits. Think about this:

When the parent becomes a "short-order cook" to please everyone, and children are allowed to eat their favorite food every night, children eat more. But when children eat a family meal, they learn to enjoy a greater variety of foods. Some of these are not their favorites, so they eat smaller portions. Start serving everyone the same meal together and make this the new pattern in your family. You and your family can decide together on the theme nights you want to have so that everyone regularly gets his or her "favorites."

Everybody wants something different...

9. The kids ate big snacks and are not hungry.

Children who are famished right after school can have a snack, but when they know that a great dinner is coming soon, they are satisfied with less at snack time. They will want to save their appetite.

Offer just enough of a snack to take the edge off before dinner. Have a piece of fruit or cheese and crackers. On cold days serve a cup of hot chocolate. Make popcorn and serve with a soda. Make cookies one weekend, freeze them, and take out just enough each day for a snack. This is one reason I wasn't big on dessert most nights of the week. If the kids and I had had a cookie for a before-dinner snack, we didn't need sweets after dinner too. More snack ideas are on page 271.

Limiting snacks and keeping to a consistent dinnertime ensures proper eating habits and helps us as parents see what our children are eating. We can get control of obesity or eating disorders before they get out of hand.

10. There is nothing to eat in the house.

This is where meal planning comes in. If you keep your pantry stocked with the basics, plan a week's worth of menus at once, and buy all the groceries you will need for those meals, you will always have on hand everything you need to make dinner. And my theme nights and the recipes in this book make it easy to plan a week's worth of menus in 10 minutes. Simply go to the chapter for each night of the week and make your selection. No more wondering what to have for dinner. Problem solved.

The kids ate big snacks and aren't hungry...

**Enough excuses!
Let's get started!**

GET THE KIDS IN ON THE ACTION!

Having your children help with meal preparations does more than just make your life less stressful at the end of the day. It adds purpose to kids' lives and gives them something constructive to do after school, a reason to tell their friends they cannot just "hang out" with them—they have something to do at home. Give them responsibility and help them rise to it and they will build self-confidence from the inside out. Make and post assignments at the beginning of each week, then also make spontaneous requests as meals are prepared. Children will come to learn that such activities are part of a family's daily life.

Single parents especially need the extra help of their children. You're all trying to make your family work. The time together in preparing, eating, and cleaning up will allow for much family communication that otherwise would not take place. Preparing and having dinner together lends itself to so many good sharing experiences that would be lost otherwise.

These girls make and proudly serve vegetable lasagna (p. 91) to their mother, aunt, and grandparents.

Teach your children the correct way to set a table

and assign that as a rotating responsibility. Dinnertime will be easier on you and they'll learn something they'll use for a lifetime.

bread or salad plate

soup bowl

Follow the diagram above to set the table for a casual meal. More formal occasions have more "rules" and that information can be found on the Web. Glasses are always above the knife. Knives and spoons are always to the right and forks to the left of the plate. The small fork is a salad fork, which would be used if a salad were served before the main course. The napkin can also be put in a napkin ring, or let the kids get creative with their napkin folding and presentation.

COOKING AND BAKING BASICS

Here are things to keep in mind as you are following the recipes and cooking. At the back of the book (p. 275-278) are lists of kitchen basics—things to have on hand to make meal preparation easier—along with some tips on shopping and menu planning. And on all the pages in between you'll find recipes that will make you hungry and eager to cook, along with do-ahead guidance and conversation starters for dinnertime talk. Remember that the pages are all color-coded so you can quickly find the recipes for each theme night. Have fun with it!

How to follow a recipe

1. Read the recipe from start to finish to avoid surprises. This way you will be sure to know how much total time to allow, if the recipe calls for equipment you don't have, or if there are cooking terms you don't understand and need to look up.

2. Gather all the necessary ingredients and equipment. If the ingredients list includes preparation instructions, such as "1 cup cooked rice," you'll know to cook the rice ahead of time so it will be ready to add to the recipe at the appropriate time.

3. For determining doneness, always rely first on descriptions in the recipe, such as "cook until the onions are soft" or "bake until the top is golden brown." Times given in the recipe usually are meant only as a guide because variations in cooktops, ovens, and other equipment can make a difference in the total time required. High elevation (above 3,000 feet) can make a difference as well. Consult a high-altitude cookbook or any of a multitude of websites devoted to the subject.

Looking for Meatless Recipes?

*For recipes without red meat, pork, poultry, or fish, look for the symbol above, or a sentence beginning "**Can be made** Meatless... "*

Meatless recipes may contain dairy.

Ingredients

Unless otherwise noted, assume that—

- for recipes calling for "coarse salt," you may use kosher salt or coarse sea salt (but not the large salt crystals for use in a salt grinder).
- eggs are large.
- fresh herbs and salad greens are washed and dried.
- garlic and onions are peeled.
- "grease the pan" means you may use cooking spray.
- you may substitute low-fat (not nonfat) versions when a recipe calls for sour cream, cream cheese, and mayonnaise.
- ingredients used in baking (such as eggs, milk, butter) should be at room temperature.
- chicken or beef broth is fat-free (and low-sodium). Broth may be purchased in a can or carton, or you may prepare your own from bouillon granules or cubes, following the directions on the package.

Preparations in the ingredient list

A recipe ingredient list may contain words such as "diced" and "chopped" that tell you how to prepare an ingredient for the recipe. The placement of these "preparation modifiers" in the ingredient line is as important as the modifier itself. Take, for example, the following two similar lines that you may see in a recipe ingredient list:

1 cup cornflakes, crushed
1 cup crushed cornflakes

The first line is telling you to take 1 cup of cornflakes and crush them; the second line is calling for 1 cup of cornflakes already crushed. The difference between the two could make a big difference in the outcome of the recipe.

Measuring accurately

- **Flour** – To ensure accuracy, which is most important when you are baking (as opposed to cooking), don't scoop the measuring cup into the flour. Instead, lightly spoon flour into a dry measuring cup and level it with the straight edge of a knife or flat metal spatula; don't shake or tap the cup. Sifting is not necessary, but many recipes in this book (for baked goods) call for sifting the flour with other dry ingredients onto a square of wax paper. This is an easy way to combine the dry ingredients and set them aside without using a separate bowl. Alternatively, though, you could forgo the sifter and stir the dry ingredients in a bowl.

- **Liquids** – Place a clear glass or plastic liquid measuring cup on a level surface and bend down to read it at eye level (or place the cup on a raised shelf). Fill the cup to the marking. Don't raise the cup to your eye; you cannot ensure a level measure holding the cup in your hand. When using measuring spoons, don't measure over the bowl because if you accidentally overfill the spoon, then too much liquid will be added. Measure over the counter instead, fill to the top of the spoon, and pour the liquid into the bowl.

- **Sugar** – Spoon granulated or powdered sugar into a dry measuring cup and level it off, just as you do with flour. For brown sugar, though, pack it into a dry measuring cup. If pressed adequately, it will remain in the shape of the cup when turned out. Powdered sugar need not be sifted, but sifting will eliminate lumps for a smoother consistency, in cake frosting, for example.

- **Shortening** – Measure shortening as for brown sugar, except use a rubber spatula to press it firmly into a dry measuring cup. Level it off with the straight edge of a knife or flat metal spatula.

- **Butter** – Use an entire 1/4 pound stick for 1/2 cup. For lesser amounts, use a sharp knife to cut off the amount needed, following the guidelines on the wrapper. Unwrapped butter can be measured like shortening, once it is softened to room temperature.

For a **measurement conversion chart**, including metrics, see page 276.

For a **measurement conversion chart**, including metrics, see page 276.

Looking for dishes to do ahead?

Recipes that can be prepared in advance or partially prepared in advance have a box similar to this:

CAN DO AHEAD

This dish may be put together ahead of time. Refrigerate until baked.

*If some portion of the recipe **must** be started ahead of time, the box will begin with **"DO AHEAD."***

See you at dinner!

ROAST CHICKEN WITH GRAVY

6 servings

I saw my Aunt Mary make this more than 40 years ago. I can still smell the chicken roasting! Mary Kay (Aunt Mary's daughter) and I have been making this since the first year we were both married. It is so simple; it's one of those staples you never get tired of fixing or eating. Take this meal to a friend in need. It makes a beautiful presentation.

While we love this roast chicken on comfort food night, it is also the perfect meal for Sunday dinner.

If your family loves chicken, roast two and serve the second one later in the week in a different way without gravy.

1   **(5-6 pound) whole young roasting chicken**
Lemon pepper
Seasoned salt
1½   **cups chicken broth, plus additional (see Note at right)**
1/4   **cup all-purpose flour**
Salt and ground black pepper

Note: Chicken broth is handy to have on hand, and it is available in a 32-ounce carton with a pouring spout. You can use the amount you need and then store the remainder in the refrigerator for 7 to 10 days.

1. Preheat the oven to 375 degrees.

2. Discard any giblets and wipe the chicken inside and out with a damp paper towel; discard the towel immediately. (This is the preferred way to "rinse" a chicken, for food safety.) Place the chicken in a shallow roasting pan or 9 x 13-inch metal baking pan. Sprinkle the chicken with the lemon pepper and seasoned salt.

3. Roast uncovered 1¼ to 1½ hours, basting with the pan drippings during cooking if desired. Or pour a little chicken broth over the chicken a couple of times to keep it moist. Check for doneness with an instant-read thermometer. The chicken is done when the thigh juices run clear when pricked deeply with a fork, or at 170 to 175 degrees. If you like the dark meat falling off the bone, roast until the thigh registers 180 degrees, but at this point the breast meat may be dry.

4. Transfer the chicken to a platter and tent with aluminum foil to keep warm while making the gravy: Leave the juices in the baking pan. Add 1½ cups of the chicken broth to the juices. In a small bowl or measuring cup, make a paste of 1/4 cup of chicken broth and the flour. Stir until smooth. Place the pan over medium-high heat and bring the juices and broth to a boil. Add the paste, stirring constantly with a whisk for 2 minutes or until the mixture is thickened. Season with the salt and pepper. Add more paste if the gravy is too thin, or add more broth or water if the gravy is too thick. Pour into a gravy dish.

5. Carve the chicken at the table and pass the gravy.

Serve with a vegetable such as **Baked Buttered Carrots** (p. 207) and a green salad. Add **corn bread** (p. 241) and **Classic Mashed Potatoes** (p. 211) or serve with baked potatoes or steamed or boiled red potatoes.

Variations:

◆ Substitute Tony Chachere's Original Creole Seasoning (p. 169) for the lemon pepper and seasoned salt.

◆ **Make roast stuffed chicken.** Prepare a packaged chicken stuffing mix or seasoned rice mix according to package directions. Spoon the hot prepared stuffing into the chicken cavity. The stuffing is done (and safe to eat) when it reaches an internal temperature of 160 degrees. Spoon it into a bowl after the chicken comes out of the oven.

◆ **Roast Cornish game hens** instead of chicken, one-half hen per person. Follow the same directions, and after roasting, cut the hen in half lengthwise, placing the cut side down on the plate.

FIRED-UP MACARONI & CHEESE

6 servings

We have been making this recipe for years and years. The cayenne and Tabasco fire up the dish and enliven it— but with just a little fire. If you don't like any fire, just omit these two ingredients.

For a touch of sophistication, use a pasta other than macaroni. I like penne.

2 cups uncooked elbow macaroni or other pasta, such as penne
1/4 cup (1/2 stick) unsalted butter
1/4 cup all-purpose flour
2 cups milk
1 teaspoon salt
1/8 to 1/2 teaspoon cayenne
1½ teaspoons Worcestershire sauce
1/8 to 1/4 teaspoon Tabasco sauce

2 cups (8 ounces) shredded sharp Cheddar cheese
1/4 cup grated Parmesan cheese

CRUMB TOPPING:
2 to 3 slices white bread
2 tablespoons unsalted butter, melted
1/4 cup grated Parmesan cheese

1. Preheat the oven to 350 degrees and grease an 8 x 8-inch baking dish.

2. Cook the pasta according to package directions; drain well.

3. Meanwhile, melt the butter over medium heat in a medium saucepan and add the flour. Stir with a spoon or whisk until the mixture is bubbly, about 1 minute. Add the milk, cooking and stirring until the mixture thickens. Add the salt, cayenne, Worcestershire sauce, and Tabasco. Stir for 1 minute.

4. Remove the pan from the heat and add the Cheddar cheese and the 1/4 cup Parmesan cheese. Cook and stir over low heat until the cheese is melted. Stir in the pasta. Transfer the mixture to the prepared baking dish.

5. To make the crumb topping, tear the bread into small pieces and pulse in the food processor to make 1 cup crumbs. Mix in the butter and the Parmesan cheese. Sprinkle over the pasta mixture. Bake for 20 to 30 minutes, until hot and bubbly and the topping is browned to your liking.

Serve with cooked fresh broccoli seasoned with a little butter, salt, and pepper.

Variation: Instead of bread crumbs, top the casserole with more grated Cheddar for a cheesy crust.

CAN DO AHEAD
This dish can be put together ahead of time. Add the crumb topping just before baking.

Meatless

CHICKEN POTPIE

6 to 8 servings

PASTRY for a double-crust pie:
2½ cups flour
1 teaspoon salt
3/4 cup shortening
1/4 cup (1/2 stick) chilled butter, cut in small pieces
4 to 6 tablespoons ice-cold water

FILLING:
2 small bone-in chicken breasts (about 1 pound)
3 Yukon gold or russet potatoes (about 1 pound), diced
2 carrots, sliced crosswise
2 teaspoons chicken bouillon granules
1/2 teaspoon salt
1/4 cup flour
1/4 cup cold water (or broth)
1/2 cup frozen peas

To me the best thing about any pie is the crust! Mine is flaky with good flavor too. When you're in the mood for comfort food, nothing beats this warm, savory dish.

CAN DO AHEAD

Make the filling and the pastry ahead of time. Assemble and bake before dinner.

1. To make the pie crust, stir the flour and salt in a large bowl. Cut in the shortening and butter with a pastry blender until the mixture resembles coarse crumbs. Sprinkle with the ice water, a tablespoon at a time, and stir with a fork to moisten all the dough. Gather the dough into a ball with your hands. Divide the dough in half. Roll out one half on a lightly floured surface and fit it into a 9-inch pie dish (deep-dish is ideal). Roll out the other half and set aside.

2. Put the chicken breasts in a large saucepan and cover with water. Bring to a boil over high heat. Decrease the heat, cover, and simmer until tender, about 18 minutes. Remove the chicken to a cutting board or plate.

3. Add the potatoes and carrots to the hot broth and return to boiling. Decrease the heat, cover, and simmer until the vegetables are tender, about 15 minutes. Meanwhile, tear or cut the chicken off the bones into bite-size pieces, discarding skin, fat and gristle. Remove the vegetables from the simmering broth with a slotted spoon and set aside with the chicken pieces.

4. Measure the broth and add water, if necessary, to make 2½ cups. Return to the pan and simmer, stirring in the bouillon and the salt.

5. Preheat the oven to 350 degrees.

6. Stir the flour into the cold water in a small bowl or measuring cup. Stir into the broth and increase the heat to medium. Stir constantly until the broth thickens.

7. Add the chicken to the broth along with the potatoes, carrots and peas. Stir to combine. Pour the filling into the pastry-lined pie dish. Cover with the top crust, seal and flute the edges, and cut a slit in the top for the steam to escape. Bake 40 minutes, or until the crust is light brown. Serve immediately.

See the photo on page 31 and "Ingredients for a Flaky Pie Crust" on page 250.

CHICKEN & NOODLES OVER
MASHED POTATOES *6 to 8 servings*

This recipe is a whole meal! It goes way back in my mother's family, back when people were often more physically active and needed hearty fare like this. It was always such a big treat that the neighbor kids wanted to eat with us every time we had it! Now we enjoy it occasionally and in small portions.

This dish does not have a "burst" of flavor; the salt and pepper make it flavorful. It is pure comfort food: not too spicy, just yummy.

1½ to 2 pounds boneless, skinless chicken breasts
4 cups chicken broth
6 medium russet potatoes (about 2 pounds), peeled and cut into 2-inch chunks
2 tablespoons butter
1/3 to 1/2 cup milk, warmed
Salt and ground black pepper
6 ounces uncooked wide egg noodles or **Homemade Egg Noodles** (recipe on next page)
1/2 cup all-purpose flour (optional)
1/2 cup water (optional)
Salt and ground black pepper
2 cups frozen peas, thawed

1. Put the chicken and broth in a large saucepan. Bring to a boil over medium-high heat. Decrease the heat, cover, and simmer 18 to 20 minutes, until the chicken is tender and no longer pink. Remove the chicken from the pot to cool, reserving the broth in the pan.

2. Meanwhile, put the potatoes in another pot and cover with water. Add a few shakes of salt and bring to a boil. Cover, decrease the heat to simmer, and continue cooking until potatoes are tender, 15 to 20 minutes. Drain.

3. Remove the pot from the heat and, with a potato masher or portable electric mixer, mash the potatoes in the pot. Add the butter, milk, and salt and pepper to taste. Cover to keep warm.

4. When the chicken is cool enough to handle, tear the meat into pieces with two forks. Stir the chicken pieces into the broth and place over high heat.

5. When the broth boils, add the noodles. When it boils again, decrease the heat to medium and cook the noodles until tender—following package directions, or 2 to 3 minutes for homemade noodles.

   NOTE: For a thicker broth, make a paste by whisking 1/2 cup flour into 1/2 cup cold water in a small bowl until smooth. Pour a little of the paste into the pot after the noodles are cooked. Stir until well-blended and boil for 1 minute, adding more thickening as desired.

6. Stir in the peas until heated through. Add salt and pepper to taste.

7. To serve, mound the mashed potatoes in the center of a platter and ladle the chicken mixture over it. Season generously with additional salt and pepper.

Can be made *Meatless*: Substitute tofu cubes and vegetable broth for the chicken breasts and chicken broth.

HOMEMADE EGG NOODLES *6 servings*

3   **eggs**
1   **tablespoon milk**
Dash of freshly ground black pepper
1   **cup all-purpose flour, plus additional**

1. Combine the eggs, milk, and pepper in a small bowl and beat with a fork.

2. Continuing to use a fork, add the 1 cup flour all at once. Add more flour a little at a time until the dough holds together but is still really sticky.

3. Gather the dough with your hands and turn it out onto a lightly floured surface. Knead the dough, adding more flour until the dough is no longer sticky. You may need as much as an additional cup of flour.

4. Roll out to 1/8-inch thickness. Using a serrated knife, cut the dough into thin strips about 3/8 inch wide and 4 inches long. As you cut the noodles, separate them so they don't stick together. Leave them to dry for at least 10 minutes (or as much as a day ahead) before adding them to the broth in step 5 on the preceding page. (These can also be boiled in salted water or chicken broth for 2 to 3 minutes to use in other ways.)

Making homemade noodles may sound complicated, but these thick and chewy noodles are fast and easy. Add them to other dishes, or serve them as is with butter, fresh Parmesan cheese, a little salt, and freshly ground black pepper. Serve with a salad and make a meal out of them!

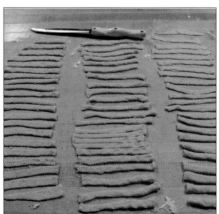

ALMOND-TOPPED CHICKEN CASSEROLE

6 servings

I got this recipe while living in upstate New York 34 years ago. My neighbor Betty and I shared many recipes, and this is one that became a classic for our family. If you have leftover chicken or turkey, this makes a quick dinner. It's like a hot chicken salad.

3 cups cooked chicken breasts, shredded or cubed (about 1 pound)
1 cup diced celery (2 to 3 ribs)
1/4 cup diced yellow onion
1 tablespoon lemon juice
1 cup cooked rice (regular or instant)

1 (10.75-ounce) can condensed cream of chicken soup
1/2 cup mayonnaise
1/2 cup chicken broth
1 cup crushed saltine crackers (about 25 crackers)
1/2 cup slivered almonds
1/4 cup (1/2 stick) butter, melted

1. Preheat the oven to 350 degrees and lightly grease a square baking dish.

2. Combine the chicken, celery, onion, lemon juice, rice, soup, mayonnaise, and broth and spoon into the prepared casserole.

3. Mix the cracker crumbs, almonds, and butter. Sprinkle over the casserole.

4. Bake uncovered for 45 minutes.

Serve with a green salad and bread.

CRUNCHY PARMESAN BAKED CHICKEN

8 servings

I had always made my own bread crumbs for all my recipes, and then my friend Joni introduced me to panko, which is Japanese-style breading. It has a coarser texture that creates a deliciously crunchy crust for chicken recipes like this. Panko is available in most supermarkets.

2/3 cup buttermilk or buttermilk ranch dressing
2 cups panko bread crumbs
1/2 cup grated Parmesan cheese

2 teaspoons garlic salt
2 pounds chicken breast tenders
1/3 cup butter
Salt

1. Preheat the oven to 400 degrees. Grease an oblong baking pan.

2. Pour the buttermilk or buttermilk ranch dressing into a wide, shallow dish or pie plate. Mix the panko, Parmesan cheese, and garlic salt in another wide, shallow dish. Roll each piece of chicken in the buttermilk and then dredge in the panko mixture to coat.

3. Arrange the chicken pieces in the prepared pan. Melt the butter in a glass measuring cup in the microwave and drizzle the melted butter over all. Bake for about 30 minutes, until the chicken is tender and no longer pink. Sprinkle with salt to taste.

Serve with a green vegetable and **Rice Pilaf** (p. 213), **Classic Mashed Potatoes** (p. 211), or fettuccine with olive oil, coarse salt, and freshly ground black pepper.

Variation: For a fast, easy dinner, simply dredge chicken tenders in panko crumbs seasoned with coarse salt. Fry in peanut or canola oil and drain on paper towels.

CHICKEN RICE BROCCOLI CASSEROLE

6 to 8 servings

1½ pounds boneless, skinless chicken breasts

8 ounces fresh broccoli, cut up (or thawed frozen chopped broccoli)

1/2 cup uncooked long-grain or calrose rice (to make 1½ cups cooked rice)

3 slices white or wheat bread, torn into pieces

3 tablespoons butter, melted

2 (10.75-ounce) cans condensed cream of chicken soup

1/2 cup mayonnaise

1/2 cup sour cream

1/4 to 1/2 teaspoon curry powder

Salt and ground black pepper

1 to 2 cups shredded Cheddar cheese

1. Put the chicken in a saucepan with water to cover; bring to boiling. Decrease the heat, cover, and simmer 18 to 20 minutes or until chicken is tender and no longer pink. Remove the chicken and reserve the stock. When the chicken is cool enough to handle, tear it into bite-size pieces. Put the pieces into a large bowl and set aside.

2. Cook the rice according to package directions. Add the cooked rice to the chicken.

3. Cook the broccoli just until tender (see Note); drain and add to the chicken-rice mixture.

4. Preheat the oven to 350 degrees and lightly grease a 9 x 13-inch baking dish.

5. Pulse the bread in a blender or food processor to the desired texture. Transfer the crumbs to a small bowl and stir in the melted butter. Set aside.

6. In a saucepan mix and heat the soup, mayonnaise, sour cream, curry powder, and salt and pepper to taste. Stir the soup mixture into the chicken-rice mixture and add reserved chicken stock to make the desired moistness (as much as a cup or more of stock).

7. Spoon into the prepared dish and top with the cheese. Sprinkle the crumb topping over all. Bake uncovered until bubbly, about 45 minutes.

This makes a great one-dish meal, or serve it with salad or hot rolls for additional texture and interest.

Note: Fresh broccoli may be cooked by boiling, steaming, or microwave cooking. Boiling uncovered in a large amount of salted water results in the mildest flavor and brightest color. For 8 ounces of cut-up broccoli, bring 2 quarts of water and 2 teaspoons salt to a rolling boil in a saucepan. Drop in the pieces and rapidly return to a boil. Boil uncovered until tender but still crisp, 2 to 4 minutes for pieces. Drain. Then, for this recipe, simply wipe out the pan and reuse it to make the sauce.

Years ago my daughter Katie and I came up with this recipe. Everyone loved it, so it became one of our standard casseroles while the kids were growing up. It's a good way to introduce children to broccoli. You can vary the proportions of mayonnaise and sour cream as desired, or leave out the mayo and use all sour cream. For a leaner version, use light mayonnaise and light sour cream.

CAN DO AHEAD

This dish may be put together ahead of time. Add the crumb topping just before baking.

STUFFING-TOPPED PORK CHOPS

6 servings

This is an all-American comfort food and one of the easiest meals to prepare. Nowadays pork chops are among the leanest of meats.

1 (6-ounce) package pork or chicken stuffing mix
6 bone-in pork chops, about 3/4 inch thick
Salt
Onion salt
Ground black pepper
1 tablespoon canola oil
1 (10.75-ounce) can condensed cream of mushroom soup
1/3 cup milk

1. Preheat the oven to 350 degrees.

2. Make the stuffing according to package directions. Set aside.

3. Season the pork chops with the salt, onion salt, and pepper. Heat the oil in a skillet over high heat and brown the chops on both sides. (This takes only a few minutes per side; the chops will bake thoroughly in the oven.) Arrange the chops in an oblong baking dish. Spoon 1/2 cup of the stuffing on top of each chop.

4. Mix the soup with the milk in a small bowl and pour over the chops. Cover with aluminum foil. Bake 35 to 40 minutes, or until pork is no longer pink.

Serve with applesauce and a couple of hot cooked vegetables. Cabbage, cauliflower, corn, green beans, spinach, tomatoes, and summer squash are good with pork.

Variation: Omit the stuffing and serve the sauce separately for spooning over baked potatoes or rice.

CONVERSATION STARTER:

You'll be starting high school next year. I hear they have some great after-school clubs and activities. What ones are you interested in joining?

CHEESY SCALLOPED POTATOES WITH HAM & CORN *6 to 8 servings*

2 pounds baking potatoes, peeled
1/4 cup (1/2 stick) butter
1/4 cup all-purpose flour
1/2 teaspoon salt
Pinch of ground white pepper

2 cups milk
2 cups shredded Cheddar cheese, divided
1 (8.5-ounce) can corn, drained
1 (1-pound) precooked ham steak, cut into bite-size pieces

We all get hungry for a ham dinner from time to time. Many nights when my children were home, I would brown a ham steak in the skillet, bake some potatoes, heat some corn, make some biscuits, and there was dinner! This casserole classic is also a good ham dinner and it was my boys' favorite casserole.

1. Preheat the oven to 350 degrees and grease a shallow oblong baking dish.

2. Thinly slice the potatoes into a large bowl.

3. Melt the butter in a medium saucepan over medium heat. Stir in the flour, salt, and pepper. Add the milk all at once and cook, stirring constantly, until the mixture thickens and bubbles. Remove from the heat and add 1½ cups of the cheese, stirring until combined. Pour the mixture over the potatoes and lightly mix.

4. Gently stir in the corn and ham. Spoon into the prepared dish.

5. Cover with aluminum foil and bake about 1 hour or until the potatoes are tender. For a browned top, remove the foil about halfway through the baking time. At the end of the baking time, sprinkle the remaining 1/2 cup of cheese over the top. Bake a few more minutes until the cheese is melted.

Serve with a green salad, hot cooked green peas or broccoli, or fresh fruit.

Variation: Omit the ham and corn from the casserole and serve the **Cheesy Scalloped Potatoes** with baked ham or **Savory Meatloaf** (p. 45) and a green salad or **Baked Buttered Carrots** (p. 207).

CAN DO AHEAD

This dish may be put together ahead of time. Refrigerate until baked.

BISCUITS & SAUSAGE COUNTRY GRAVY

4 to 6 servings

Dinner in 20 minutes! My recipe feeds four hearty appetites, and you can double it very easily. We always served this at dinnertime, but in the South it is a traditional food for breakfast. It is fast, easy, and delicious— and a real comfort food. If you're short on time, bake refrigerator biscuits instead of homemade.

Old-Fashioned Biscuits
   or Buttermilk Biscuits (p. 240)
8   ounces sage- or maple-flavored bulk sausage
1/4 cup (1/2 stick) butter

1/3 cup all-purpose flour
2   cups milk
1   cup water
1   teaspoon salt
1   teaspoon ground black pepper

1. Prepare the biscuits and bake them while you make the gravy.

2. Cook and stir the sausage in a small skillet over medium heat, crumbling it with a wooden spoon. Drain the fat, if necessary.

3. Melt the butter in a medium saucepan over medium heat. Stir in the flour, stirring constantly to prevent scorching. Cook until the roux begins to darken slightly. Slowly whisk in the milk, water, salt, and pepper. Continue stirring until the gravy thickens and comes to a simmer. Stir in the sausage.

4. Break the warm biscuits in half and cover with the gravy.

Serve with colorful fruits or vegetables on the side, such as a green salad, fresh berries or canned peach slices, carrot and celery sticks, or a hot cooked green vegetable or corn.

CONVERSATION STARTER:

I enjoyed meeting Allison this weekend. I'll bet she'll become a good friend for you. Tell me...what do you look for in a friend?

SAVORY MEATLOAF

4 to 6 servings

3 slices white or wheat bread
1 pound ground beef
1 egg, beaten
1 cup ketchup, divided
1/3 cup milk

1/2 teaspoon salt
1/4 teaspoon ground black pepper
1 teaspoon ground sage
Brown sugar, for sprinkling atop
  (optional)

1. Preheat the oven to 350 degrees.

2. Cut or break the bread into pieces and pulse in a blender or food processor to make crumbs (1½ cups).

3. In a large bowl combine the meat, egg, and bread crumbs. Add 1/2 cup of the ketchup, the milk, salt, pepper, and sage. Mix well with a fork.

4. Place the meat mixture in a 9 x 5-inch loaf pan (see Note) and shape it with a fork. Spread the remaining 1/2 cup of ketchup over the top. Sprinkle with brown sugar, if desired. Bake uncovered for 1 hour.

Serve with a vegetable and your choice of a side dish: **Cheesy Scalloped Potatoes** (p. 43), baked potatoes, **Classic Mashed Potatoes** (p. 211), rice or **Rice Pilaf** (p. 213), or noodles.

Variations:

◆ Substitute 3/4 cup toasted wheat germ for the bread crumbs.

◆ Use half ground beef and half ground pork.

◆ Mix in 3/4 cup partially cooked diced carrots.

◆ In place of the ketchup topping, mix 3 tablespoons honey with 1/4 cup prepared mustard. Spread half of the mixture over the meatloaf before baking. Heat the other half in the microwave just before serving and pass as a sauce with the baked meatloaf.

◆ Bake the loaf in a shallow baking pan. Spread mashed potatoes over the top and sides. Sprinkle with grated Cheddar cheese and return it to the oven until the cheese melts. Cut into slices and serve immediately.

◆ Bake the loaf in a 9 x 13-inch pan, and after 40 minutes of baking, pour one 8-ounce can of tomato sauce and one 8-ounce can of peas, undrained, around the meatloaf. Return the pan to the oven to continue baking. This makes a yummy sauce that can be spooned over mashed potatoes. My former neighbor Alice shared this idea with me, and it became a favorite of Steve's.

Note: As an alternative to the loaf pan, form the meat mixture into a loaf and place it in a shallow baking pan. Meatloaf baked this way will have a crustier outside.

Of course I learned to make meatloaf from my mom. She makes great meatloaf, but my kids didn't like the onions in her recipe, so I took them out and changed things just a bit. I like this even better! (If you like onions, simply add 1/4 cup diced to the meat mixture.) The ketchup and brown sugar topping makes it especially good, and the variations are excellent as well. The leftovers make great meatloaf sandwiches for the next day!

CAN DO AHEAD

This dish may be put together ahead of time. Refrigerate until baked.

BEEF STROGANOFF
8 servings

I love this meal! And it's so easy and great to serve company. My daughter-in-law Kim made this dish for us once with filet mignon, and it was a real treat!

CAN DO AHEAD

Steps 1 and 2 can be done ahead of time.

2	tablespoons butter
1/2	medium white onion, chopped
2	pounds beef sirloin
1	pound mushrooms, sliced
2	cups beef broth
1¼	teaspoons salt
1	teaspoon ground nutmeg
1/2	teaspoon dried basil
1/8	teaspoon cayenne
1/8	teaspoon ground black pepper
2	tablespoons cream or milk
2	cups sour cream
1	(12-ounce) package extra-wide noodles or other pasta

1. Melt the butter in a large skillet over medium heat. Add the onion and cook and stir until it is soft.

2. Trim the fat from the meat and cut the meat into 1/4-inch strips. Add to the pan and cook and stir until browned. Add the mushrooms, broth, salt, nutmeg, basil, cayenne, and pepper. Bring to a boil and immediately decrease the heat to low. Simmer until all but about 1/2 cup liquid remains, about 40 minutes.

3. Meanwhile, cook the noodles according to package directions, drain, and set aside.

4. Stir the cream and sour cream into the meat mixture. Cook 1 minute more. Serve immediately over the cooked noodles.

Serve with a green vegetable or a green salad. When you're serving a heavy dish like stroganoff, it's not necessary to serve bread, although a slice of crusty bread adds a crunchy texture to this "soft" meal.

Variation: Add 1/4 cup Madeira wine with the beef broth. Remember, the alcohol cooks away as the sauce simmers. (Paul taught me that Madeira complements many Italian dishes, stews, and sauces.)

COUNTRY-FRIED STEAK WITH MILK GRAVY

4 to 6 servings

2 eggs
2 tablespoons milk
1/4 pound (1 package) saltine crackers
1½ teaspoons salt
1½ teaspoons ground black pepper
4 to 6 cube steaks (1 to 1½ pounds)
1/3 cup canola oil

GRAVY:
About 2 tablespoons pan drippings (supplement with canola oil or butter if necessary)
2 tablespoons all-purpose flour
1 cup milk

Country-fried steak is an American favorite and a comfort food for us. Our boys could never get enough of it. You can make it easily right at home; just make sure you cook the meat on low heat. You can't hurry this dish.

1. Whisk the eggs in a wide, shallow dish, such as a cake pan or pie plate. Whisk in the milk.

2. Crush the crackers finely in the food processor, or put them in a resealable plastic bag and crush with a rolling pin, to make about 1 1/2 cups crumbs. Put the crumbs in a second wide, shallow dish. Stir in the salt and pepper.

3. Dip each steak in the egg mixture on both sides and then in the cracker crumbs to coat both sides.

4. Heat the oil over medium-high heat in a large skillet (or two medium skillets). When the oil is hot, brown the steaks on both sides. Immediately decrease the heat to the lowest setting.

5. Cover and continue to cook over the lowest heat about 1 hour, turning the steaks halfway through, until the meat is tender. Remove the steaks to a platter lined with paper towels.

6. To make gravy, place the skillet with pan drippings over medium heat. Whisk in the flour until well-blended. Whisk in the milk and bring to a boil, scraping up browned bits in the pan. Decrease the heat and simmer until thickened, 3 to 5 minutes. Season with salt and pepper to taste. Spoon the gravy into a small dish and serve with the steaks.

Serve with mashed potatoes and your choice of vegetable. A green vegetable or salad would also add color to the plate.

Variation: As an alternative to cube steak, use top round and pound with a meat mallet to 1/2-inch thickness.

BEEF STEW WITH DUMPLINGS

6 to 8 servings

This is one of our favorite meals. In the wintertime there is nothing better. If you have never put dumplings in your stew, you must try it. I think you will end up loving this stew as much as we do.

CAN DO AHEAD

This stew may be cooked ahead of time. Refrigerate. Reheat stew and cook dumplings right before serving.

2	tablespoons canola oil
1½	pounds beef sirloin, cut into 1½-inch cubes
6	cups hot water, divided
2	teaspoons Worcestershire sauce
2	garlic cloves, minced
1/2	medium onion, chopped
3	bay leaves
1	tablespoon salt
2	teaspoons sugar
1	teaspoon ground black pepper
1	teaspoon paprika
1/4	teaspoon ground cloves
6	carrots, peeled, quartered crosswise, then halved lengthwise
4	medium russet potatoes, peeled and quartered
1	(15-ounce) can corn, undrained
1/2	cup all-purpose flour
1/2	cup cold water

DUMPLINGS:

1	cup all-purpose flour
2	teaspoons baking powder
1/2	teaspoon salt
1/2	cup milk
2	tablespoons canola oil

1. Heat the oil in a Dutch oven or large, heavy-bottomed pot over medium heat. Thoroughly brown the meat, turning often with a wooden spoon. The meat should almost stick to the pan but not be burned.

2. Pour 4 cups of the hot water into the pot. Add the Worcestershire sauce, garlic, onion, bay leaves, salt, sugar, pepper, paprika, and cloves. Bring to a boil. Decrease the heat, cover, and simmer for 1 1/2 hours, stirring occasionally to keep the ingredients from sticking. Remove the bay leaves.

3. Add the carrots, potatoes, corn, and the remaining 2 cups of hot water to the stew. Bring to a boil, decrease the heat, cover, and cook until the vegetables are almost done, 20 to 30 minutes.

4. Meanwhile, make the dumplings: Combine the dry ingredients in a small bowl. In a glass measuring cup, combine the milk and oil and then add this all at once to the flour mixture. Stir just until moistened.

5. Make a paste of the 1/2 cup flour and the cold water in a small bowl; stir until smooth. Pour into the stew and stir with a wooden spoon to thicken the stew, about 2 minutes. If you like stew with more liquid, add water to make the desired consistency.

6. Drop the dumpling dough by teaspoonfuls on top of the bubbling stew. (You'll have about 14 dumplings.) Decrease the heat, cover, and simmer about 10 minutes or until the vegetables are done. Serve immediately.

Serve the stew with a salad.

Variation: Omit the dumplings and cook the stew in a slow cooker on medium heat 4 to 5 hours. Serve with hot rolls or corn bread.

THREE-BEAN CHILI WITH SAUSAGE

8 to 12 servings

1 (14.5-ounce) can diced tomatoes, undrained
1 pound lean ground beef
1 pound maple-flavored bulk sausage
1/4 medium onion, diced
1/4 cup red wine vinegar
1 (46-ounce) can tomato juice
1 (15-ounce) can black beans, undrained
1 (15-ounce) can pinto beans, undrained

1 (16-ounce) can kidney beans, undrained
3 tablespoons chili powder
1/4 cup packed brown sugar
1/4 teaspoon cayenne (optional)
2 teaspoons salt
1 teaspoon paprika

Shredded Cheddar cheese (optional)
Sour cream (optional)

1. Optional step: Crush the tomatoes with their juice in a blender and set aside.

2. Brown the beef, sausage, and onion in a large pot over medium-high heat. Drain the fat. Add the vinegar and cook for 1 minute to reduce the liquid. Add the tomatoes, tomato juice, beans, chili powder, brown sugar, cayenne, salt, and paprika. Decrease the heat and simmer for 1 hour.

3. Serve in bowls and top with a sprinkle of cheese and 1 teaspoon of sour cream if desired.

When the kids were growing up, I almost always served my chili with hot home-made cinnamon rolls. At first, I did it mainly for me because chili is not one of my favorite foods. The cinnamon rolls made the chili much more of a treat. And I love the flavor combination. This is the same chili that I use for my Navajo Tacos (p. 113).

Serve with **Cinnamon Rolls** (p. 236), corn bread, or biscuits and a salad. (Steve's favorite way to eat chili is with a square of **Buttermilk Corn Bread** (p. 241) in the bowl and the chili ladled over and then topped with a sprinkling of pepper Jack or Cheddar cheese and a dollop of sour cream.)

Can be made *Meatless*: Omit the meats and double the beans.

CAN DO AHEAD

This dish may be put together ahead of time. Refrigerate. Reheat and serve.

CHICKEN FAJITA SOUP

About 10 cups

With its sautéed chicken, tomatoes, and bell pepper, this Southwest-spiced soup tastes like a chicken fajita in a bowl! The first time I ate it, my daughter-in-law Lisa had made it for us for lunch. You'll find that it makes a healthy way to end the day as well.

1	pound boneless, skinless chicken breasts
1	medium onion
1	teaspoon butter
4	cups chicken broth
2	cups beef broth
1	(14.5-ounce) can diced tomatoes
1/4	cup chopped green bell pepper

1 to 2 tablespoons chili powder
1/2 teaspoon ground cumin
Salt and ground black pepper

Tortilla chips
Grated Cheddar cheese
Avocado slices
Lime wedges

1. Cut the chicken into bite-size pieces. Chop the onion. Melt the butter in a large pot. Cook and stir the chicken and onion over medium-high heat until the onion is soft and the chicken is no longer pink.

2. Stir in the chicken broth, beef broth, tomatoes, bell pepper, chili powder, and cumin. Bring to a boil, then decrease the heat and simmer for 20 minutes. Season with salt and black pepper to taste.

3. Serve in bowls and top with the tortilla chips, cheese, and avocado slices. Pass the lime wedges.

CONVERSATION STARTER:
If you had $100, how would you spend it? How about a million dollars?

PEPPER JACK POTATO SOUP

About 10 cups

3   strips bacon
1   tablespoon olive oil
1/4 medium yellow onion, diced
1   garlic clove, crushed
1   carrot, peeled and diced
1/2 green bell pepper, diced
1/2 red bell pepper, diced
1½   cups chicken broth
2   cups cubed russet potatoes
     (about 8 ounces)

1/4 cup (1/2 stick) butter
1/4 cup all-purpose flour
1   (12-ounce) can evaporated
     fat-free milk
8   ounces pepper Jack cheese,
     shredded
1/2 teaspoon ground white pepper
1/2 teaspoon salt
1/2 teaspoon ground thyme

This may be my favorite soup in the world! Sometimes I make it with cream or half-and-half for richer flavor (instead of the evaporated milk), but I think you'll find that the cheese gives all the richness you'll love.

1. Fry the bacon until crisp; drain. Crumble and set aside.

2. Heat the oil in a soup pot over medium-high heat. Add the onions, garlic, carrots, and the green and red bell pepper; cook and stir just until the onions are soft. Add the broth and bring to a boil. Decrease the heat and simmer about 20 minutes or until the carrots are cooked.

3. Meanwhile, boil the potatoes in a medium saucepan until they are just tender, about 10 minutes. Drain and add to the soup with the bacon. Wipe out the pan if necessary and use it for the next step.

4. Melt the butter over low heat. Add the flour and turn the heat up slightly and whisk until the mixture is bubbly. Add the milk, stirring constantly until the mixture thickens. Add to the soup.

5. Stir in the cheese and continue to cook until the cheese melts. Do not boil. Add the white pepper, salt, and thyme. Ladle into soup bowls and serve.

Can be made *Meatless*: Omit the bacon and use vegetable broth (although the bacon gives the soup extra flavor).

CONVERSATION STARTER:
You've had the same curfew for a couple of years now and you've been very responsible. Let's talk about the pros and cons of making it an hour later now.

CARROT POTATO SOUP WITH GINGER

7 to 9 cups

Thanks to my friend Sheila for sharing this unique and wonderfully delicious soup recipe. Dad and the kids will love it as much as you will!

1/4 cup (1/2 stick) butter
1 pound carrots, peeled and cut into 1/2-inch slices
1 small white onion, peeled and cut into large chunks
4 to 6 cups chicken broth (see Note)
1 Yukon gold potato, peeled and cut into 1-inch chunks

1/2 teaspoon grated fresh ginger
1 teaspoon salt
1/2 teaspoon white pepper
1/4 cup heavy cream or half-and-half

1. Melt the butter in a large saucepan or soup pot over medium heat. Cook and stir the carrots and onion until the onion is just starting to brown, about 8 minutes.

2. Stir in the broth and potato. Increase the heat and bring to a boil. Decrease the heat to simmer and cook, covered, until the vegetables are soft and the flavors are blended, about 40 minutes. Add the ginger.

3. Puree in batches in a blender or food processor until smooth. (Or use an immersion blender in the soup pot.) Stir in the salt, white pepper, and cream and serve immediately.

Serve with **French Baguette** (p. 225), **Italian Bread** (p. 224), or **Bruschetta** (p. 81) and a green salad, if desired.

Note: Use just 4 cups of broth for a more distinct carrot flavor. The more chicken broth, the milder the flavor.

CONVERSATION STARTER:

Let's set some goals tonight. Where do you see our family in one year? Five years?

CHICKEN SALAD CROISSANT SANDWICHES FOR A CROWD *15 sandwiches*

2 pounds boneless, skinless chicken breasts, or about 5 cups shredded cooked chicken

1½ cups mayonnaise

2 tablespoons minced white onion

1 tablespoon chicken bouillon granules

4 celery ribs, minced

Salt and ground black pepper

2 cups whole cashews

15 small croissants

Our family and friends have been serving these sandwiches for over 25 years. They are a real crowd-pleaser. This recipe serves a small crowd, or you can easily double or triple it for larger groups. Plan ahead to allow the chicken salad to refrigerate for at least 2 hours before making sandwiches.

1. Cook the chicken by your preferred method: poach, grill, or broil. Or simply cut chicken off the bones of a roast chicken from the deli.

2. Tear the meat into bite-size pieces. In a large bowl combine the chicken with the mayonnaise, onion, bouillon, and celery. Mix thoroughly; season with salt and pepper to taste. Refrigerate for at least 2 hours.

3. Fold the cashews into the chicken salad mixture just before serving.

4. Split the croissants in half lengthwise and spoon the salad mixture onto one half of each croissant. Top with the other half.

Serve with baked beans and melon slices or a fruit platter.

Variation: Substitute **Liz's Crescent Dinner Rolls** (p. 234) for the croissants.

DO AHEAD

Make the chicken salad at least 2 hours ahead of time, and up to one day ahead. Add the cashews just before making the sandwiches.

CROQUE MONSIEUR *"croak mess-yur"*

4 servings

A little taste of Paris right at our own tables! Steve and L.J. ordered this specialty all over France the last time we were there. It is one of our favorite French dishes, and my rendition tastes exactly like the ones we ate. It's the Gruyère cheese that makes all the difference. It's the same cheese that tops French onion soup, and it melts so beautifully.

1 tablespoon butter
1 tablespoon flour
3/4 cup milk
Pinch each salt, pepper, and nutmeg
8 slices French, Italian, or sourdough French bread, about 1/2 inch thick

4 (1/8 inch-thick) slices deli ham
8 to 10 ounces Gruyère cheese, shredded (2 to 2½ cups) divided
Softened butter, for buttering the bread

1. Melt the butter in a small saucepan over medium heat. Add the flour and cook and stir until bubbly. Add the milk all at once and cook, stirring constantly, until the sauce thickens. Add the salt, pepper, and nutmeg. Remove from the heat.

2. Place 4 bread slices on a baking sheet. Top each with a slice of ham and about 1/4 cup Gruyère. Top with the remaining bread.

3. Preheat the broiler to low broil and adjust a rack to 6 inches from the heat. Butter the sandwiches on both sides (outsides). Place them under the broiler until deep golden brown, about 2 minutes per side. Watch closely to prevent burning.

4. Spoon one-fourth of the sauce (about 3 tablespoons) over each sandwich. Top each one with 1/4 cup of the remaining cheese. Broil until the cheese begins to brown, about 2 minutes.

Serve the sandwiches with a green salad or fruit platter.

Variation: Croque Madame
Fry an egg over-easy in a small skillet and place the fried egg on top of the sandwich as soon as it comes out of the oven. This is how I see most French people eat this sandwich.

SPAGHETTI CARBONARA ALLA MARIO

2 servings

My sister-in-law Toni is a beautiful Italian, and she and I were always on the hunt for the best carbonara wherever we went. Not any-more! This recipe from Mario Pierallini is the best! While in Lucca, Italy, we dined and cooked along with Mario, the head chef of the family. He says the black pepper just makes this dish!

4	ounces uncooked spaghetti
1	egg plus 1 egg yolk
4	strips bacon
	or 2 slices pancetta
	(Italian bacon), diced
1	tablespoon olive oil

1	garlic clove, minced
1/4	teaspoon salt
1/8	teaspoon ground black pepper
1/4	cup freshly grated Parmesan
	cheese (see Note p. 67)
	Crushed red pepper

1. Cook the spaghetti according to package directions.

2. Meanwhile, beat the egg and egg yolk in a small bowl. Set aside.

3. Cook the bacon in a large saucepan over medium-high heat until it is cooked through, not crisp. Remove it from the pan with a slotted spoon and drain it on paper towels. Leave the bacon fat in the pan and add the olive oil. Heat. Add the garlic and cook for about 30 seconds, just until you smell the aroma. Remove from the heat. Return the bacon to the pan.

Italian pancetta has a unique flavor. If you can find it, it's worth the splurge.

4. When the spaghetti is cooked, lift it out of the water with tongs and put it in the saucepan with the bacon. Measure 1 cup of pasta water and discard the rest. Place the saucepan over medium-high heat. Pour the hot pasta water over the spaghetti and use tongs to turn the spaghetti over several times. Add the beaten eggs and continue stirring quickly to cook the egg.

5. When the water is almost evaporated, add the salt, black pepper, and cheese. Continue to stir until well-mixed. When the cheese is mostly melted, take the pan off the heat.

6. Divide the carbonara between two plates and serve immediately. Pass the crushed red pepper.

Italians would have this as a course by itself, but to make a whole meal, serve with Italian bread and a green vegetable or salad of your choice.

Variation: You may use 1 cup of milk in place of the water. But the dish will have more egg flavor if you use water.

SPAGHETTI AND MEAT SAUCE

8 servings

This spaghetti has been a favorite meal in our home for many years. The kids would come home from school and smell the sauce cooking, and the boys could not resist grabbing a piece of bread and dipping it into the sauce as a snack before dinner. I can still see them today in this ritual and it brings back many happy memories. This meal also became a tradition every Halloween. Before the kids left for trick-or-treating, they filled up on this delicious dinner. Everyone loved eating Mom's homemade spaghetti. The ingredient that makes this special? Brown sugar!

3   (14.5-ounce) cans diced tomatoes, undrained
2   tablespoons plus 1 teaspoon olive oil, divided
1/3 cup chopped white onion
3   garlic cloves, minced
1½ pounds lean ground beef
1   (6-ounce) can tomato paste
3   tablespoons brown sugar

1½ teaspoons dried oregano
1   teaspoon salt
1/2 teaspoon dried basil
1/2 teaspoon dried thyme
1   bay leaf
2   cups hot water
1   pound uncooked spaghetti
Freshly grated Parmesan cheese (optional) (see Note p. 67)

1. Optional step: Put the tomatoes and liquid in a blender and pulse 4 or 5 seconds to crush. Set aside.

2. Heat 2 tablespoons of the oil in a large pot or skillet over medium heat. Add the onion and garlic and cook and stir until the onion is soft but not brown. Increase the heat to medium-high and add the meat. Continue to cook, stirring until the meat is browned. Stir in the tomato paste with a wooden spoon. Cook until the mixture starts sticking to the pan, about 5 minutes. Add the reserved tomatoes, brown sugar, oregano, salt, basil, thyme, and bay leaf. Mix well. Stir in the water. Bring to a boil, decrease the heat, and simmer uncovered about 2 hours, stirring periodically and adding more hot water if the sauce gets too thick.

3. Twenty minutes before serving, cook the spaghetti according to package directions. Drain.

4. Put the spaghetti in a bowl, sprinkle in the remaining 1 teaspoon of oil, and combine. Serve the sauce in another bowl. Pass the cheese.

Serve with a tossed green salad, corn or green beans, and **Garlic Bread** (p. 227).

CAN DO AHEAD

This sauce can be made ahead of time. Cook the spaghetti while you reheat the sauce.

Variations:

◆ Use just 1 pound of ground beef and add 1/2 pound of bulk Italian sausage.

◆ Substitute **Classic Italian Meatballs**, on the next page, for the ground beef. Add the meatballs to the sauce while the spaghetti is cooking.

Can be made *Meatless*.

CLASSIC ITALIAN MEATBALLS

About 24 (2-inch) meatballs

4   slices white or wheat bread
1   pound ground beef
2   eggs, beaten
1/3 cup milk
1   teaspoon salt

1/4 teaspoon dried oregano
Dash ground black pepper
2   tablespoons olive oil, for
     frying (optional)

1. Tear the bread into uniformly small pieces, put in a blender or food processor, and pulse to make fine crumbs.

2. In a medium bowl, mix the meat with the bread crumbs. Add the eggs, milk, salt, oregano, and pepper. Mix with a fork until smooth. With your hands, form about 24 meatballs onto a sheet pan. Or use a medium spring-release ice cream scoop to form uniform balls.

3. To fry the meatballs, heat the oil in a large skillet over medium-high heat. Add the meatballs in batches, turning them often until cooked through. To bake, preheat the oven to 375 degrees. Bake in the sheet pan about 20 minutes or until no pink remains.

Try these flavorful meatballs on their own, in a tomato sauce, or in a submarine sandwich. They make a great meatball sandwich on my Italian (or French) bread for another "Italian Night experience."

CONVERSATION STARTER:

I've noticed you haven't been eating much at dinner lately. Is everything okay?

SPAGHETTI WITH QUICK TOMATO SAUCE

4 servings

This sauce reminds me of something my mother made years ago, only she served it with just bread rather than pasta. If you have your own garden with vine-ripened tomatoes, or access to a local farmer's market or farm stand, you can enjoy this sauce all summer long. (See Variations.) Be sure to use fresh basil for the fullest flavor.

Another reason I love to make this sauce in the summertime is that it's quick and delicious without heating up the whole kitchen. Just remember, this is not meant to replace a slow-simmered sauce; it is just another option.

8 ounces uncooked spaghetti	1/4 teaspoon coarse salt
1/4 cup olive oil	1/3 cup thinly sliced fresh basil, or 2 teaspoons dried
6 to 8 garlic cloves, minced	
2 (14.5-ounce) cans diced tomatoes, undrained	Grated Parmesan cheese (see Note, p. 67)
1/4 teaspoon crushed red pepper (optional)	

1. Cook the spaghetti according to package directions.

2. Meanwhile, heat the oil in a large skillet over medium heat. Add the garlic and cook about 30 seconds. Add the tomatoes, crushed red pepper, and salt. Stir and cook over medium-high heat about 10 minutes.

3. Reserving some of the water, drain the pasta and add it to the sauce. Using tongs, coat the pasta with the sauce. If it is too dry, add some reserved pasta water. Cook over medium heat another 5 minutes. Add the basil and cook 1 minute.

4. To serve, divide among four serving plates and pass the cheese.

Serve with a tossed green salad and **Italian Bread** (p. 224).

Variations:

◆ Substitute 6 to 8 medium vine-ripened or Roma tomatoes, peeled and diced (about 3½ cups) for the canned tomatoes.

◆ Add 6 ounces cooked bulk Italian sausage to the sauce with the tomatoes.

◆ Serve the sauce over fresh pasta.

CONVERSATION STARTER:

Let's have a vegetable garden this summer! We can grow our own tomatoes and basil for this dish and our pizzas and bruschetta. We can go to the nursery Saturday morning to get starts and seeds. What other herbs and vegetables shall we plant?

Meatless

BOLOGNESE SAUCE WITH PASTA

8 servings

3   tablespoons olive oil
1/2   medium yellow onion, minced
1   carrot, peeled and
      finely shredded (about 1/2 cup)
1   celery rib, including leaves, diced
1   teaspoon coarse salt
1   (6-ounce) can tomato paste
1   pound ground beef
1   pound ground pork
1   cup red wine

3   bay leaves
1   teaspoon ground black pepper
3   (14.5-ounce) cans diced
      tomatoes, undrained
1   pound uncooked spaghetti,
      fettuccine, linguine, or penne

Grated Parmesan cheese

When I am craving real Italian food, this is the recipe I reach for. The name Bolognese means a thick, full-bodied meat sauce that's a staple of Bologna in northern Italy. Whatever pasta you choose, you will not be disappointed. Your family and friends will come running! Be sure to plan ahead because the sauce simmers for a couple of hours.

CAN DO AHEAD

This sauce can be made ahead of time. Cook the pasta while you reheat the sauce.

1. Heat the oil in a large pot or Dutch oven over medium heat. Stir in the onion, carrot, celery, and salt. Cook, stirring, until the onion is soft, about 4 minutes.

2. Stir in the tomato paste and cook another 5 minutes. Let the tomato paste stick to the pan a bit and become a little brown to provide a rich flavor.

3. Crumble in the meat and continue cooking, stirring to break it up until all the meat liquid has evaporated and the meat is lightly browned, about 10 minutes.

4. Pour in the wine and cook, scraping the meat bits from the bottom of the pan, until the liquid has evaporated, 3 to 4 minutes.

5. If desired, puree the tomatoes in a blender or food processor. Pour into the meat mixture and add the bay leaves and pepper. Bring to a boil. Decrease the heat and simmer, stirring occasionally, until the sauce is a rich, dark red color, 2 to 3 hours. The longer you cook the sauce, the better it will become. (A layer of oil will float to the top toward the end of cooking. It can be spooned off or, as is done traditionally, stirred into the sauce.) While the sauce is cooking, add hot water if the sauce becomes too thick.

6. About 30 minutes before serving, cook the pasta according to package directions. Drain the pasta, reserving the water.

7. When the sauce is done cooking, remove the bay leaves and add the pasta. Stir to coat the pasta with the sauce and cook until bubbly. Add some of the pasta water as necessary (which helps the sauce stick to the pasta) for the desired consistency. Remove from the heat and stir in the cheese to taste. Season with additional salt and pepper to taste.

8. To serve, transfer the pasta mixture to a large pasta bowl. Pass additional cheese.

Serve with a tossed green salad and hot **Italian Bread** (p. 224).

SPAGHETTI WITH CHEESY TOMATO CREAM SAUCE

4 servings

My sister Sue taught us how to make this recipe. It saves us over and over again on Italian night when we need a quick dinner. It's a great dinner anytime! For a variation, use gnocchi (Italian dumplings) in place of the pasta.

1/4 cup olive oil
4 garlic cloves, minced
1/2 small white onion, minced
2 (14.5-ounce) cans diced tomatoes, undrained (see Note)
1/2 cup grated Parmesan cheese, plus additional for sprinkling
1/2 cup cream or half-and-half
1/4 cup low-fat ricotta cheese, about 2 ounces

20 fresh basil leaves, or 1/2 teaspoon dried
1/4 teaspoon coarse salt
1/4 teaspoon ground black pepper
1/4 teaspoon crushed red pepper (optional)
8 ounces uncooked spaghetti or the pasta of your choice

1. Heat the oil in a medium saucepan over medium-high heat. Cook and stir the garlic and onion until you smell the aroma. Remove from the heat and add the tomatoes, 1/2 cup of the Parmesan cheese, cream, ricotta, basil, salt, black pepper, and crushed red pepper, if using. Cook over low heat until the sauce coats the back of a spoon, 10 to 15 minutes.

2. Meanwhile, cook the pasta according to package directions. Drain.

3. Divide the pasta among four plates and spoon the sauce over each. Serve, passing the additional cheese.

Serve with a green vegetable or a salad and your favorite Italian bread.

Note: For a smoother sauce, puree the tomatoes first in a blender for a few seconds.

CONVERSATION STARTER:

You had a pretty good report card this time. That B+ in math is great! But I know you could do better in science. What can we do to help you with that?

Meatless

BOW-TIE PASTA WITH CHERRY TOMATOES & FRESH BASIL *6 to 8 servings*

1   pound uncooked bow-tie pasta
1½   pounds cherry tomatoes
1/3 cup chopped fresh basil
1/4 cup capers, drained
1/3 cup olive oil
1   large garlic clove, minced
15   pitted black olives, sliced
1/2 cup grated Parmesan cheese (see Note)
Crushed red pepper
Coarse salt and ground black pepper

1.   Cook the pasta according to package directions.

2.   Meanwhile, slice the tomatoes in half and place them in a large skillet. Add the basil, capers, oil, garlic, and olives. Set aside while the pasta cooks.

3.   Drain the pasta. Place the tomato mixture over medium-high heat and cook until heated through. Stir in the pasta. Sprinkle on the Parmesan cheese. Add a few shakes of crushed red pepper or pass with the pasta. Season to taste with salt and pepper. Serve immediately.

Serve with Italian or French bread or **Garlic Bread** (p. 227) with cheese.

What I love about Italian cooking is that you don't need much in the kitchen to make a great meal—tomatoes, garlic, olive oil, and fresh herbs. It's fast and easy and healthy. Add a piece of good bread and you have a meal. This recipe from my friend Ann makes the kind of light pasta you eat in a restaurant and wish you could make at home. Now you can!

A Note About Parmesan:

If you can find it, for a real treat buy fresh chunks of Parmigiano-Reggiano cheese imported from the Emilia-Romagna region of Italy, then grate it yourself right before using. The flavor is incomparable! Some consider this the "king" of Italian cheeses.

Meatless

PENNE WITH SAUSAGE, RED POTATOES, AND GREEN BEANS *4 servings*

8	ounces uncooked penne pasta	1	tablespoon butter
4	small red potatoes, quartered	1	pound fresh green beans, trimmed and cut in half (see Note)
8	ounces low-fat spicy bulk Italian sausage	1	tablespoon coarsely chopped fresh parsley
1/4	cup minced yellow onion		Salt and ground black pepper
2	small garlic cloves, minced	1/2	cup grated Romano, Asiago, or Parmesan cheese, plus additional
1	cup chicken broth		
1	tablespoon olive oil		

1. Cook the pasta according to package directions. Drain.

2. Steam the potatoes or cook them in boiling salted water until tender. At the same time, steam the beans or cook in the microwave until tender, 6 to 12 minutes.

3. Meanwhile, brown the sausage in a Dutch oven or large pot over medium heat. Add the onion and garlic; cook and stir until the onion is soft and the sausage is completely cooked. Pour in the broth and simmer for 3 minutes. Stir in the oil and butter until the butter melts. Add the green beans, potatoes, and pasta. Mix well with a large spoon. Add the parsley and salt and pepper to taste.

4. Decrease the heat to low and sprinkle 1/2 cup of the cheese over the mixture. Cover the pan and cook a few more minutes until the cheese is melted.

5. Serve immediately in the same pot or spoon the mixture into a large, shallow serving bowl or deep platter. Pass the extra cheese.

Note: As a speedy alternative to preparing fresh beans, heat 1 (14.5-ounce) can of cut green beans, drained, in the microwave and add them with the potatoes and pasta.

Can be made *Meatless*.

I got this recipe from Ann Luther, one of the best cooks I know. She and I became close friends 34 years ago in New York. We cooked for each other's families, traded recipes, and spent many hours together bargain hunting antiques with our babies. This family favorite has hot sausage to spice it up for our taste buds; you may use the sausage of your choice.

RED-AND-WHITE MOSTACCIOLI *("little mustaches")*

10 to 12 servings

1   pound uncooked mostaccioli or other tubular pasta
Alfredo Sauce (p. 71)
1   (26-ounce) jar meatless spaghetti sauce
        or 3 cups homemade sauce, divided (see Note)
3   cups shredded mozzarella cheese, divided

1.   Preheat the oven to 350 degrees.

2.   Cook the pasta according to package directions; drain.

3.   Meanwhile, prepare sauce of Fettuccine Alfredo (omit the pasta).

4.   Spread a thin layer of spaghetti sauce in a 9 x 13-inch baking dish. Layer half the pasta, half the Alfredo sauce, half the spaghetti sauce, and 1½ cups of the cheese. Repeat the layering with the remaining pasta, Alfredo sauce, spaghetti sauce, and cheese.

5.   Cover with aluminum foil and bake about 30 minutes or until it is hot and bubbly.

Serve with a tossed green salad and Italian or French bread.

Note: You may use meat sauce or meatless; I prefer meatless. When I make my own spaghetti sauce (p. 62 made meatless), I often double the recipe so I can freeze half of it to have on hand for this recipe. But purchased sauce is almost as good.

One day many years ago, before I had ever been to Italy, my sister-in-law Kathy in Phoenix told me about how she mixed her white sauce with her red sauce for pasta. That led me to devise this dish, Alfredo sauce layered with spaghetti sauce and served over mostaccioli pasta. This dish has become a legend in our home. When the kids were barely 12 years old, they were making it when I was out of town, and they still make it. It is one of my easiest and best recipes.

CAN DO AHEAD

This dish can be made ahead of time. Refrigerate until ready to bake. Lower the oven temperature 25 degrees and add 15 minutes to the baking time.

CONVERSATION STARTER:

There's a lot of talk about living "green" – recycling, reusing, buying local products, cutting back on gas use, etc. What can we as a family do to make a difference?

LASAGNA BOLOGNESE WITH BÉCHAMEL SAUCE

8 to 10 servings

This is my favorite lasagna. When I bite into it, my taste buds transport me right back to Bruno's Restaurant on the Costa del Sol, Spain. (We ate some of the finest Italian food in Spain.) The béchamel (white) sauce makes all the difference. I love it mixed with bolognese (meat) sauce in this recipe. The fresh Parmesan cheese—not the mozzarella and ricotta in a typical American lasagna—gives it just enough cheese flavor. I make my own pasta for this recipe, duplicating the wide, flat noodles I remember from Italy. This is a time-consuming recipe, so get your kids to help you with it. For me every bite of this lasagna is well worth the effort. And the leftovers are even better!

Bolognese Sauce (p. 65)
1 pound uncooked lasagna noodles (see Note)
3/4 cup (1½ sticks) unsalted butter
3/4 cup all-purpose flour
4¾ cups milk, warmed

1/8 teaspoon ground nutmeg
1/2 teaspoon salt
1½ cups freshly grated Parmesan cheese
1/4 cup (1/2 stick) unsalted butter

1. Prepare the Bolognese Sauce and set aside.

2. Preheat the oven to 400 degrees and grease a 10½ x 15½-inch casserole dish. Or make two lasagnas with two greased square pans. Bake one and freeze the other.

3. Cook the pasta according to package directions. (If you're making home-made pasta, have it ready to cook as soon as the béchamel sauce is done.)

4. Meanwhile, make the béchamel sauce: Melt the butter in a large saucepan over medium heat. Stir in the flour and cook, stirring, about 3 minutes. Add the milk a little at a time, stirring constantly with a whisk to avoid lumping. When all the milk is mixed in, add the nutmeg and salt.

5. Continue cooking, stirring constantly, until the sauce thickens and becomes smooth. Remove from the heat and let stand while the pasta cooks.

6. Drain the pasta and lay it out on a cookie sheet to prevent it from sticking together as it cools.

7. To assemble the lasagna, spread a thin layer of bolognese sauce (just a few tablespoons) in the prepared casserole, then one-third of the pasta, 2 cups of the bolognese sauce, 2 cups of the bechamel sauce, and 1/2 cup of the Parmesan. Repeat layering two more times. (Refrigerate or freeze any left-over bolognese sauce to serve over pasta for another meal.) Dot the top with the butter to keep the lasagna moist during baking. Bake 20 to 30 minutes until golden brown and bubbly.

CAN DO AHEAD

You can freeze the lasagna before you bake it. Let it thaw completely in the refrigerator before baking and bake 10 to 15 minutes longer than directed.

Serve with a tossed green salad and **Italian Bread**, homemade (p. 224) or from the bakery.

Note: Substitute your own fresh pasta (p. 76) for the packaged lasagna noodles.

EASY AMERICAN LASAGNA

8 to 10 servings

1   **pound mild bulk Italian sausage or ground beef**
1   **(26-ounce) jar meatless spaghetti sauce or marinara sauce (see Note)**
1   **pound uncooked lasagna noodles**
1   **(15-ounce) package ricotta cheese**
1/2 **cup grated Parmesan cheese**
2   **eggs**
1/4 **teaspoon ground black pepper**
4   **cups (1 pound) shredded mozzarella cheese**
3   **tablespoons butter (optional)**

I started making this quick and easy lasagna during my first year of marriage. My husband thought I was a wonderful cook! He loved it and so did our friends—and they still do!

1. Brown the meat in a large skillet. Drain off the fat. Stir in the spaghetti sauce and simmer for 10 minutes.

2. Remove 16 noodles from the package and cook according to package directions. Drain. Lay out the cooked pasta in a single layer on a 15-inch-sheet of aluminum foil to cool. (The foil will be reused to cover the baking dish.)

3. Preheat the oven to 350 degrees. Grease a 9 x 13-inch baking dish.

4. Mix the ricotta cheese, Parmesan cheese, eggs, and pepper in a large bowl.

5. To assemble the lasagna, spread one-quarter of the meat sauce in the prepared baking dish. Arrange four noodles lengthwise over the sauce, overlapping the edges. Spread one-fourth of the cheese mixture and sprinkle 1 cup of the mozzarella cheese over the pasta. Repeat the layers three more times, ending with the mozzarella. Dot with the butter around the edges, if desired.

6. Cover with the foil and bake 35 to 45 minutes or until bubbly. Let stand 5 minutes before serving.

Serve with a tossed green salad and hot Italian bread.

Note: If desired, substitute 3 cups of homemade sauce for the purchased sauce. Two choices include my Spaghetti Sauce (made meatless), page 62, and a double recipe of my Marinara Sauce, page 140.

CAN DO AHEAD

You can freeze the lasagna before you bake it. Let it thaw completely in the refrigerator before baking and bake 10 to 15 minutes longer than directed.

FRESH LASAGNA NOODLES

About 2 pounds, or 8 servings

Fresh lasagna noodles have so much more flavor than dried noodles purchased from the store, and rolling out the dough using a pasta machine can be a fun family activity.

The rule of thumb for making fresh pasta is one egg to 3/4 cup flour and a pinch of salt, so you can easily decrease or increase this basic recipe for your needs.

*Remember these easy proportions:
5 eggs = 6 servings;
6 eggs = 8 servings;
7 eggs = 10 servings;
9 eggs = 12 servings.*

4½ **cups all-purpose flour**
6   **large eggs, at room temperature**
1/4 **teaspoon plus 1 tablespoon salt**

1. Measure the flour into a large bowl. Make a well in the center and break the eggs into the well. Add the 1/4 teaspoon of salt. Beat the eggs with a fork and gradually mix in the flour. The result should be ragged, sticky dough.

2. Turn the dough onto a lightly floured surface and knead until it is well-mixed, about 5 minutes. If the dough is too sticky, add flour. If the dough is too dry, add a little water. A good mixture will not stick to your fingers. Cut the dough into four pieces. Cover them with plastic wrap so they do not dry out.

    Variation: The dough may also be mixed in a food processor and then kneaded for 3 to 4 minutes before rolling out.

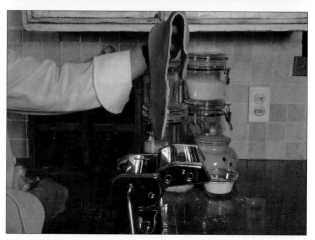

3. Roll one piece of dough through the pasta maker five times, beginning at the setting #1 and ending at #5. Add a little flour if the dough starts to stick on the counter as you roll it thinner and thinner. Roll the dough to about double the length of the lasagna pan.

4. Lay the dough out on the counter and cut lengths to fit the pan. Repeat with the other pieces. Note: If the dough is too soft, you may have difficulty rolling it. Knead in a little flour, but be careful not to get the dough too dry.

5. Bring a large pot of water to a rapid boil. Add 1 tablespoon salt. Cook the noodles a few at a time just until they get soft and slightly sticky.

6. Remove the noodles with a slotted or pasta spoon and lay them out on a dish towel or cookie sheet to prevent them from sticking together as they cool.

CHICKEN MARSALA WITH MUSHROOMS

4 servings

This dish is an old Italian favorite and one of my favorite meals. I love the mild taste of the wine that comes through. Remember that the alcohol cooks out as the sauce simmers.

4   boneless, skinless chicken breasts, or 1 to 1½ pounds chicken tenders
Salt and ground black pepper
1/4   cup plus 1 tablespoon all-purpose flour, divided
2   tablespoons olive oil

1/4   cup (1/2 stick) butter
8   ounces mushrooms, sliced
1   cup chicken broth
1¼   cups Marsala wine
8   ounces uncooked bow-tie pasta
1   tablespoon butter

1.   Using a heavy meat mallet, pound the chicken to 1/4 inch thick. (I place the chicken in a plastic bag and pound it flat.) Cut away any gristle. Season both sides with salt and pepper. (Cut flattened breasts in half if necessary to make portions easier to handle.) Spread 1/4 cup of the flour in a pie pan. Dredge both sides of the chicken in the flour and shake off the excess.

2.   Heat the oil in a large skillet over medium-high heat. When the oil is hot, place the chicken in the oil and sear both sides until lightly browned. The chicken will not take very long to cook because it is so thin. Remove the chicken to a platter.

3.   Add the 1/4 cup butter to the hot skillet and after it melts, sauté the mushrooms lightly. Stir the remaining 1 tablespoon flour into the chicken broth in a small bowl. Stir this and the wine into the mushrooms. Cook the sauce uncovered until the liquid is reduced by half.

4.   Meanwhile, cook the pasta according to package directions. Drain and return to the cooking pot. Stir in the 1 tablespoon butter until it melts.

5.   Return the chicken to the skillet for just a minute or two before serving. Divide the pasta onto individual plates, place the chicken atop, and pour the sauce over all. Serve with a tossed green salad, green beans, or broccoli, and French or Italian bread.

Variations:

◆   Use veal instead of chicken.

◆   Use madeira wine in place of marsala.

CHICKEN PICCATA WITH CAPERS

4 servings

4   thin boneless, skinless chicken breasts, or 1 to 1½ pounds chicken tenders
1/2 cup all-purpose flour
1/2 teaspoon salt
1/8 teaspoon ground black pepper
1   garlic clove, minced
2   tablespoons olive oil

1/4 cup (1/2 stick) butter, divided
1   cup white wine
     Juice of 1 lemon
3/4 cup chicken broth
4   ounces sliced mushrooms (optional)
1/4 cup capers, drained

1. Remove any extra fat or gristle from the chicken. Mix the flour, salt, pepper, and garlic in a resealable plastic bag. Shake each piece of chicken in the flour mixture.

2. In a large skillet over medium-high heat, heat the oil and 2 tablespoons of the butter until melted. Brown the chicken on both sides until light brown, about 4 minutes per side. Remove the chicken to a platter.

3. Leave all the frying juices in the pan, add the wine, stir, and bring to a boil. Immediately add the lemon juice, broth, and the remaining 2 tablespoons butter.

4. Place the chicken and mushrooms in the pan, cover, and simmer 10 to 15 minutes. Add the capers and cook covered 2 to 3 minutes. Remove the chicken to a platter and keep warm in a 175-degree oven. To thicken the sauce (if desired), add a dusting of flour and whisk until smooth. Increase the heat and simmer briskly to reduce the liquid and concentrate the sauce.

5. Spoon sauce over each chicken breast and serve immediately.

Serve with a green vegetable or tossed green salad, plus fettuccine or rice. If you serve fettuccine, sprinkle the cooked pasta with a little olive oil, fresh Parmesan cheese (see Note, p. 67), and fresh parsley.

Variation: Replace the chicken with fish, such as tilapia or halibut.

I love most anything with wine added to it. The alcohol evaporates as you cook and leaves just the taste. Capers also give this dish its special flavor. Don't be afraid to use them; they are very mild. This is a favorite recipe of my friend Deb, a great cook. From start to finish you can have this meal ready in about 30 minutes.

BAKED CHICKEN AND POTATOES ITALIANO

6 to 8 servings

I love this Italian meal because it is simple and light— a piece of chicken, a couple of potatoes, and some vegetables. Yet this is so delicious; it tastes just like you ordered it in Rome. Your oven does all the work for you. The fresh rosemary is what makes the dish authentic. You may substitute dried, but the rosemary is a must!

6	medium russet potatoes (about 2 pounds), peeled and quartered lengthwise
2	medium white onions, thickly sliced
1/4	cup olive oil, divided

6	chicken thighs
6	chicken drumsticks
2	tablespoons fresh rosemary leaves, or 2 teaspoons dried

Coarse salt
Freshly ground black pepper

1. Preheat the oven to 400 degrees.

2. Place the potato and onion pieces in a sheet pan or other large baking pan. Drizzle 2 tablespoons of the oil over them and stir to coat.

3. Remove the skin from the chicken pieces if desired. Rub the remaining 2 table-spoons of oil over the chicken and place in the pan between the potatoes and onions. Sprinkle the rosemary on the chicken. Sprinkle the salt and pepper generously over all.

4. Bake for 30 minutes. Turn the potatoes and onions and continue baking until the chicken is cooked through and the vegetables are tender, 15 to 25 more minutes. Transfer to a large platter and serve immediately.

Serve with green vegetables and butter beans and your choice of bread, if desired.

Variation: This recipe can be made with bone-in chicken breasts in place of thighs and drumsticks if you prefer white meat—one chicken breast per serving.

CONVERSATION STARTER:

Isn't this chicken dish great? You could have the same thing in Rome. That's where the Sistine Chapel is. Do you remember who painted the ceiling there? Can you imagine spending four years on your back on scaffolding painting that fresco?

FRESH TOMATO BRUSCHETTA WITH BASIL

3 to 4 servings

2   large hothouse or vine-ripened tomatoes, coarsely chopped
2   tablespoons olive oil
2   teaspoons chopped fresh basil
1/2 loaf crusty Italian bread, cut into 1/2-inch-thick slices
2   whole garlic cloves, cut in half (optional)
Olive oil, for brushing on the toasted bread
1/4 cup freshly grated Parmesan cheese
Coarse salt and freshly ground black pepper

1. Combine the tomatoes, oil, and basil in a medium bowl. Set aside.

2. Preheat the broiler to low broil and adjust the oven rack to the middle position. (Broiling on a higher rack will broil the bread too fast.)

3. Arrange the bread on a cookie sheet, place it under the broiler, and toast it on both sides to light brown. Watch closely so the bread doesn't burn.

4. Remove the pan from the oven. Rub the cut side of the garlic, if using, over one side of each slice of bread. Brush a tiny amount of oil over each slice. Divide the tomato mixture and spread it evenly over the slices; sprinkle evenly with the cheese.

5. Put the pan under the broiler and broil just until the cheese is melted and the tomato mixture is hot.
    Season to taste with salt and pepper and serve immediately.

For years we have all been hooked on this light, meatless meal, especially for lunch. As an alternative to Italian bread, I sometimes use my own French baguettes—they make the cutest little rounds, instead of big slices. You can use whatever you have in your kitchen.

Variations:

◆ Top each toast slice with one leaf of fresh basil, a thin slice of tomato, and a sprinkling of freshly grated Parmesan, mozzarella, or Cheddar cheese. Broil.

◆ Lay a trimmed spear of cooked asparagus on each bread slice before sprinkling on the cheese (my favorite!).

You can vary bruschetta in countless ways, like this one described at left.

CREAMY TOMATO BASIL SOUP

About 12 cups

I got this recipe from my friend Ann and then tweaked it quite a bit. It is as good as any soup you will eat in a restaurant. Everyone who tastes it wants more. It is that good! You can use prepared marinara sauce, or make your own from my recipe (p. 140).

1/2 cup (1 stick) butter
1 cup all-purpose flour
4 cups chicken broth
3½ cups half-and-half
1½ cups marinara sauce

1 (14.5-ounce) can diced tomatoes or 8 to 10 small vine-ripened tomatoes, diced
2 tablespoons chopped fresh basil, or 1/2 teaspoon dried
Coarse salt and ground black pepper

1. Melt the butter in a large saucepan over medium heat. Whisk in the flour and cook and stir for 5 minutes to slightly brown the mixture. Whisk in the broth. Increase the heat and cook and stir until thickened. Decrease the heat to low, stir in the half-and-half, and simmer for 20 minutes.

2. Stir in the marinara sauce, tomatoes, and basil, and cook until heated through. Season to taste with salt and pepper. Serve as is chunky-style, or puree in a food processor or blender if you prefer a smooth soup.

Serve with a salad and crackers or hot **corn bread** (p. 241), **Fresh Tomato Bruschetta with Basil** (p. 81), **Italian Bread** (p. 224), **French Baguettes** (p. 225), or **Garlic Bread** (p. 227).

Can be made *Meatless*. Substitute vegetable broth for the chicken broth.

CONVERSATION STARTER:
Did you read about the robots being developed that will have personalities? What do you think about that? What does it mean to be human?

WEDNESDAY
FISH &
MEATLESS

I learned from a nutritionist many years ago about the impor-tance of fish in our diet—at least one night a week, preferably two. While raising our family, however, buying good fish was out of our budget. I could feed my large family a fresh fish dinner only about once a month.

We tried fish sticks and frozen fillets but no one really craved them. So we made tuna casserole, which was a big favorite of the kids. Dad requested it too.

My need to keep the budget down and the variety up led me to combine two concepts into one: Fish & Meatless. Homemade macaroni and cheese became Emaly's favorite, and each Wednesday she never failed to request it.

With a theme like Fish & Meatless, Wednesday also became a good night for the breakfast foods that we all love so much. Breakfast at night sometimes tastes even better. Homemade waffles (p. 101), pancakes (p. 102), French toast (p.100), scrambled or fried eggs, and hash browns were a huge hit. We had this about once a month. We all enjoyed it, especially in the wintertime—all of us, that is, except Dad, so we planned this meal mostly when he was out of town.

Waffles are one of those meals that you can fix anytime—anytime you need a fast meal. All you need are 10 minutes and a good waffle iron. Our older kids could follow these simple recipes and put these ingredients together quickly if I was out of town.

Homemade tastes great. You have everything on hand. Homemade waffles and pancakes don't call for anything other than flour, milk, butter, salt, and sugar—and syrup. To this day my children crave my homemade waffles and pancakes!

This chapter includes more than a dozen wonderful fish or meatless recipes, and you can find many more meatless recipes in other chapters.

You can eat meatless or fish as many times a week as you would like. It's now possible to purchase good fresh, affordable salmon, which is our family's favorite fish. Nowadays more and more markets are carrying all kinds of fresh fish.

If you have a vegetarian in your family, maybe you'll choose to have fish/meatless three out of the five nights a week at home. On the other two nights you could prepare a "regular" meal, and the vegetarian in the family could eat leftovers. Or have brown rice, vegetables, and fruit as a vegetarian option no matter what else you're cooking.

Your family will love our Fish & Meatless night!

Liz

MAC & CHEESE KIDS CRAVE

6 servings

When my kids were little, we couldn't live without this cheesy, saucy recipe. My daughter Emaly begged for it every Wednesday! There is nothing fancy about it—it's just plain macaroni and cheese—but kids love it. Today I make it for the grandkids.

1½ cups uncooked elbow macaroni	1/8 teaspoon ground black pepper
3 tablespoons butter	2 cups milk
2 tablespoons all-purpose flour	2 cups shredded Cheddar
1/2 teaspoon salt	or Colby cheese

1. Preheat the oven to 350 degrees and lightly grease a square baking dish.

2. Cook the macaroni according to package directions. Drain and set aside.

3. Melt the butter in a medium saucepan over medium heat. Blend in the flour, salt, and pepper. Add the milk; cook and stir until the mixture is thick and bubbly. Decrease the heat to low and add the cheese. Stir until the cheese is melted.

4. Combine the cheese sauce with the macaroni and place in the prepared baking dish. Bake 35 to 40 minutes or until heated through. The finished dish may be seen on page 83.

Serve with your choice of vegetable.

CAN DO AHEAD

This dish can be made ahead and refrigerated. When ready to bake, bring to room temperature and bake as directed.

LINGUINE IN CLAM SAUCE

4 servings

8	ounces uncooked linguine	1	tablespoon butter
1/4	cup olive oil	1	tablespoon all-purpose flour
3	garlic cloves, minced	1/4	cup chopped fresh parsley
2	(6.5-ounce) cans chopped clams in clam juice, undrained		Freshly grated Parmesan cheese, for sprinkling

1. Cook the linguine according to package directions; drain.

2. Meanwhile, heat the oil in a saucepan over medium heat. Cook and stir the garlic for 30 seconds; do not burn it. Add the clams and juice, increase the heat, and cook until the mixture comes to a boil. Decrease the heat to low.

3. Melt the butter in a small bowl in the microwave. Stir in the flour. Add this to the clam mixture and stir for 1 minute. Add the parsley, increase the heat, and bring to a boil; remove from the heat. (The sauce will thicken a little so it will stick to the linguine.)

4. Put the linguine in a large bowl. Pour the clam sauce over and toss. Serve immediately and pass the Parmesan cheese.

Serve with a green salad and French bread.

If you like clams, you will enjoy this easy meal. And you'll want to soak up every last drop of sauce with French bread! Canned clams are readily available year-round, but if you have access to fresh clams, then substitute them along with bottled clam juice.

FRIED RICE, CANTONESE STYLE

4 servings

2	eggs	4	cups cooked long-grain white rice
1½	teaspoons salt	1	teaspoon Kitchen Bouquet browning sauce or soy sauce (see Note)
1/4	cup canola oil		
2	tablespoons minced onion	1	cup bean sprouts

1. Beat the eggs and salt with a fork in a small bowl.

2. Heat the oil in a stir-fry pan, wok, or skillet. Stir in the onion and egg mixture. Scramble until the eggs are quite dry.

3. Add the rice, browning sauce, and bean sprouts. Stir until the ingredients are heated and well-blended, about 10 minutes. Transfer to a bowl for serving.

Note: I learned in China not to use soy sauce because it tends to make the rice too soft, but you may use it if you prefer its flavor.

Variation: This recipe is meatless, but you can add 1/2 cup diced pork, ham, chicken, shrimp, or beef to the rice mixture. Use whatever you have left over!

Fried rice is a way that the Chinese people use their leftover rice, and Cantonese is a style of Chinese cooking that is typically based on mild spices. Fried rice is one of the fastest dishes to put together, and the variations are endless.

FISH TACOS

4 servings

8   white corn
     or taco-size flour tortillas

Buttermilk Ranch Dressing (p. 198),
    or bottled ranch dressing

1   pound tilapia
3   tablespoons olive oil
Salt and ground black pepper

CONDIMENTS:
Diced tomatoes
Sprigs of fresh cilantro
Sliced avocado
Shredded cabbage
Tabasco sauce

I like to try fish tacos wherever in the world we are traveling, and it's easy to do because they are popular everywhere. No wonder—they are easy to prepare and healthful since they're low in fat and calories. Most of the calories are in the dressing, so use it in moderation.

1. Preheat the oven to 325 degrees. Wrap the tortillas in aluminum foil and heat in the oven 20 to 30 minutes.

2. Meanwhile, make the dressing and set aside.

3. Prepare the condiments and put them in individual serving bowls and place them on the dinner table.

4. Heat the oil in a large skillet over medium heat and fry the fish. Cooking time will depend on the thickness of the fish. A thin fillet may need only 2 to 3 minutes on each side; a thicker fillet may need 4 to 5 minutes on each side. The fish is done when it flakes easily with a fork. The outside should be crunchy, the inside soft. Remove the fish to a plate and season with the salt and pepper.

5. To serve, pass the tortillas, fish, condiments, and dressing.

Serve with **Santa Fe Lime Rice** (p. 123), black beans, and a bowl of crunchy red, orange, and yellow bell pepper strips.

Variations:

◆ Use sour cream instead of the dressing: spread it on the warm tortillas, then add the fish and toppings.

◆ For crisp corn tortillas, fry them in hot canola oil following the instructions on page 110, step 2, using about 1/2 cup of oil.

◆ Omit the tomatoes, cilantro, avocado, and cabbage, and replace with **Mango Salsa** (p. 124).

EASY SKILLET SALMON

4 servings

I love grilled salmon, but on a cold and snowy winter evening, grilling is not an option, and that's where this recipe comes in. This is my favorite way to cook salmon in the kitchen.

1	tablespoon olive oil
4	salmon fillets, about 4 ounces each
2	tablespoons fresh lemon juice

Coarse salt and freshly ground pepper

1. Heat the oil in a large skillet over low heat. Place the salmon, skin side down, in the pan, pour the lemon juice over the fillets, and sprinkle with the salt and pepper.

2. Cook until the fish flakes easily with a fork, 10 to 12 minutes. Peel away the skin before serving and top with a drizzling of olive oil.

Serve with rice or **Garlic Mashed Potatoes** (p. 211), broccoli or asparagus, and French bread.

ROAST SALMON WITH VEGETABLES

4 servings

We are always coming up with different ways to prepare fish. Feel free to substitute other vegetables, such as broccoli, cauliflower, and asparagus.

4	medium potatoes	1	tablespoon lemon juice
2	small zucchini	2	tablespoons butter, melted
1	red bell pepper	1/2	teaspoon coarse salt
4	salmon fillets, about 4 ounces each	1/4	teaspoon pepper
		1/2	teaspoon dried tarragon leaves

1. Scrub the potatoes and cut them in half crosswise. Put them in a medium saucepan with cold water to cover and bring them to boiling. Decrease the heat to medium, cover, and cook just until tender, 20 to 30 minutes; drain.

2. Meanwhile, preheat the oven to 450 degrees. Grease a 9 x 13-inch baking pan.

3. Cut the potatoes into thick slices. Cut the zucchini and bell pepper in half lengthwise, then into 2-inch pieces.

4. Place the salmon in the prepared pan and drizzle with the lemon juice. Arrange the potato, zucchini, and bell pepper around the fish. Drizzle the butter over all and sprinkle with the salt, pepper, and tarragon. Bake 15 to 20 minutes, until the salmon flakes easily with a fork and the vegetables are tender.

For a grilled version of this meal, see page 159.

ROAST SALMON WITH TARRAGON

4 servings

4   salmon fillets, about 4 ounces each
3   tablespoons olive oil
Coarse salt and ground black pepper
Chopped fresh tarragon, or dried (optional)
White wine or fresh lemon juice, for sprinkling on salmon

Roasting is an easy, no-fuss way to prepare salmon, but be sure to remove the fillets from the oven before the centers are completely opaque. The fresh tarragon makes this dish delightfully unique.

1.   Preheat the oven to 425 degrees.

2.   Arrange the salmon in a baking dish. Drizzle the oil over the fish and season with the salt and pepper. Sprinkle with the tarragon.

3.   Roast about 10 minutes, sprinkle with the wine or lemon juice, and continue roasting 8 minutes or until the fish flakes easily with a fork.

Serve with rice pilaf, packaged long-grain and wild rice, brown rice, or steamed red potatoes. Steam or boil broccoli and top with a little butter, salt, and pepper. Add French bread.

CONVERSATION STARTER:
Tell me about something you learned in school today that you didn't know when you left the house this morning.

BLUEBERRY CROISSANT FRENCH TOAST

4 to 8 servings

2	cups frozen blueberries	4	medium or 8 small croissants, sliced lengthwise
3	eggs		
1	cup milk	3	tablespoons unsalted butter, divided
1	teaspoon sugar	1	tablespoon canola oil
1	teaspoon vanilla extract	3	heaping tablespoons brown sugar
1/4	teaspoon salt	1/3	cup maple syrup

*Breakfast foods
are some of our
favorite Wednesday
suppers.*

*When we were
visiting our friends
Ann and David,
Ann served us this
great treat. It
looked amazing on
the plate and tasted
even more amazing!
Every bite was a
blueberry feast.
Bacon, from
their own pigs,
complemented it
perfectly. I will
never forget that
meal—and you
won't either when
you make this
wonderful dish.*

1. Remove the blueberries from the freezer and allow to thaw on paper towels. (They need not completely thaw.)

2. Meanwhile, in a shallow dish or pie plate, beat the eggs, milk, sugar, vanilla, and salt with a whisk until blended. Place both halves of one croissant into the egg mixture and soak them without oversaturating, about 1 minute. Transfer the halves to a platter, allowing the excess batter to drain back into the dish. Spread 1/4 cup of the blueberries on one croissant half (2 table-spoons berries for small croissants). Top with the other croissant half and press down firmly. Repeat with the remaining croissants and reserve the remaining blueberries for the sauce.

3. Preheat the oven to 200 degrees.

4. Heat 1 tablespoon of the butter and the oil in a large skillet over medium heat. When the butter begins to bubble, add the filled croissants and pour any remaining batter over them, if desired. Cook until they are brown, 4 to 6 minutes. Turn them and cook the other side until brown. Turn again as necessary until there is no egg mixture leaking and the egg has finished cooking.

5. Transfer the croissants to a large, clean plate or platter and place in the oven to keep warm while you make the sauce.

6. In the same skillet, melt the remaining 2 tablespoons of butter over medium heat. Add the brown sugar and let the mixture foam. Add the syrup and the remaining blueberries. Simmer about 4 minutes. (The blueberries will create more juice.) Place the croissants on individual plates; cut large croissants in half for smaller servings, if desired. Quickly ladle the sauce evenly over each croissant and serve immediately.

Variations: Replace the frozen blueberries with fresh blueberries, raspberries or blackberries in season. For a lower-fat version, substitute French bread for the croissants.

QUICK & EASY
EGG SUPPERS

Eggs are one of the easiest, quickest meals to prepare. And there are so many ways to fix them! Here are just a few possibilities.

◆ **Scrambled eggs, omelettes** or a **frittata** (an Italian omelette that usually has the ingredients mixed with the eggs rather than being folded inside): Add your choice of small chunks of cheese, chopped herbs, sautéed mushrooms, leftover cooked vegetables and/or meats. Serve with slices of tomato sautéed in a little butter, or with a green salad and my **Honey Oat Wheat Bread** (p. 229) or **Hearth Bread** (p. 230), toasted.

◆ **Poached eggs or soft boiled eggs:** Serve on toasted bread or English muffins, or place on top of freshly steamed asparagus and grate a little Parmesan over all. (Soft boiled eggs take 3 to 4 minutes after the water comes to a boil.)

◆ **Baked eggs:** Preheat the oven to 325 degrees. Break one to two eggs into a buttered custard cup. Dot with butter or pour a teaspoon of cream over the top. Bake for 12 to 18 minutes until set, season with salt and pepper, and serve. Serve with steamed spinach or broccoli. **Variations:** Put a tablespoon or two of salsa in the custard cup before adding eggs. • Top with buttered bread crumbs or grated cheese before baking. • Add chopped basil or tarragon before serving. • Bake in a toast "cup" using a muffin pan. Trim off crusts and butter both sides of slices of bread. Press into muffin cups. Bake for about 5 minutes until bread is very lightly toasted. Break eggs into toast cups. Bake as above.

◆ **Creamed hard-boiled eggs or Deviled Eggs** (p. 272): Quarter the eggs. Fold gently into béchamel sauce (use the recipe from **Lasagna Bolognese,** p. 74) or condensed cream of mushroom or cream of celery soup that has been heated with a little milk. Stir in a little curry powder for a twist. Serve on English muffins or **Old-Fashioned Biscuits** (p. 240), with fresh fruit or **Reds & Greens Salad** (p. 191).

*Sauté **mushrooms** (p. 155), sliced or whole, and serve alongside or mixed in to scrambled eggs or an omelette.*

THE FOOD NANNY RESCUES DINNER

THURSDAY
MEXICAN NIGHT

It was only natural for our family to include Mexican Night as one of our themes. With Mexico as close as it is to the south of us, no wonder Mexican food has caught on in our country to the extent it has. How would we ever get along anymore without salsa? I know that in our family we would not be happy without it! We love our Mexican food.

I've learned so much about Mexican dishes and techniques from a lovely Mexican family Steve and I frequently spend time with. One evening while her husband was at work, Zulma joined me at a friend's home to show me how she makes fresh tortillas (p. 108), then she and sons Max and Diego stayed to sample my chicken tacos.

I grew up in California where we could get wonderful Mexican food. Most of the time we just wanted crispy fried beef tacos. My mother especially loved them; my dad, not so much. So a girls' night out would usually mean a great taco someplace with chips and salsa.

The best chips and salsa I ever ate were in Laguna Beach, California, in a café perched on a cliff above the beach. It serves its salsa with a big, fresh slice of avocado on the side. The chips are amazing as well.

Today we have become much more sophisticated in fixing Mexican food in our own homes. Cilantro is now in grocery stores across America, when only 15 years ago it was hard to find. Fajitas have become well-known among Americans. Of course enchiladas, burritos, tortilla soup, taco salad, taco soup, nachos, quesadillas, and chicken tacos have all become household words and favorite foods.

In this chapter I have included some authentic Mexican recipes, like my chicken tacos, my Mexican beans and rice, carne asada tacos, homemade tortillas, and sopaipillas. These recipes are the real deal. You must try them. They are not difficult. My directions are easy to follow. I have also included Navajo tacos, which originated in the American Southwest, instead of Mexico, but the flavors are similar.

If I were to take a poll of my family for their consistently favorite dinner, they would probably vote for the chicken tacos. Enjoy!

Liz

HOMEMADE CORN TORTILLAS
Twelve 6-inch tortillas

Rather than buying tortillas, try making them yourself with masa harina (corn flour). These are surprisingly quick and easy to make. You don't even need a special press; just press them out very flat with a rolling pin. Masa harina has a finer texture than cornmeal. It can be found along with other flour and cornmeal products in large grocery stores and Mexican-American markets. It can be stored in the freezer for up to six months, so have it on hand for anytime you want these fresh tortillas.

1   cup masa harina (corn flour)
1   cup plus 2 tablespoons hot water

1. Mix the masa harina with the water in a small bowl. Cover with plastic wrap and let stand for 30 minutes.

2. Divide the dough evenly into 12 mounds. Roll into balls and cover each with plastic wrap to keep them from drying out as you're working with them.

3. To press, place one ball between two sheets of medium to heavy plastic cut into a circle slightly larger than a finished tortilla. (A gallon-size resealable freezer bag works well.) Use a tortilla press or roll out using a rolling pin until the dough is as thin as possible without breaking apart when you peel it from the plastic. (These will never be as thin as the store-bought ones.) Practice a couple of times; you can reuse the dough.

4. Cook in a small heavy skillet or griddle (cast iron is ideal) over high heat about 45 seconds per side. No oil is necessary. Transfer tortillas to a cloth-lined basket and cover with cloth, or wrap tortillas in a large sheet of aluminum foil and keep warm in a 250-degree oven.

Serve these for open-face tacos or as an accompaniment with **Mexican Beans & Rice** (p.122) or **Beef & Bean Taco Soup** (p. 120). They also make a delicious quick snack with a little butter and honey or cinnamon and sugar.

Using a rolling pin, at left, to roll out tortillas between plastic sheets; and using a tortilla press, opposite.

TACO SALAD

6 servings

This is my family's favorite taco salad because of its mix of warm and cold ingredients. You may vary the ingredients in so many ways. Try black beans instead of kidney beans. Try pepper Jack cheese in place of Cheddar. Have fun experimenting if you like.

1 pound lean ground beef
1 (15-ounce) can kidney beans, drained
1 (15-ounce) can corn, drained
1 (2.25 ounce) can sliced black olives, drained
1 (1.2-ounce) packet taco seasoning

1 head romaine lettuce, torn into bite-size pieces
2 cups shredded Cheddar cheese
2 vine-ripened tomatoes, diced
Buttermilk Ranch Dressing (p. 198), or bottled ranch dressing
Corn chips, coarsely crushed
Fresh Salsa (p. 125)

1. Brown the meat in a large saucepan over medium heat. Drain off the fat. Add the beans, corn, olives, and taco seasoning. Stir and cook until heated through. Keep warm.

2. Combine the lettuce, cheese, and tomatoes in a large salad bowl. Add the meat mixture and toss lightly to combine. Serve immediately.

3. Pass the salad dressing, corn chips, and salsa.

Can be made *Meatless*: Omit the meat and add more beans.

CONVERSATION STARTER:
What does it mean to be a citizen? How can we be better citizens of this country?

INDIAN FRY BREAD
Up to 12 servings

White Bread (p. 228)
3 cups canola oil
Butter
Honey

Jam or jelly
Peanut butter
Cinnamon/sugar
Flavored syrup

Prepare White Bread to the point of dividing the dough into thirds. Set aside two of the sections to bake into loaves later. Use the remaining third of the dough for this recipe, proceeding as follows:

1. Pinch off pieces of dough about the size of a dinner roll and stretch them and roll out to flatten into a disk about 4 inches in diameter. Make about four disks at a time and set them on the counter.

2. In a medium skillet over medium-high heat, heat the oil to 360 degrees on a candy thermometer. The oil should bubble when you drop the dough into it. (The oil may splatter, so be sure that little children are not underfoot.) Fry one disk at a time until light brown. Flip with tongs and fry on the other side until light brown. The dough will puff up a little.

3. Drain the fried pieces on triple paper towels set on a dish or plate. Keep warm in a 200-degree oven while you fry all the pieces.

4. If desired, let the kids begin eating while you are frying. Have the toppings already on the table before you begin, and let the fry bread cool slightly before serving.

CONVERSATION STARTER:

Native Americans didn't originally make fry bread in their villages, only after they were forced onto the reservations. Can you imagine our family being forced out of our home like that?

Fry bread was created in the 1800s, when Native Americans were forced onto reservations and given rations of flour and lard by the government. So the Native Americans made dough and fried it in the lard. Many of us here in the West have made "Indian fry bread" a family tradition using white bread dough. (In Utah it became known as "scones," though obviously very different from the English version.) With peanut butter and jam or jelly, this was dinner on an occasional meatless night when my husband was out of town. My kids were in heaven!

SOPAIPILLAS

About 18 sopaipillas

If you have not tried sopaipillas for dessert with Mexican foods, you're missing a real treat! They are much like the Indian fry bread on the preceding page, except this recipe is a biscuit dough rather than a yeast dough, so it is quicker to make.

2 cups all-purpose flour	1 tablespoon shortening
1 tablespoon baking powder	3/4 cup lukewarm water
1/2 teaspoon salt	Canola oil, for frying

1. Combine the flour, baking powder, and salt in a medium bowl. Cut in the shortening with a pastry blender. Gradually add the water, stirring with a fork. The mixture will be a little crumbly.

2. Turn the dough onto a lightly floured surface and knead lightly until the dough is smooth. Divide the dough in half and let stand for 10 minutes.

3. Roll one half of the dough into a rounded square to 1/8-inch thickness. Cut into thirds vertically and horizontally to make 9 pieces. Repeat with the other half of the dough.

4. Pour the oil to 1 inch deep in a small skillet and heat over medium heat. (The oil is hot if it bubbles when a bit of dough is dropped into it.) Stretch the dough squares slightly before dropping into the hot oil, as shown below left. Cook about 30 seconds on each side. Remove with tongs and drain on paper towels.

Serve warm with honey and/or honey butter.

Variation: Roll the hot sopaipillas in a mixture of 1 tablespoon sugar and 1/2 teaspoon cinnamon.

FRIDAY PIZZA NIGHT

It was over 25 years ago that my family started making pizza our Friday night tradition. Our children were young then and looked forward to the weekends and a break from school. Dad was usually working Friday night so it was up to Mom to corral everyone's happy extra energy. Once in a while we would go out for pizza, which was fun. But for the most part, staying home on Friday night and watching "Dallas" together on TV was much more fun than going out. But we still wanted our pizza!

Because we lived out in the country, we could not order in from the local pizza parlor. So I started making pizza from scratch. I found my first pizza crust recipe in some old Italian cookbook I had. It was a pleasant surprise to find out how easy it was to make.

At first we made our pizza on cookie sheets. In those days hardly anyone even sold pizza pans. One day I got the idea to go to our local Pizza Hut and ask to buy some of their pans. The store manager had never had such a request. Nobody made pizza at home! He sold me five pizza pans: two large, two medium, and one small. Our homemade pizza was getting more sophisticated!

I experimented with different sauces. At first I used tomato sauce, but now I use fresh or canned tomatoes. The kids' favorite pizza was pepperoni and cheese. That became the standard. Later, our oldest son would make pizza on Friday nights for all his football buddies.

If my husband was home and we could have a "date night," this was the night we went out together. I would either make the pizza earlier in the day or order it in. We served the pizza on special yellow plates that became a tradition with our pizza, along with root beer. If Steve and I happened to go out with the kids on Friday night, guess where we went? Out for pizza! It became the Friday night tradition. We all loved it!

I will never forget the first time we ate pizza in Italy. We were with our good friends Jeni and Richard, who took us to Italy our first time. When I tasted the Margherita, I knew it was my favorite. Named for Italy's Queen Margherita in 1889, this pizza is the colors of the Italian flag: red sauce, green basil, and white (mozzarella) cheese, with olive oil.

From that day, I was driven to find the perfect recipe for my family. When we got home, Jeni and I made pizza all the time, experimenting. It was so fun. We used pizza stones; Jeni even had at one time a real wood-burning pizza oven. That didn't last long, but the pizza memories sure did.

Pizza has become a favorite meal for many people around the world. It is nutritious because it is the bread, dairy, vegetables, and protein that you need for a balanced diet. It is easy to eat, easy to find, and prepared in many shapes and sizes. Everyone can find a pizza they love.

As I have traveled around the world, I have tasted and eaten just about every kind of pizza there is. I love the pizza in Manhattan, Chicago, and San Francisco, each with its own style and taste. One of the best pizzas we ever ate was in Cairo, Egypt. But my favorite pizza in the world is in Italy. I prefer the thin crust with a light sauce and no meat.

Very popular in the United States right now are gourmet pizzas, such as chicken BBQ and Thai with peanut sauce. I love the cheese mixture of Gouda, mozzarella, and Gruyère. Alfredo pizza with chicken and ham is excellent.

Even salad may top a pizza, as on a "club" pizza: Chicken, bacon bits, and ham go on the bottom with a little cheese. After baking, you toss green salad mixed with mayonnaise on top. Another of my favorite pizzas is pear with gorgonzola cheese, topped with my Pear Gorgonzola Salad (p. 187).

On the next page are the most desired pizzas in Italy. You may find a favorite of yours, or these fresh ideas may get you thinking about what your family would prefer. Experiment and have fun with these ideas and my recipes. Surely there is a pizza for you!

Today I am still experimenting with new pizza sauce recipes and of course with gourmet pizza. Where can you go in the world and get a better meal that you can eat with your hands? But remember that Europeans usually use their fork!

Liz

P.S. Do you have room for a small garden? Make a pizza garden! Kids will love growing and harvesting their pizza ingredients. See page 146 for a diagram.

POPULAR ITALIAN PIZZAS

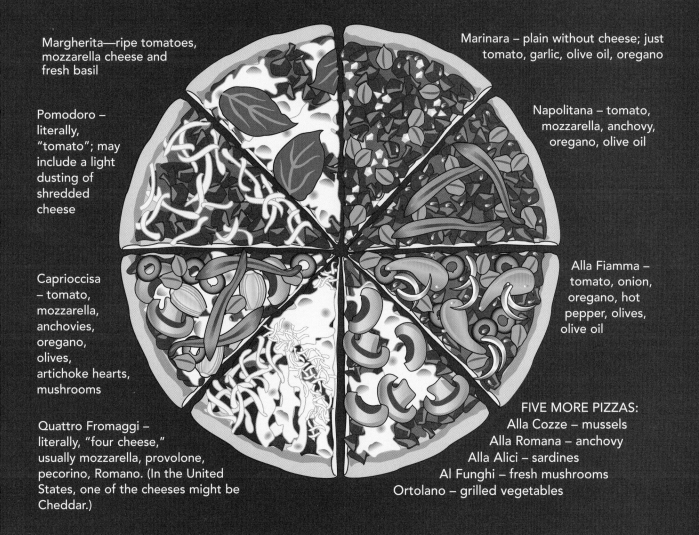

Margherita—ripe tomatoes, mozzarella cheese and fresh basil

Pomodoro – literally, "tomato"; may include a light dusting of shredded cheese

Caprioccisa – tomato, mozzarella, anchovies, oregano, olives, artichoke hearts, mushrooms

Quattro Fromaggi – literally, "four cheese," usually mozzarella, provolone, pecorino, Romano. (In the United States, one of the cheeses might be Cheddar.)

Marinara – plain without cheese; just tomato, garlic, olive oil, oregano

Napolitana – tomato, mozzarella, anchovy, oregano, olive oil

Alla Fiamma – tomato, onion, oregano, hot pepper, olives, olive oil

FIVE MORE PIZZAS:
Alla Cozze – mussels
Alla Romana – anchovy
Alla Alici – sardines
Al Funghi – fresh mushrooms
Ortolano – grilled vegetables

Quattro Stagione – divided into four sections representing your four favorite ingredients. The classic is tomatoes over the whole pizza, then one section mozzarella, one artichoke hearts, one prosciutto, and one mushroom or olive. Olive oil is drizzled over the entire pie.

134

BASIC PIZZA DOUGH

One 16-inch medium-crust pizza or two 12-inch thin-crust pizzas or four 8-inch thin-crust pizzas

1	tablespoon active dry yeast	1/4	teaspoon salt
1	cup warm (105-115 degrees) water	3 to 4	cups all-purpose flour or half all-purpose and half whole wheat (see Note)
2	tablespoons olive oil		
1	tablespoon honey		

1. Mix the yeast and water in a small bowl, cover, and let stand until foamy, 5 to 10 minutes.

2. Mix the oil, honey, salt, and yeast mixture in a large mixing bowl. If using a food processor, add 1 cup of flour at a time, up to 3 cups, mixing well after each addition. You may have to stir in the third cup of flour by hand, depending on your machine. Or mix in all 3 cups of flour by hand with a wooden spoon.

   If the dough seems too wet, mix in more flour, 1/4 cup at a time, until the dough is soft. Turn the dough onto a floured surface and knead in more flour, 1/4 cup at a time, until the dough is moderately stiff and somewhat firm to the touch, about 6 minutes.

3. Lightly grease pizza pan(s) or a cookie sheet(s) with oil. If you are making two or more thin-crust pizzas, divide the dough. With a rolling pin, roll out the dough on a floured surface. Gently stretch the dough to fill the pan(s).

4. Let the dough rise (it will not rise very much) while you make sauce and continue with the pizza recipe of your choice.

Note: I like this pizza crust best with half all-purpose flour and half whole wheat. I now keep my whole wheat flour in a canister right beside my all-purpose, so I can dip into and add whole wheat to almost any bread dough or pancake or waffle batter.

Our oldest son, David, used to make this for his classmates when he was in high school. Lizi used this recipe at college. She could mix it up in no time by hand because the recipe does not make a large amount. I have experimented with many pizza doughs, but I always go back to this one given to me by a long-ago friend whose daughter Katie played with my Emaly; it is our favorite.

THICK-CRUST PIZZA DOUGH

One 17 x 12-inch pizza or two medium pizzas

You will marvel at how easy it is to make this pizza dough using the food processor. It takes little more than 10 minutes tops!

1 tablespoon active dry yeast
1/4 cup warm (105–115 degrees) water
4 cups all-purpose flour
1/4 cup olive oil
2/3 cup water

1. Preheat the oven to 425 degrees. Lightly grease a 17 x 12-inch sheet pan (see Note). The sides should be at least 1" high.

2. Dissolve the yeast and water in a small bowl and let stand 5 to 10 minutes.

3. Blend the flour, yeast mixture, and oil in a food processor until crumbly. Add the water with the blade running until the dough forms a ball.

4. Press the dough into the prepared pan. Top with pizza sauce and your favorite toppings. Bake 20 to 30 minutes on a lower rack.

Note: For a medium pizza, use a 9 x 12-inch baking pan such as the ceramic Mamma Ró dish below. Divide the dough in half and place the extra in an airtight freezer container and freeze it for up to several weeks. When ready to use, thaw the dough and then stretch it to the desired dimensions.

CONVERSATION STARTER:
Which colleges interest you? What is it about them that's appealing?

EASY PIZZA SAUCE YOUR KIDS WILL MAKE

About 1 cup sauce; enough for one 16-inch pizza

1   (8-ounce) can tomato sauce
1/2 teaspoon dried basil or oregano
1/4 teaspoon garlic salt
1/8 teaspoon ground black pepper
Pinch of sugar (optional)

Mix the tomato sauce, basil, garlic salt, and pepper in a small bowl.

FRIDAY
PIZZA NIGHT

This is the sauce I started out with over 30 years ago. I made it up. My kids loved it then, and my boys still prefer it. David now makes this sauce at home with his own kids.

BASIC PIZZA SAUCE

About 1 1/2 cups sauce; enough for one 16-inch pizza or two 12-inch pizzas

2   (14.5-ounce) cans diced tomatoes, drained well
2   teaspoons dried oregano
3   tablespoons olive oil
1/2 teaspoon salt

1. Put the tomatoes in a sieve and push the juice out with a spoon. Put the drained tomatoes in a food processor or blender and pulse to crush them.

2. Pour the tomatoes into a bowl and mix in the oregano, oil, and salt.

This is the sauce that I have used over and over for many years. It is the quickest to prepare and the taste is almost as good as the sauces you spend hours on. I have tried them all—including recipes from Julia Child and every Italian cookbook I have. This recipe is as good as any. Make extra and keep it in the refrigerator for up to 4 days or frozen for up to 3 months.

CONVERSATION STARTER:

Have you been worried about a friend who might be taking drugs? What would you like to say to her?

CHOOSE-A-FLAVOR PIZZA

One 16-inch pizza

Use this versatile recipe to mix and match meat, cheese, and other toppings to suit your fancy. Sauté the mushrooms in 1 tablespoon each olive oil and butter, if desired, before placing atop the pizza. Or keep things simple with a basic cheese pizza.

Olive oil, for greasing the pizza pan
Basic Pizza Dough (p. 135)
Basic Pizza Sauce (p. 137)

3   cups shredded mozzarella
     cheese, divided

8   ounces pepperoni slices,
     fully cooked bulk sausage,
     or Canadian bacon slices
Sliced mushrooms, diced green bell
     pepper, sliced black olives,
     or pineapple tidbits

1. Preheat the oven to 425 degrees and lightly oil a 16-inch round pizza pan.

2. Place the prepared pizza dough in the pan and spread the sauce over the crust.

3. Sprinkle on 2½ cups of the cheese, and place the meat or vegetables of your choice on the cheese. Top with the remaining 1/2 cup of cheese.

4. Bake 15 to 20 minutes on the lowest oven rack.

Serve with a tossed green salad.

Variation: For a three-cheese pizza, use 1½ cups mozzarella, 1 cup smoked Gouda cheese, and 1 cup Gruyère cheese.

Can be made *Meatless*: Simply omit the meat and top only with vegetables and cheese.

CONVERSATION STARTER:
*Let's talk about what to do
for our vacation this summer.
I'd like to plan something really
educational this year...
and fun, of course!*

MARINARA SAUCE

About 2 cups sauce

1	(14.5-ounce) can diced tomatoes, or 4 fresh tomatoes, peeled and diced (about 2 cups)
4	small garlic cloves, minced
2	sprigs fresh oregano, or 1 teaspoon dried

Many consider marinara sauce to be a tomato sauce with onions, garlic, and herbs. Yet marinara pizza normally consists of tomato, garlic, olive oil, and oregano. That's why I call this sauce marinara, even though it doesn't have onions, although you may certainly add some. Try this as a quick all-purpose tomato sauce for pizza or pasta or for dipping breadsticks.

1. Crush the tomatoes in a blender. Pour into a small saucepan and stir in the garlic and oregano. Cook over low heat about 5 minutes.

2. Use as a pizza or pasta sauce or as a dipping sauce for breadsticks.

MARINARA PIZZA

One 16-inch pizza

Basic Pizza Dough (p. 135)
Marinara Sauce
Olive oil

1. Prepare the pizza dough and set aside.

2. Preheat the oven to 425 degrees and lightly oil the pizza pan.

3. Prepare the marinara sauce.

4. Stretch the dough to fit the prepared pan. Spread the sauce over the dough and bake on the lowest oven rack 15 to 20 minutes.

CONVERSATION STARTER:

It's difficult for our aging neighbor Mr. Smith to mow his lawn these days. Would one of you do that this weekend? We could make cookies for him, too. What kind shall we make?

ARUGULA PIZZA WITH FRESH MOZZARELLA AND CHERRY TOMATOES
One 12-inch thin-crust pizza

1/2 recipe **Basic Pizza Dough** (p. 135)

Fresh mozzarella cheese, or shredded regular mozzarella
Fresh baby arugula, torn into pieces
Fresh cherry or grape tomatoes, halved
Olive oil, for drizzling
Salt and ground black pepper (see Note)

1. Preheat the oven to 450 degrees. Oil a pizza pan with olive oil.

2. Prepare the dough and place it on the prepared pan.

3. Slice the fresh mozzarella cheese and place it on the crust, or top with shredded regular mozzarella.

4. Bake the pizza on the lowest oven rack for 12 to 15 minutes or until the crust is brown on the bottom and the cheese is melted. Remove from the oven and immediately pile the arugula pieces onto the hot melted cheese and top with the tomatoes. Drizzle on a little olive oil. Season lightly with salt and pepper. Serve immediately.

The first time I ate this pizza in Italy, I just could not believe how much I loved the nutty flavor! But you have to love arugula. This pungent salad green is an acquired taste. If you want to try something special and different, take a chance on this pizza. It is so fresh, so healthy, so good for you.

A Note About Pepper:
If you have a pepper mill, freshly ground peppercorns will offer a more "lively" flavor than pre-ground pepper. If you do use pre-ground pepper, buy only small amounts, as the flavors fade away over time, just as with other dried herbs and spices.

BBQ CHICKEN PIZZA

One 16-inch pizza

Basic Pizza Dough (p. 135)

3/4 pound boneless, skinless chicken breasts

1 cup plus 2 tablespoons sweet barbecue sauce, divided

1/4 cup shredded smoked Gouda cheese

3½ cups shredded mozzarella cheese, divided

1/4 cup thinly sliced red onion

3 tablespoons chopped fresh cilantro

1/4 green bell pepper, chopped (optional)

This recipe will show you how easy it is to prepare popular restaurant-quality pizza right at home.

1. Prepare the pizza dough and place it in an oiled pizza pan and set aside.

2. Grill or broil the chicken breasts until barely done. Cut them into strips or chunks. Mix the chicken with 2 tablespoons of the barbecue sauce.

3. Preheat the oven to 425 degrees.

4. To assemble the pizza, spread the remaining 1 cup of barbecue sauce over the pizza crust. Sprinkle with the Gouda cheese and top with 3 cups of the mozzarella cheese. Sprinkle the chicken and onions over the cheese. Top with the remaining 1/2 cup of mozzarella cheese. Bake 10 minutes on the lowest oven rack. Remove pizza from oven and sprinkle with the cilantro. Return to oven and bake until the crust is light brown, 5 to 10 minutes more.

5. Slice, and serve.

Variation: Instead of grilling, cut the raw chicken breasts into strips or chunks. Heat 2 tablespoons of olive oil over medium heat and cook and stir the chicken until tender and no longer pink. Continue as above.

AUTHENTIC MARGHERITA PIZZA

One 16-inch pizza or two 12-inch pizzas

When I am thinking about authentic Italian pizza, I make this recipe. Remember, Margherita means red sauce, green basil, and white cheese—the colors of the Italian flag!

In Italy the cheese on top of the pizza is sliced rather than shredded. And it is usually fresh mozzarella cheese.

Basic Pizza Dough (p. 135)

2   pounds very ripe Roma or hot-house tomatoes
1/4   teaspoon salt
1/4   cup olive oil
8   ounces fresh mozzarella cheese, thinly sliced

2   tablespoons freshly grated imported Parmigiano-Reggiano (optional, see Note, p. 67)
Coarse salt and ground black pepper
14   small fresh basil leaves or 7 large, torn into pieces

1.   Oil the pizza pan(s) and set aside.

2.   Prepare the pizza dough, roll it out, and place it in the prepared pan(s).

3.   Preheat the oven to 450 degrees.

4.   Peel (optional, see Note) and dice the tomatoes, discarding the seeds, and combine with the salt and 1/4 cup oil in a bowl. Spread over the crust.

5.   Bake 15 to 20 minutes on the lowest oven rack. Remove pizza from oven and arrange the mozzarella and the Parmesan, if using. Sprinkle with salt and pepper and drizzle on additional olive oil. Return to oven till bubbly, 5 to 10 minutes. Top with basil and serve immediately.

Note: A simple way to peel tomatoes is by scalding them in boiling water. Here's how: Bring water to boil in a medium saucepan. On the bottom of each tomato, cut a shallow X with a paring knife; do not cut the flesh. With a large slotted spoon, drop each tomato in the boiling water. When the skin begins to curl back at the X, after 15 to 30 seconds, remove the tomatoes and place them in ice water to stop the cooking. Then simply peel off the skin.

PIZZA BIANCA

One 12-inch pizza

Olive oil, for oiling pan and
    spreading on dough
Basic Pizza Dough (p. 135)

3   **tablespoons olive oil**
4   **garlic cloves, minced**
2   **fresh oregano sprigs**

1.   Preheat the oven to 425 degrees. Lightly oil the pizza pan with olive oil.

2.   Prepare the dough and place it on the pan. Spread a thin layer of oil over the dough.

3.   Mix the 3 tablespoons oil, garlic, and oregano. Spread the mixture over the dough and bake on the lowest oven rack for 15 minutes.

TRY A PIZZA STONE

Pizza crust browns especially well and "crisps" better when baked on a baking stone or tiles. Preheat the oven with the stone inside for 30 minutes. Sprinkle cornmeal or semolina flour (or both) on a pizza peel or paddle and assemble the pizza on that. After the oven has preheated for 30 minutes (so the stone is hot), brush the stone with olive oil or a little cornmeal. Slide the pizza off the peel onto the stone. Bake according to the recipe.

sliding a BBQ Chicken Pizza off the peel onto the pizza stone

Bianca is the Italian word for "white," so in pizza lingo it refers to a pie with white sauce or simply no sauce at all, like this one. Some call this the "garlic lover's pizza," because that's just about all it is. You might think it wouldn't have enough flavor, but it does! And you can always top it with still more garlic or other herbs, such as rosemary. I like to serve it alongside a Margherita pizza. They complement each other—one with sauce and cheese and one without.

GROW A PIZZA GARDEN

We have planted all kinds of gardens through the years, but this idea is by far the most fun! I saw this garden growing at a Montessori pre-school in our area. What do you grow in a pizza garden? All the vegetables and herbs for topping your pizza, of course!

Have the kids help you plant seeds or seedlings. Take turns watering and weeding to keep it growing and beautiful. Harvest the vegetables with the kids so they can see the "fruits" of their work. Then have fun preparing and eating super-fresh homemade pizzas!

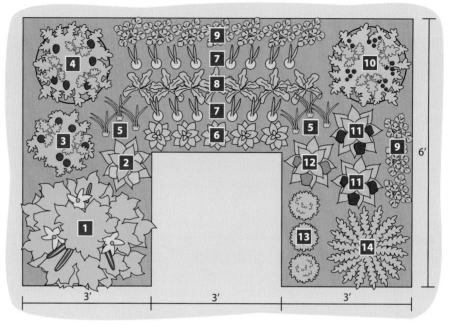

1	Zucchini Squash	8	Arugula
2	Yellow Bell Pepper	9	Cilantro
3	Patio Tomato	10	Cherry Tomato
4	Roma Tomato	11	Red Bell Pepper
5	Garlic	12	Green Bell Pepper
6	Genovese Basil	13	Globe Basil (with tiny leaves)
7	Onions	14	Oregano

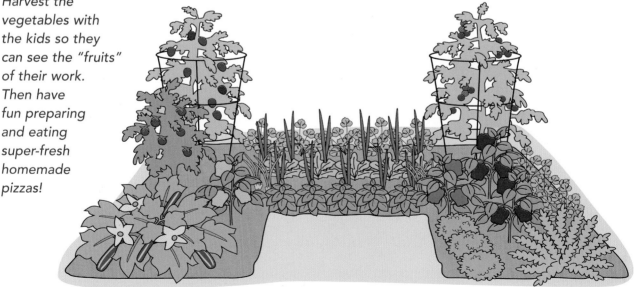

SATURDAY GRILL NIGHT

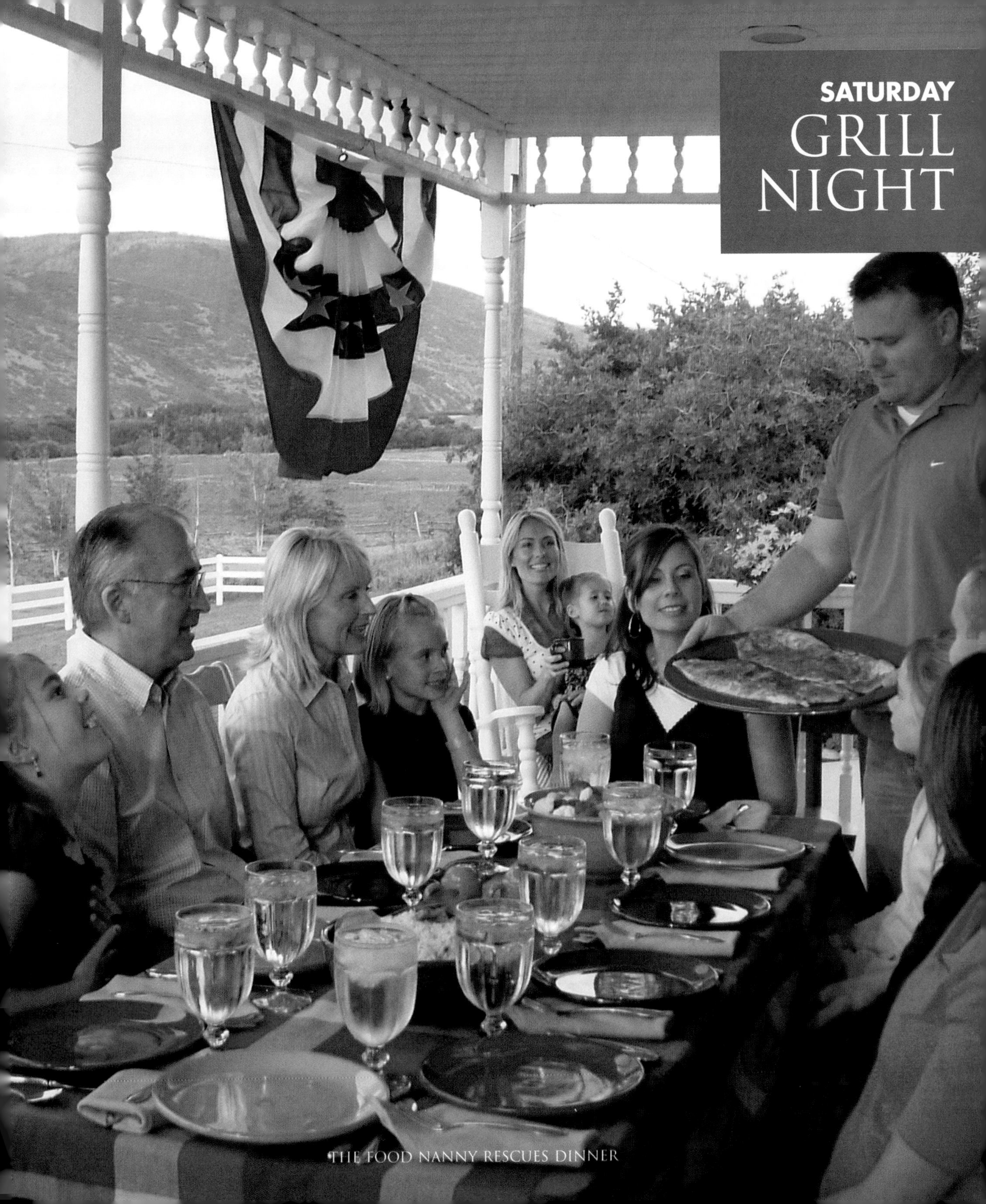

SATURDAY
GRILL
NIGHT

Saturday was one of those days I dreaded as a mom. It just wasn't a lot of fun for me. I believed that the kids needed to learn to work on this day, and I hoped to teach them a work ethic that would pay off one day. So I gave all of them chores around the house. For me, this meant more work—prying teenagers out of bed, keeping them on task, getting their rooms cleaned, breaking up fights. It just wasn't a lot of fun.

But the part I did enjoy was the end of the day. If we chose not to go to a movie in the afternoon or chose not to do a family activity that would take us away for dinner, then in the summertime especially, we always looked forward to barbecued hamburgers. Dad did a great job on the burgers, although he was not always home on Saturday nights, so Mom did the barbecue until the kids got old enough to help.

If our family was not all home for Saturday dinner, we chose to eat hamburgers out.

That's what everyone wanted—

148

pizza on Friday night, hamburgers on Saturday, at home or out. In those days it was Pizza Hut for pizza and Chili's for hamburgers. We hit all the fast-food places for hamburgers too. Love them! This is what I loved so much about Friday and Saturday nights— free nights for Mom. It was wonderful.

Of course circumstances don't allow you to go out every Friday and Saturday. If Steve and I decided to go to a movie or out to dinner by ourselves on Saturday night, we would either go get the hamburgers and bring them home or make sloppy joes for the kids. Everyone loved sloppy joes, including us adults. But most of the time our Saturday dinnertime meant wonderful hamburgers right off the grill, even in wintertime, with sloppy joes a close second.

As the children got older, we would sometimes grill fish on Saturday night, especially salmon. This was a delicious change, and just as easy. It was great to get fish into our diet more often. We also grilled chicken and turkey and the best steaks. Or the kids would take over in the kitchen and prepare a recipe they liked.

I could eat a grilled hamburger every week, but when you're looking for a change of pace, try one of my other great barbecue-inspired recipes.

Liz

SATURDAY
GRILL NIGHT

GRILLED HAMBURGERS
4 burgers

This "recipe" is simplicity itself, more a reminder of what to make sure you have on hand when everyone's hungry for a burger. I think the best burgers are made from ground chuck. Its slightly higher fat content makes juicier and more flavorful burgers, with only a few more calories per 4-ounce patty.

1	pound ground beef
1	teaspoon coarse salt
1/2	teaspoon ground black pepper
4	hamburger buns

CONDIMENTS:
Ketchup
Mustard of your choice
Mayonnaise

Pickles
Sliced red onion
Sliced tomatoes
Lettuce leaves

1. Heat the grill to medium-high.

2. Spread the meat in a shallow pan and mix in the salt and pepper. Delicately form the meat into patties; do not press the meat together really hard. This way air will be able to get in through the spaces during cooking and the meat will cook faster.

3. Brush the grill with cooking oil. Cook the patties until they look juicy and brown around the edges. Flip them only once and continue cooking to the desired doneness, 5 to 7 minutes total cooking time for medium.

4. Place the bun halves atop the grill, cut side down, just to warm them. Place the burgers between the buns and serve with the condiments.

Variations:

◆ **Teriyaki Burgers:** Mix 1/2 cup teriyaki sauce into the meat before forming patties. Grill the burgers along with 4 fresh pineapple slices, brushing the meat and pineapple with additional teriyaki sauce as they cook.

◆ Mix in a splash of Worcestershire sauce or soy sauce with the meat before forming patties.

◆ Slice onions and brush with oil, and then grill alongside the hamburgers until caramelized and tender, 10 to 15 minutes.

◆ Replace the ground beef with ground turkey, veggie burgers, or chicken burgers.

◆ For a *Meatless* alternative, grill portobello mushrooms brushed with a mixture of olive oil and balsamic vinegar.

BBQ DOGS YOUR WAY

4 hot dogs

4	hot dogs or Polish sausages	**CONDIMENTS:** Ketchup
4	hot dog buns, white or wheat	Mustard Sweet relish or hot dog relish Grated onions

1. Heat the grill to medium.

2. Place the hot dogs on the grill and turn them often until they are well-seared, about 3 minutes each side.

3. Serve on the buns with the condiments.

Serve with potato chips, baked beans, or potato salad.

Variations:

◆ **For a Chicago dog,** grill as above and top with cut-up tomato, diced cucumber, yellow peppers, and diced onion.

◆ **Pan-Fried or Boiled Hot Dogs:** Don't feel like grilling? Place a medium skillet on low heat. Turn the hot dogs frequently while they cook. The low heat will give the hot dogs enough time to plump and get juicy. They taste almost as good as those from the barbecue if you have the patience to cook them slowly. Alternatively, place the hot dogs in a medium saucepan and add enough water to cover. Boil until they are done, 3 to 4 minutes. Tuck the dogs into a bun and serve with your choice of condiments.

Like hamburgers, this "recipe" is about as easy as it gets! Our favorite hot dogs are Nathan's—we have eaten them for years in every airport around the country!—although we also enjoy Polish dogs for a change.

CONVERSATION STARTER:

Let's start a regular physical activity as a family. What sounds good – hiking, biking, rollerblading, walking…?

SLOPPY JOES

6 sandwiches

July 24 is Pioneer Day in Utah, and we have a derby in our town. We always have a big, big party with all our friends from Salt Lake who come to see the derby. For years we barbecued hamburgers with all the works, until one year when it was raining. We switched to sloppy joes and from then on everyone wanted my joes. We have several great recipes, and this one is my daughter Aimee's favorite.

1	tablespoon butter		1	tablespoon red wine vinegar
1/4	cup chopped onion (optional)		2	teaspoons chili powder
1	pound lean ground beef		1	teaspoon salt
1	cup ketchup		1/2	teaspoon ground black pepper
1/2 to 1	cup water		6	hamburger buns
1/4	cup packed brown sugar			Butter, for buttering the buns
2	tablespoons Worcestershire sauce			(optional)

1. Melt the 1 tablespoon butter in a medium saucepan or skillet over medium heat and cook and stir the onion until soft. Add the meat and cook and stir until it is thoroughly cooked. Drain and return to the pan.

2. Add the ketchup, 1/2 cup of the water, brown sugar, Worcestershire sauce, vinegar, chili powder, salt, and pepper. Simmer for 20 minutes, adding more water as needed for the desired consistency.

3. Butter the buns, if desired, and toast them under the broiler. Watch closely to be sure they don't burn. Spoon the meat mixture onto the bottom halves of the buns and cover with the tops. Or prepare open-face sandwiches. Serve immediately.

Serve with your favorite beans, potato chips, black olives, and carrot sticks.

Variations:

◆ Use half ground turkey and half lean ground beef. These are also great on whole wheat buns or bread.

◆ For cheese sloppy joes, prepare open-face sandwiches, top one half of each with a slice of cheese, and place them under the broiler just until the cheese is melted.

CAN DO AHEAD

Make the sloppy joe mixture ahead of time. Reheat to serve.

CONVERSATION STARTER:
I remember when we...
(tell the story of something funny that happened to your family).
What funny things do you remember?

BBQ-STYLE BRISKET

6 to 8 servings

DRY RUB:
2 to 3 tablespoons brown sugar
2   tablespoons seasoned salt
1   tablespoon chili powder
1   teaspoon garlic salt
1/2 teaspoon paprika
1/2 teaspoon ground black pepper
1/4 teaspoon ground ginger

1/4 teaspoon ground nutmeg
1/4 teaspoon dry mustard
1/4 teaspoon ground cloves

1   (3 to 5-pound) beef brisket
     or chuck roast
BBQ Sauce (recipe follows)
     or bottled sauce

1. Preheat the oven to 300 degrees.

2. Make the dry rub by mixing the brown sugar and seasonings in a small bowl. Rub the mixture over the meat and place it fat side up in a Dutch oven or a large pot.

3. Cover the pan tightly with a lid or aluminum foil and cook until the meat is fork-tender, 2$\frac{1}{2}$ to 3 hours.

4. Just ahead of serving time, prepare the BBQ Sauce and keep warm, or heat your favorite sauce and keep warm.

5. When the brisket is done, transfer it to a cutting board. Trim away the fat and slice the meat.

Top with the warm **BBQ Sauce**. Serve with **Classic American-Style Potato Salad** (p. 196), baked potatoes, potato chips, or **Acini di PePe Salad** (p. 197), a tossed green salad, or a vegetable tray.

BBQ SAUCE

About 2 cups

1/4 cup packed brown sugar
1   cup ketchup
1/2 cup water
1   teaspoon celery seed

3   tablespoons Worcestershire sauce
1   tablespoon dry mustard
1/4 teaspoon ground black pepper

Combine all the ingredients in a small saucepan and simmer about 30 minutes.

I first learned how to cook brisket in Granbury, Texas, and then made up this recipe as I went along over the years. The leftovers are delicious smothered with BBQ Sauce and made into sandwiches on hoagie rolls.

CAN DO AHEAD

Allow at least three hours for prepping and roasting the brisket or do it a day or two ahead and reheat.

GRILLED STEAK

4 servings

A good steak doesn't need much of anything, except attention at the grill to make sure it doesn't overcook. That's why I like to make sure everyone is ready to eat, the table is set, and the side dishes are ready before I grill the meat.

4   (6-ounce) bone-in T-bone or rib-eye steaks, 1 inch thick (see Note)
1   garlic clove, cut in half, or garlic powder (optional)
Seasoned salt

1.   Place the steaks on a platter and let them come to room temperature. About 10 minutes before grilling, rub the cut side of the garlic clove over one side of the steak or shake on a little garlic powder. Sprinkle both sides generously with the seasoned salt.

2.   Heat the grill to medium-high for 1 minute and place the steaks on it. Grill rib-eye 9 to 14 minutes for medium-rare to medium; T-bone 15 to 19 minutes. Turn the steaks about halfway through the cooking time. The most accurate test for doneness is using an instant-read thermometer inserted horizontally into the center: medium rare is 145 degrees, medium is 160, and well-done is 170 degrees. Remember that the meat will continue to cook after you remove it from the grill, adding 5 to 10 degrees of doneness.

     With practice you may master the "poke test" for doneness: Gently push the top of the steak with your finger. The resilience will tell you the degree of doneness. A soft, squishy steak will be rare or raw in the center. A firm, springy steak will be well-done. For medium-rare, look for a steak that feels gently yielding; for medium, a steak that's semi-firm.

3.   Let the steaks rest a couple of minutes before serving to help the meat retain more juices when sliced, then serve immediately.

Serve with baked potatoes, brown rice, steamed or boiled red potatoes, or **Homemade Egg Noodles** (p. 39) with olive oil; **Reds & Greens Salad** (p. 191); and another vegetable.

Note: I find that bone-in steaks have more flavor, although boneless rib-eye is also a tasty cut. If using boneless steak, serve 4-ounce portions.

Variation: As Americans, we tend to think that thicker is better for steak, but you might like to try doing as the Italians do: Have your steak cut thin. The butcher can cut both rib-eye and T-bone thin. Serve the thinner steak with more vegetables, and then the meal is more about the vegetables than the meat. Remember, a thinner steak will cook much faster, so don't ever leave it alone on the grill. It will be done before you know it.

GRILLED MARINATED LONDON BROIL
WITH SAUTÉED MUSHROOMS *6 to 8 servings*

2   garlic cloves, minced
1   tablespoon chopped fresh parsley, or 1 teaspoon dried
1   tablespoon chopped fresh basil, or 1 teaspoon dried
2   pounds beef flank steak

Salt and ground black pepper
1/2   cup soy sauce
1   tablespoon butter
8   ounces mushrooms
Garlic salt, for seasoning mushrooms

Flank steak is the traditional cut for London broil. Because it is a tougher cut of meat, I used to be afraid of it. I wondered how to cook it. Then our friend Stan gave me this recipe for a tasty marinade. The trick with London broil is cooking the meat no more than medium-rare and then slicing it thinly across the grain for serving. This recipe is very quick to make, but you do have to allow time in advance for marinating.

1. In a small bowl mix the garlic, parsley, and basil. Rub the mixture into the steak and season with the salt and pepper.

2. Pour the soy sauce into a resealable plastic bag. Add the steak to the bag and turn to coat. Marinate in the refrigerator, turning the bag occasionally, about 2 hours. (Note: You may decrease the marinating time, although the cooked meat may not be as flavorful.)

3. Drain the meat and bring the marinade to a boil in a small saucepan. Allow the meat to come to room temperature while heating the grill to medium-high.

4. Grill the meat until it is pink and juicy in the middle, 6 to 10 minutes per side. Baste with the marinade while the meat is cooking. Remove from the grill while the meat is still very pink; it will continue to cook. Transfer the meat to a cutting board to rest 5 minutes before slicing.

5. Meanwhile, heat the butter in a small skillet over medium heat. Cook and stir the mushrooms for a few minutes. Sprinkle with garlic salt.

6. Thinly slice the meat across the grain and place it on a platter. Spoon the mushrooms over the top.

Serve with baked potatoes or Italian bread and **BLT Salad** (p. 186) or a green vegetable.

DO AHEAD

Place meat in marinade about 2 hours ahead of time

Grilled steaks and the London Broil are always better when sautéed mushrooms are added.

GRILLED GARLIC-BUTTER CHICKEN

4 servings

Our friend Rick made up this recipe. We all love the way it makes the chicken crispy on the outside and moist on the inside.

4 small bone-in chicken breasts or 8 thighs, drumsticks or wings	1/4 teaspoon onion salt
1/4 cup (1/2 stick) butter, melted	1/4 teaspoon dry minced onion
1/4 teaspoon salt	1/4 teaspoon ground black pepper
1/4 teaspoon garlic salt	Juice of 1/2 lemon

1. Heat the grill to medium. Place the chicken pieces in a shallow dish.

2. Melt the butter in a small bowl in the microwave. Add the salt, garlic salt, onion salt, onion, pepper, and lemon juice. Brush the chicken on both sides with the butter mixture. Reserve remaining mixture for basting during grilling.

3. Place the chicken on the grill and cook, basting often, until tender and no longer pink, 10 to 15 minutes per side for breasts and thighs; 8 to 12 minutes per side for drumsticks and wings.

Serve with **Reds & Greens Salad** (p. 191), **Acini di Pepe Salad** (p. 197), macaroni salad, or potato salad; corn on the cob or steamed potatoes; and corn bread.

Variation: Substitute salmon steaks for the chicken pieces. Grill 4 to 6 minutes per 1/2-inch thickness. Serve with lemon wedges.

GRILLED MARINATED TURKEY BREAST

8 servings

This marinade is especially good on turkey, but you may substitute 8 boneless, skinless chicken breasts.

1/2 cup lemon-lime soda (such as 7UP®)	1/4 teaspoon garlic powder
1/4 cup canola oil	1/4 teaspoon horseradish
1/4 cup soy sauce	1 (3-pound) boneless turkey breast, cut into pieces

1. Combine the soda, oil, soy sauce, garlic powder, and horseradish in a large resealable plastic bag. Add the turkey breast and mix well. Refrigerate 3 to 4 hours before grilling.

2. Drain the turkey and discard the marinade. (If you want to baste with the marinade, be sure to boil it a few minutes before using.)

3. Grill breast pieces about 15 minutes on each side, or to an internal temperature of 165 degrees.

Serve with potato salad, macaroni salad, **Baked Beans with Maple and Cocoa** (p. 210), fruit with **Fruit Dip** (p. 273), or vegetables with **Dill Dip** (p. 272).

Variation: As an alternative to grilling, bake the turkey breast at 350 degrees 15 to 20 minutes per pound, until the meat releases clear juices when pricked deeply with a fork, or to an internal temperature of 165 degrees.

GRILLED CHICKEN WITH DAD'S SWEET BBQ SAUCE *6 servings*

1 (8-ounce) can tomato sauce
1/2 to 1 cup packed brown sugar
1 teaspoon prepared mustard

1 teaspoon cider vinegar
6 to 12 chicken parts of your choice
Salt and ground black pepper

1. Combine the tomato sauce, brown sugar, mustard, and vinegar in a small saucepan. Bring the sauce to a boil and then decrease the heat to simmer. Cook, stirring occasionally, for 30 to 45 minutes until thickened.

2. Preheat the grill to medium. Trim excess fat from the chicken pieces and remove the skin if desired. Wipe the chicken with damp paper towels; discard the towels immediately to prevent cross-contamination. Season with salt and pepper. Place the chicken on the grill and cook until the chicken is tender and no longer pink: 10 to 15 minutes per side for breasts and thighs, 8 to 12 minutes per side for drumsticks and wings.

3. Pour half of the sauce into a bowl to pass at the table; set aside. Baste the chicken with the remaining sauce only during the last few minutes of cooking, to prevent the sauce from burning.

Serve immediately with **Rice Pilaf** (p. 213) or **Grilled Vegetables in Chicken Broth** (p. 159). Any remaining sauce may be stored, covered, in the refrigerator for up to one week.

When I was growing up, my dad was great on the old-fashioned potbelly grill with coals that you waited for hours to get perfectly ready. He rolled whole onions, corn on the cob, and just about anything he felt like in aluminum foil and placed them individually on the grill to cook. They were done to perfection and delicious! Today we love remembering this great man and his BBQ sauce. He basted most of his meats and salmon with this sauce.

CONVERSATION STARTER:
I've been really enjoying the classical music that's been playing here in the house, but I know there's other music you might enjoy, too. Let's take turns choosing. What appeals to you?

GRILLED SALMON

4 servings

4	salmon fillets, about 4 ounces each*	Lemon pepper
2	tablespoons softened butter	Brown sugar

1. Heat the grill to medium-high.

2. Layer two large sheets of aluminum foil and fold in the edges to make "sides." Place the salmon fillets on the foil sheets. Spread a thin coating of the butter on the fillets. Sprinkle on a dusting of the lemon pepper. Make a few shallow slits in each fillet and sprinkle on the brown sugar.

3. Place the salmon fillets on the grill, cover, and cook 4 to 6 minutes per 1/2-inch thickness, or until the fish flakes easily when tested with a fork. Serve immediately.

Serve with **Grilled Vegetables in Chicken Broth**, below, and **Garlic Bread** (p. 227) wrapped in foil and heated on the grill or in a 350-degree oven for 15 to 20 minutes.

*To serve 8 or more, purchase an entire half salmon, rather than individual fillets.

I got started using brown sugar with my salmon because of our good neighbor Richard, who is a great fisherman and a good cook. This became my kids' favorite salmon dinner. They love the sweetness and tartness that the lemon pepper/ brown sugar combination gives the salmon.

GRILLED VEGETABLES IN CHICKEN BROTH

4 to 6 servings

1½	cups chicken broth, plus additional if needed	1	small zucchini, diced
6	red potatoes, quartered	1	small red bell pepper, cut into strips
8	ounces fresh mushrooms, cut in half	1	tablespoon butter
			Salt and ground black pepper

1. Heat the grill to low and have a 10 x 10-inch sturdy foil baking pan available.

2. Pour the broth into the pan. Add the potatoes, mushrooms, zucchini, bell pepper, and butter. Season with salt and pepper. Cover tightly with foil, leaving one corner slightly open so you can check on the vegetables.

3. Place the pan on the grill and cook until the vegetables are tender, about 25 minutes. Check while they are cooking to see if you need more broth. (Be careful not to burn yourself from the steam.)

Serve with any grilled fish or meat, or with rice for a meatless meal.

The first time we had these grilled veggies was at the home of our relatives Debbie and Tom. What a great idea, I thought. We have been grilling our own ever since, especially when we have fresh ones straight out of our garden. You're going to love this fast, healthful way to eat vegetables. Feel free to substitute other vegetables for the ones listed here.

MARINATED GRILLED VEGETABLES

6 servings

SATURDAY
GRILL NIGHT

1   eggplant
2   small zucchini and/or summer
      squash
1   each red and yellow bell
      pepper
1   bunch asparagus

2 to 3 garlic cloves, chopped
3   tablespoons olive oil
Salt and freshly ground black
      pepper (see Note)
Fresh herbs of your choice,
      such as rosemary, oregano,
      marjoram, savory, or thyme

Dave and Robin make these vegetables year-round on their backyard grill. The vegetables are great with BBQ chicken or a simple grilled steak...or make a whole meal of them!

1. Heat the grill to medium-high.

2. Cut eggplant and squash into 1/2-inch-thick slices. Cut bell peppers into quarters and remove seeds. Break tough ends off the bottom of the asparagus spears.

3. Mix garlic and oil in a large bowl. Add the vegetables and toss to coat. Season with salt, pepper, and herbs.

4. Grill, turning as needed, until slightly charred and beginning to go limp. As each vegetable nears being done, move it to the upper rack to keep warm.

Serve with brown rice or **Simple Parmesan Risotto** (p. 212) as a meatless meal, or with the grilled variation of **Sweet & Sour Baked Chicken** (p. 162) and **Rice Pilaf** (p. 213).

Note: If you have one, use a pepper mill filled with whole peppercorns to grind the pepper over the vegetables. Freshly ground pepper is much more flavorful than pepper purchased pre-ground.

Variation: Add onions, mushrooms, and/or prawns.

SWEET & SOUR BAKED CHICKEN

3 to 6 servings

This isn't really barbecue, but it's an easy Saturday supper, so I've included it here. Aimee taught us how to make this dish, and all our girls make it a lot for their families. It couldn't be much easier to make, and the chicken comes out so tender and tasty.

6	drumsticks or thighs
1	cup packed brown sugar
1	(8-ounce) can pineapple chunks with juice, undrained
1/4	cup soy sauce
1	teaspoon dry mustard

1. Preheat the oven to 300 degrees.

2. Place the chicken pieces in a 9 x 13-inch baking dish. (You may remove the skin if desired.)

3. In a small bowl combine the brown sugar, pineapple, soy sauce, and dry mustard. Pour the sauce over the chicken.

4. Bake 60 to 70 minutes, turning the chicken halfway through the cooking time. The chicken is done when the juices run clear, or if you prefer them well-done, when the meat falls off the bone.

5. Transfer the chicken to a platter and pour the sauce into a small bowl.

Serve with brown or white rice. Spoon the sauce over the chicken and rice. Add **BLT Salad** (p. 186), **Reds & Greens Salad** (p. 191), or **Pear Gorgonzola Salad** (p. 187) and a cooked vegetable if desired, such as peas and carrots or cauliflower.

Variations:

◆ Substitute chicken breasts for the legs and remove them from the oven when the flesh is no longer pink. You could also make this with a mix of legs and breasts, but be aware that the breasts may dry out while you wait for the legs to finish cooking.

◆ **Grill the chicken, along with fresh pineapple slices.** Marinate the chicken (briefly or all day) in the sauce from step 3. Pour 1/4 cup of the sauce into a separate cup and brush it onto the chicken and the pineapple as they grill. Boil the remaining sauce and place it in a bowl to serve at the table.

SUNDAY FAMILY TRADITIONS

We all love our Sundays, whether we spend them going to church, sleeping in, kicking back, cooking, resting, or playing. For many people, Sunday is a day spent with family and friends. For others, it might be the only quiet day all to yourself to recharge your spirits. You make the choice; you set the mood. However you define your Sunday, you might consider it a "tradition day." This can include traditions in Sunday dinner.

Before Steve and I had children, we automatically incorporated our own families' traditions on Sunday. For dinner it was roast beef, mashed potatoes, and gravy. No one cooked a better roast beef than my Aunt Jean. She taught me that there was no easier meal to put together than a roast beef, vegetables, and potatoes. Just put it all in one roaster pot and let it cook for 4 to 5 hours in the oven at 300 degrees.

Steve used to say to me, "Why don't you cook something easier on Sunday?" I would answer, "There is nothing easier than putting a roast in my roaster pan, adding a few onions, carrots, potatoes, and sweet potatoes to the pot, and letting it cook for a few hours." This meal is also healthful—a small portion of meat and mostly vegetables. Steve could never disagree and besides, it was everyone's favorite meal. So we have kept that tradition in our family.

I know that families everywhere have all kinds of traditions for Sunday dinner. Many Italians choose lasagna, stuffed shells, or chicken and roasted vegetables. We knew a family from Poland who ate stuffed cabbage rolls every Sunday.

While traveling in Spain, we learned that paella (pronounced pie-AY-uh)—a saffron-flavored rice combined with meat, seafood and vegetables—is a Sunday tradition there, with the men traditionally in charge of cooking it. I just love it that the men are in charge of Sunday dinner! That is a tradition in itself. We all need to learn from the Spanish!

I will never forget the Sunday we visited the Rock of Gibraltar. When we were there, the main roadway into Gibraltar actually crossed the airport runway. (Movable barricades closed the road when aircraft landed or departed.) Unforgettable! It was one of those days with a chill in the air but plenty of sunshine. We found the perfect little out-door café. Brent and Toni, Mike

SUNDAY FAMILY TRADITIONS

SUNDAY FAMILY TRADITIONS

and Sally, and Steve and I feasted on the most wonderful fish and chips—a must-eat while you're there. This was another wonderful "Sunday feast."

Wherever you live or wherever you're visiting, think about how you can make Sunday different. Especially when you are home, make Sunday meaningful. When your children are young, it's a day for bonding with one another, a day to spend with family, a quieter day. Make it a day full of family tradition and lasting memories that will carry you and your family throughout your lives.

I love Sunday dinner. When our children were growing up, we made Sunday dinner special. We had the table-cloth on the dining room table and the table set before we went to church.

We ate our Sunday dinner as soon as we got home, which was just after noon. Everyone was famished!

Then we spent the afternoon discussing hot topics, reading, and resting. Sometimes we got together with close friends in the evening for a snack.

If you have to work on Sundays, this can put a crimp in getting together with family and friends. But don't let your job or your spouse's ruin Sunday tradition. It can still be special. Make it special for those who are home. Use your better dishes, if you have some. Use your dining room if you have one.

I have given you some great choices for Sunday dinner. If you do not have a tradition on Sunday, start one. This could be your first family tradition in the making.

Liz

SUNDAY FAMILY TRADITIONS

LOUISIANA-STYLE BRAISED PORK LOIN WITH GRAVY *8 to 10 servings*

1   (3 to 4-pound) boneless
    pork roast
1   tablespoon butter (optional)
1   tablespoon olive oil (optional)
1   small white onion, diced
1   small green bell pepper, diced
Tony Chachere's Original Creole
    Seasoning (see intro at right)

1/2 cup plus 3 tablespoons
     canola oil
4   cups chicken broth
1/2 cup all-purpose flour
Dash of Kitchen Bouquet browning
     sauce (optional)

1. Preheat the oven to 400 degrees.

2. To brown the roast (optional), heat the butter and olive oil in a Dutch oven or large pot over high heat. Brown the meat well on all sides. Remove the roast to a plate.

3. Mix the onion and bell pepper in a small bowl. Sprinkle generously with the Creole seasoning. Add 3 tablespoons of the canola oil and mix.

4. With a sharp knife, cut four or five cross-wise slits in the top of the roast, each about $1^1/2$ inches deep. Return the roast to the Dutch oven or a roasting pan. Stuff the onion-pepper mixture into the slits. Rub any excess mixture over the roast.

5. Pour the broth into the pan, but not over the roast.

6. Cover with a tight-fitting lid or aluminum foil and bake $1^1/2$ to $2^1/2$ hours, to an internal temperature of 160 degrees. Remove to a cutting board and cover with foil to keep warm.

7. To make gravy, place the pan with the chicken broth and meat juices over medium-high heat. In a small bowl, whisk the remaining 1/2 cup canola oil and the flour until the mixture is very smooth, the consistency of pancake batter. Whisk the mixture into the broth, stirring until the gravy boils and thickens. Season generously with additional Creole seasoning and add a few drops of Kitchen Bouquet, if desired. Simmer for 5 minutes. The gravy should have the consistency of heavy cream.

8. Slice the roast, transfer the meat to a serving platter, and drizzle gravy over the slices or pour it into a gravy bowl and pass with the roast.

Serve with **Classic Mashed Potatoes** (p. 211) and a hot cooked vegetable—buttered carrots, green beans, or any Southern vegetable, such as collard greens or turnips. This is also good served with tossed green salad and **Buttermilk Corn Bread** (p. 241).

While traveling in Louisiana, we came upon a tiny restaurant in Lafayette, the St. Landry Cafe, where we ate this special pork roast. I met the owner and asked about her secret for the roast. She smiled and went back into the kitchen to get me my own shaker of Tony Chachere's Original Creole Seasoning. I was so excited! Back at home I did not have any measurements, so by trial and error I came up with this recipe. My family and friends think this is divine! I will never forget those precious cooks at the St. Landry Café (although I don't know if the restaurant is still there). Thank you for sharing your secret recipe with me.

TRADITIONAL POT ROAST DINNER

9 to 10 servings

This is an easy meal to get ready for Sunday when everyone is going to be home, so it became our standard traditional Sunday roast. It all cooks in the same pot and there is hardly any mess to clean up. It takes less than 30 minutes of prep time and you never have to check on it while it's cooking. You can mix homemade rolls as the meat is roasting and have them ready to bake when the roast comes out of the oven.

1/3 cup all-purpose flour
1 teaspoon garlic powder or other favorite seasoning
1 teaspoon salt
1 teaspoon ground black pepper
1 (3½ to 4-pound) boneless chuck, rump, or shoulder roast
2 tablespoons olive oil

1 cup beef broth
5 large carrots, peeled and quartered
5 red potatoes, scrubbed
1 large yellow onion, quartered
2 sweet potatoes or yams, peeled and quartered

1. Preheat the oven to 275 degrees.

2. Mix the flour, garlic powder, salt, and pepper, and rub on the meat.

3. In a Dutch oven or large pot, heat the oil over medium heat. Brown the meat on all sides; drain the fat. Add the broth; bring to a boil and boil about 1 minute. Remove the pot from the heat.

4. Add the carrots, red potatoes, onion, and sweet potatoes. Cover tightly with a lid or aluminum foil and place in the oven. Roast for 5 hours. (Alternatively, roast at 325 degrees for 3 hours; roasting at lower temperature for longer time produces more meat juices.)

5. Transfer the meat to a large platter and surround it with the vegetables. Cover with foil to keep warm. When ready to serve, slice the meat on a cutting board and return it to the platter.

6. Meanwhile, make **Pan Gravy for Pot Roast** on the next page. Transfer to a bowl or gravy dish and serve with the roast and vegetables.

Serve with a tossed green salad and **Liz's Crescent Dinner Rolls** (p. 234), **corn bread** (p. 241), or **Old-Fashioned Biscuits** (p. 240).

Variation: When you are hungry for mashed potatoes, exclude the potatoes from the roasting pot and make **Classic Mashed Potatoes** (p. 211).

Leftovers Tip: You can use up leftover roast beef the next night by cutting the meat into chunks and making more gravy, if necessary, from gravy mix. Add the meat to the hot gravy in a saucepan on top of the stove until heated through. Serve over mashed potatoes. Add a vegetable of your choice. You may also use leftover roast for French dip sandwiches.

DO AHEAD

Start this dish at least 4 hours ahead of time, or up to 6 hours ahead of time to allow for roasting time—see step 4.

EASY POT ROAST DINNER

4 to 6 servings

1	(2-pound) boneless chuck or shoulder roast	4	red potatoes, scrubbed and quartered
1	cup cold water	1/2	large yellow onion, cut in half
1	(1-ounce) packet brown-gravy mix	1	yam, peeled and quartered
4	large carrots, peeled and cut in half		

1. Preheat the oven to 300 degrees. Place the roast in a Dutch oven, roasting pan, or oblong metal baking pan.

2. Stir the water and gravy mix together in a small bowl and pour over the roast. Add the carrots, potatoes, onion, and yam. Cover tightly with a lid or aluminum foil, place in the oven, and roast for 3 hours. The long cooking time at low heat will ensure the roast will be tender.

3. Remove from the oven, place the roast and vegetables on a platter, and cover with foil to keep warm. When ready to serve, slice the meat on a cutting board and return it to the platter.

4. Meanwhile, make **Pan Gravy for Pot Roast**, below. Transfer to a bowl or gravy dish and serve with the roast and vegetables.

Here's an even easier version of a pot roast dinner. Even the kids could make this for their parents for a change. Practically all it takes is desire!

DO AHEAD

Start this dish at least 4 hours ahead of time to allow for roasting time.

PAN GRAVY FOR POT ROAST

About 2 cups

Pan juices from pot-roasting meat
Beef broth (optional)
1/4 cup all-purpose flour
1/2 cup cold water
Dash of Kitchen Bouquet browning sauce

Note: Always have gravy mix packets on hand. (My favorite is mushroom.) If you think your gravy needs a little zip, you can always add gravy mix and adjust. Or if your family likes more gravy than your meat drippings yield, simply make additional gravy from the mix.

1. After removing meat from the pan, pour pan juices into a 2-cup measuring cup. Tilt the measuring cup and spoon off the fat that rises to the top. If necessary, add beef broth or water to total 1 1/2 cups of liquid. Return the juices to the pan.

2. Whisk the flour and water together in a small bowl or measuring cup and add to the pan juices. Cook and stir over medium-high heat until thickened and bubbly. Cook and stir 1 minute more. Add the browning sauce to make the gravy a rich dark brown. Season to taste.

3. When ready to serve, pour into a gravy dish and serve with the pot roast.

I think this is the easiest way for inexperienced cooks to make gravy from meat drippings. I like to use flour for thickening; I prefer the taste that the flour gives compared with other thickeners.

CROCK-POT ROAST BEEF DINNER

8 to 12 servings

Using a slow cooker, such as a Crock-Pot, is a great, easy way to fix dinner, especially meats. Make this recipe, go to work or away for the day, and come home to a great meal! If eight servings are too many, simply halve the recipe. My children cut roasts in half and freeze the remainder for another time. You need not have a large group to enjoy a roast.

1   **(4-pound) beef sirloin roast**
Garlic salt
1/3 **cup packed brown sugar**
3   **tablespoons cider vinegar**
1   **tablespoon soy sauce**
1   **tablespoon Worcestershire sauce**
1   **(10.75-ounce) can condensed cream of mushroom soup**

1   **(1-ounce) packet onion soup mix**
1   **cup beef broth**
5   **large carrots, peeled and cut into 1-inch pieces (optional)**
6   **red potatoes or medium russets, scrubbed and quartered (optional)**

1. Place the roast in a slow cooker. Sprinkle with the garlic salt.

2. In a medium bowl, mix the brown sugar, vinegar, soy sauce, Worcestershire sauce, mushroom soup, onion soup mix, and broth; pour over the roast.

3. Add the carrots and/or potatoes to the slow cooker if it is large enough to hold them.

4. Cook on high heat 5 to 6 hours or on low heat for 10 to 12 hours.

If you choose not to add the carrots or potatoes to the slow cooker, then two good side dishes are mashed potatoes and **Reds & Greens Salad** (p. 191).

Variation: Use a pork roast.

DO AHEAD

Start this dish at least 6 hours ahead of time, or up to 12 hours ahead of time (see step 4).

TRI-TIP ROAST WITH RED POTATOES

6 to 8 servings

1   boneless 2-pound tri-tip roast (see Note at right)
2   tablespoons olive oil
6 to 8 medium red potatoes
Salt and ground black pepper
3   tablespoons minced white onion or shallot
1¼ cups red wine
1/4 cup chicken broth
5   tablespoons unsalted butter, cut in pieces

2   tablespoons minced fresh parsley, plus additional for garnish
2   tablespoons unsalted butter, melted

Note: This flavorful cut is more readily available than it once was, or try calling around. It is worth the search.

1. Preheat the oven to 400 degrees.

2. Place the roast in a shallow metal pan, pour on the oil, and rub it thoroughly over the entire surface of the meat. Roast in the oven for 45 to 60 minutes. Check for doneness with a meat thermometer: 135 degrees for medium rare, 150 degrees for medium-well. The temperature will continue to rise 5 to 10 degrees after the meat is taken out of the oven; do not overcook.

3. Meanwhile, scrub the potatoes and with a paring knife peel only around the middle of each potato, to make a skinless "band." The peel can look jagged. Place the potatoes in the steamer insert of a large saucepan. (Note: As an alternative to steaming, you may boil the potatoes in water, but they retain their red and glossy skins better when they are steamed.) Add water up to the bottom of the steamer insert; bring the water to a boil. Decrease the heat to medium and steam the potatoes until they are done, about 20 minutes. Remove from the heat and keep warm.

4. When the meat is done, set it on a platter and sprinkle with salt and pepper to taste. Cover with aluminum foil to keep warm. Let rest for 10 minutes.

5. Place the roasting pan over medium-high heat. Add the onion to the pan juices and cook and stir about 2 minutes. Add the wine and broth. Boil 3 to 5 minutes until more than half the wine has evaporated. Remove from the heat and add the 5 tablespoons of butter and the 2 tablespoons of parsley.

6. Cut the roast into 1-inch-thick slices and place them on a large platter. Reheat the sauce and pour it down the center of the slices. Place the potatoes around the meat. Drizzle the melted butter over the potatoes and sprinkle on additional parsley.

Surround the roast with a beautiful display of steamed vegetables, such as carrots cut on the diagonal into chunks, whole green beans, and broccoli and cauliflower.

This is the fanciest of all the dinners I make. We have fun cooking this meal for our family and friends. We all look forward to the meat and the wonderful flavor that the sauce gives it. It's the butter that makes the difference! You can have this roast on the table in an hour and it tastes as if you spent all day.

SLOW-COOKER BARBECUED RIBS
6 to 8 servings

Sometimes I'm tied up all day and need to have dinner going while I'm away, so I always like a good recipe for the slow cooker. This is a great one!

DO AHEAD

Start this dish at least 4 hours ahead of time, or up to 8 hours ahead of time (see step 2).

4	pounds country-style pork ribs
1	(10.75-ounce) can condensed tomato soup
1/2	cup cider vinegar
3/4	cup packed brown sugar
1	tablespoon soy sauce
1	teaspoon celery seed
1	teaspoon chili powder

1. Trim excess fat from the ribs and put them in a slow cooker. Combine the soup, vinegar, brown sugar, soy sauce, celery seed, and chili powder in a medium bowl and pour over the meat.

2. Cover the pot and cook at low setting 7 to 8 hours, medium setting 5 to 6 hours, or high setting 3 to 4 hours.

Serve with baked potatoes, potato salad, or rice, and vegetables.

Variations:

◆ Brown the ribs before slow cooking: After trimming excess fat from the meat, place the ribs on a rack in a broiler pan under the broiler. Then place the ribs in the slow cooker and proceed.

◆ Put scrubbed small whole red potatoes under the ribs and cook the meat and potatoes together.

◆ Use the same recipe with beef ribs.

CONVERSATION STARTER:

Start a Sunday Tradition by having each person at the dinner table talk about one thing they appreciate. Throughout the week they'll think about what they'll choose.

BBQ BEEF SANDWICHES

6 to 8 sandwiches

1   tablespoon vegetable oil
1   (3-pound) boneless beef shoulder or chuck roast
1   cup barbecue sauce
1/2 cup cider vinegar
1/2 cup chicken broth
1/4 cup packed brown sugar
1   tablespoon prepared mustard
1   tablespoon Worcestershire sauce

1   tablespoon chili powder
1/2 medium yellow onion, minced
2   garlic cloves, crushed
1½ teaspoons dried thyme
6 to 8 hamburger buns
Butter (optional)
6 to 8 slices Swiss cheese (optional)

My daughter Katie makes this meal the best. We all look forward to these special sandwiches— a pleasant change from regular roast beef. You can make this recipe with a smaller roast, but use the full amount of sauce and roast for a shorter time.

DO AHEAD

Start this dish at least 4 hours ahead of time.

1. Preheat the oven to 275 degrees.

2. Heat the oil in a Dutch oven or large pot over medium-high heat and brown the meat well, turning often, about 15 minutes. In a bowl combine the barbecue sauce, vinegar, broth, sugar, mustard, Worcestershire sauce, chili powder, onion, garlic, and thyme. Pour over the meat and bring to a boil. Cover tightly with a lid or aluminum foil and roast in the oven for 3 to 4 hours. Remove the meat and shred it with a fork. Return the meat to the pot and keep warm.

3. Butter the hamburger buns, if desired, and broil them until they are barely brown around the edges. Place one slice of Swiss cheese, if using, on the bottom bun and place under the broiler just until the cheese has melted.

4. Fill the buns with the meat and serve.

Serve with **Classic American-Style Potato Salad** (p. 196) and **Baked Beans with Maple and Cocoa** (p. 210) or canned baked beans.

Variation: For a leaner version, place the shredded meat in a large saucepan rather than returning it to the sauce it cooked in. Add bottled barbecue sauce to make the desired "sauciness." Place over medium heat and cook until heated through. Broil unbuttered buns, omit the cheese, and fill the sandwiches with the meat mixture.

CRUNCHY-FRIED CHICKEN WITH GRAVY

6 servings

I love to make this fried chicken for my sons and sons-in-law: David, Brent, Joey, Colin, Aaron, Rich, and Chris. We count our many blessings and have a wonderful day together. This dinnertime experience is truly a labor of love. This meal says we're all home together, safe and hungry.

3½ pounds chicken parts
3/4 cup all-purpose flour
1 teaspoon salt
Ground black pepper
2 eggs
1/4 cup milk
1 package saltine crackers
(1/4 box), finely crushed

Canola oil, for frying

GRAVY:
2 cups milk
1/2 cup flour
1/2 cup water
1 teaspoon salt
1/2 teaspoon pepper

1. Trim the chicken parts of extra skin or remove the skin from the breasts, thighs, and drumsticks. In a pie plate or other shallow dish, combine the flour, salt and a sprinkling of pepper. In another pie plate, whisk the eggs with the milk; sprinkle with salt and pepper. In a third pie plate, spread the cracker crumbs. Roll one piece of chicken in the flour mixture. Shake off the excess and dip it in the egg mixture. Dip it in the cracker crumbs, covering all sides. Set it on a large sheet of aluminum foil or waxed paper. Continue this process until all the pieces are coated.

2. In a skillet that is large enough so the chicken will not be crowded (or in two medium skillets), pour in the oil to about 1/2 inch deep. Heat the oil over medium-high heat until it is 360 degrees on a deep-fry thermometer.

3. Place the chicken in the oil. Avoid crowding, which creates too much steam and will not allow the chicken to fry to the desired crispness. Turn the chicken after 5 minutes, turn again after 5 minutes; continue turning until the chicken has cooked 20 minutes. Adjust the heat as needed so the oil bubbles steadily around the chicken but doesn't brown the chicken too quickly. Watch the oil level; don't let it get too low. If necessary, add more oil while the chicken is frying. You should end with the same amount of oil you started with.

4. While the chicken is frying, line a 9 x 13-inch baking dish with paper towels.

5. Remove the fried chicken to the baking dish. (The paper towels will soak up excess oil from the chicken.) Place the dish in a warm oven (about 170 degrees) until serving time.

6. To make the gravy, drain the oil from the skillet, leaving about 2 teaspoons in the pan. Place over medium heat and pour in the milk. In a small bowl, make a paste with the flour and the water. As the milk begins to heat, pour in the paste and continue stirring with a whisk until the gravy thickens. Add the salt and pepper. Bring to a boil and continue boiling for 2 minutes. Decrease the heat to simmer and adjust the seasonings. If the gravy is too thick, add more milk. If too thin, make more paste.

7. When ready to serve, transfer the chicken to a platter and pour the gravy into a gravy dish.

Serve with mashed potatoes and corn on the cob when in season—or canned or frozen corn, peas and carrots, or broccoli—or a salad. For a lighter meal, omit the mashed potatoes and gravy and serve the chicken with steamed or boiled red potatoes, rice, noodles, **Buttermilk Corn Bread** or **Northern-Style Corn Bread** (p. 241), or **Buttermilk Biscuits** (p. 240).

Variations:

◆ **Crisp-Fried Chicken** In place of the three pie plates, measure 1 cup flour, 1 teaspoon salt, 1/4 teaspoon ground black pepper, and 1 teaspoon paprika into a small paper or plastic bag. Shake to blend the seasonings. Put two pieces of chicken in the bag at a time and shake so the chicken is coated with the flour mixture. Fry as directed in the main recipe, but decrease the heat a little after the chicken is browned on both sides.

◆ **Southern-Style Gravy** This gravy method is customary in the American South. In place of the paste with water and flour, make a roux of canola oil and flour. It adds calories, but oh, does it taste good! In place of salt and pepper, add 1 teaspoon Tony Chachere's Original Creole Seasoning (see p. 169).

◆ **Buttermilk Fried Chicken** Place the chicken in a large bowl. Pour in 2 cups buttermilk and add 1 teaspoon salt. Refrigerate at least one hour. When ready to fry the chicken, mix 1 cup flour, 1 teaspoon paprika, and 1/2 teaspoon pepper in a shallow dish. Remove one piece of chicken at a time from the buttermilk; let excess drain. Roll chicken in flour mixture and fry as directed in the main recipe.

◆ **Single-Serving Oven-Fried Chicken** Wash and pat-dry two pieces of chicken of your choice. In a small bowl mix 2 tablespoons wheat germ seasoned with garlic salt and garlic powder. Roll the chicken in the mixture. Bake skin side up (if skin is left on) in a 400-degree oven for 40 to 50 minutes, or until tender and no longer pink. My friend Barbara, who is the master at eating healthy, has been making this chicken for years. It is delicious! The wheat germ mixture is also good on pork and fish.

ROAST TURKEY AND STUFFING

6 servings

Traditional Bread Stuffing (p. 214),
    Corn Bread Stuffing (p. 215),
    or 1 (6-ounce) package
    stuffing mix
1   (8-pound) fresh turkey,
    or frozen, thawed

4   cups chicken broth
1/2 cup canola oil
1/2 cup all-purpose flour
Salt and ground black pepper

1. Prepare the stuffing.

2. Unwrap the turkey, save the wrapper, and discard the giblets. Wipe the cavity with damp paper towels and discard the towel immediately (to prevent cross-contamination). Place the turkey in a large, shallow casserole dish or roasting pan. Fill the cavity with the stuffing. Cover the turkey loosely with aluminum foil and roast according to the wrapper's directions for a stuffed turkey.

3. Remove the stuffing from the turkey and place it in a serving dish. Remove the turkey from the pan and place on a platter or cutting board. Cover with the foil to keep it warm and let it stand for 15 to 20 minutes before carving.

4. To make the gravy, discard any bones or skin remaining in the drippings. (You can strain the drippings and return them to the pan.) Place the pan over medium-high heat and heat the drippings. Add the broth.

5. In a small bowl, make a roux of the oil and flour and mix until smooth. Pour into the pan and stir with a whisk until the mixture is smooth. Season with salt and pepper to taste. If the gravy is too thin, add more roux.

Serve with any of the following side dishes to complement your turkey dinner:

    Classic Mashed Potatoes (p. 211)
    Caramelized Sweet Potatoes and Yams (p. 216)
    Swiss Green Bean Bake (p. 206)
    Cheesy Broccoli Rice Bake (p. 208)
    Parmesan-Topped Creamed Corn (p. 206)
    Liz's Crescent Dinner Rolls (p. 234)
    Buttermilk Corn Bread or **Northern-Style Corn Bread** (p. 241)
    Cranberry sauce (fresh or canned)

Variation: Bake a turkey breast; make the stuffing separately and bake it in a casserole dish.

EASY CHICKEN CORDON BLEU
4 servings

2	slices white or wheat bread	4	slices deli ham
4	small boneless, skinless chicken breasts	6	thin slices Swiss cheese
Salt		8	tablespoons (1 stick) cold butter

I have always loved Chicken Cordon Bleu, but most recipes are much too complicated. Not this one. My friend Cherrie gave me this recipe some years ago. She said it's a family favorite, and it has become a favorite of ours as well.

1. Tear the bread into uniform pieces and pulse in a blender to make crumbs. Set aside.

2. If you are using frozen chicken breasts, while they are still slightly frozen, place the breasts between sheets of wax paper or resealable plastic bags and pound with a meat mallet to 1/8-inch thickness; don't pound too thin or the breast could fall apart in rolling. If you are using fresh breasts, remove the extra fat and cut into the breast to remove the gristle. Then pound to flatten. Lay the flattened breasts side by side on a platter, sheet pan, or a sheet of wax paper.

3. Preheat the oven to 350 degrees and grease a small baking dish.

4. Sprinkle each breast with salt. Add 1 slice of ham, 1 slice of cheese, 1 tablespoon of butter, and a sprinkling of bread crumbs. Roll up the breasts tightly and tuck in the ends. Place them seam side down in the prepared baking dish. When you have all the breasts in the baking dish, top each with 1 tablespoon of the remaining butter and 1/2 slice of the remaining cheese.

5. Bake 40 to 50 minutes, basting occasionally. Cover the dish with foil when the chicken browns, to prevent it from drying out. The chicken is done when it is tender and no longer pink. Serve immediately.

Serve with **Rice Pilaf** (p. 213), packaged quick rice, or baked potatoes, with green beans or broccoli for the vegetable. You don't need a salad with every meal. Just make sure you have plenty of vegetables to go with your main course. The chicken and the vegetables are plenty, or serve the chicken with salad and a roll.

Variations:

◆ Substitute baked ham slices or prosciutto and Mozzarella cheese.

◆ To make this for a crowd, double or triple the recipe and proceed as follows: Pound the breasts first, stack them with wax paper or foil between to separate them, and put them in the fridge until all the breasts are flattened. Then take out four breasts at a time, assemble them, and place them side by side on a jelly roll pan. Continue with four more until all are ready to bake.

CHINESE STIR-FRY

6 servings

This stir-fry makes me think of the one we had on the East King riverboat in China. We were traveling down the Yangtze River toward the Three Gorges Dam project, all the while eating the most wonderful Chinese food prepared by the cooks on the boat. This recipe is not exactly the same, but it is quick and easy. Brown rice is better than white—and better for you—but you can substitute white if you prefer.

1½ pounds boneless, skinless chicken breasts
1 tablespoon canola or peanut oil
1/2 cup chicken broth, divided
1/2 cup snow peas
1/4 cup each sliced red, yellow, and green bell pepper
1/2 cup sliced fresh mushrooms

2 cups cooked brown or white rice
2 tablespoons sugar
2 teaspoons grated fresh ginger, or ground
1/2 cup soy sauce
2 teaspoons cornstarch

1. Cut the chicken into bite-size strips. Heat the oil in a large skillet or wok over high heat. Swirl the oil to coat the pan. Stir-fry the chicken until it is no longer pink. Cover, reduce the heat, and simmer for 6 minutes.

2. Meanwhile, heat the cooked rice, if necessary, to warm it for serving.

3. Combine the remaining 1/4 cup broth, sugar, ginger, soy sauce, and cornstarch in a small bowl. Pour over the chicken and vegetables and cook over medium heat until thickened and bubbly. Serve immediately over rice.

Variations: Substitute or add vegetables of your choice: onion wedges or green onion pieces, sliced water chestnuts, bamboo shoots, asparagus pieces, broccoli florets, bias-sliced carrots, or chopped Chinese cabbage.

Can be made *Meatless*: Use tofu and vegetable broth in place of chicken and chicken broth.

CONVERSATION STARTER:

Do you kids realize that in China right now the Yangtze River, which is the third-longest river in the world, is rising and millions of homes are going under water because of the big dam that is going in? People there have had to find new homes. What would that be like for us, say, if we had a flood, or a fire? What kind of home would we look for?

CHINESE SUNDAES KIDS WILL LOVE

6 servings

1   cup uncooked calrose rice (see Note)
1/4 teaspoon salt
1   pound grilled or broiled boneless, skinless chicken breasts, or 3 cups chopped cooked chicken
Coarse salt and freshly ground pepper
1   (5-ounce) can ready-to-eat chow mein noodles
2   celery ribs, diced
1/2 cup slivered or chopped raw almonds

1   (20-ounce) can pineapple tidbits, drained
2   (11-ounce) cans mandarin oranges, drained, or fresh orange segments
1/2 cup coconut
1   (6-ounce) jar maraschino cherries, drained
1   (10.75-ounce) can condensed cream of chicken soup
1   cup sour cream
1/2 cup milk

My daughter-in-law Shana loves this dish—as do the rest of us. Jared requests it. It's fun to fix and to serve. I love all the combinations of the different flavors, especially the crunchy noodles with all the toppings.

1. Cook the rice according to package directions, adding the 1/4 teaspoon salt to the boiling water. Keep warm.

2. Meanwhile, grill or broil the chicken breasts, 6 to 8 minutes per side until no longer pink. Season to taste with coarse salt and freshly ground black pepper. Cut into bite-size pieces. Keep warm.

3. Place the noodles, celery, almonds, pineapple, oranges, coconut, and cherries in individual serving bowls.

4. To make the sauce, mix the soup, sour cream and milk in a small saucepan. Stir occasionally over medium heat until heated through. Transfer to a bowl.

5. Set up as a buffet or pass the ingredients for everyone to make their "sundaes" on dinner plates or in large bowls. Start with the a bed of chow mein noodles and add rice, chicken, celery, pineapple, oranges, coconut, and almonds. Drizzle sauce over all and top with a cherry!

Note: Calrose rice is available in the Asian foods section of many supermarkets, or you may substitute any short- to medium-grain rice.

Can be made *Meatless*.

SLOW-COOKED CHICKEN NOODLE SOUP

About 12 cups

The slow cooker can be a lifesaver for all of us. Sometimes it is the difference between getting a meal on the table and not. This is a light chicken noodle soup that is perfect for an afternoon meal on a lazy Sunday.

DO AHEAD

Start this dish at least 5 hours ahead of time, or up to 11 hours ahead of time to allow for cooking time—see step 2.

2½ to 3 pounds chicken parts (see Note)
1   medium onion, chopped
4   carrots, sliced
2   celery ribs, sliced
2   tablespoons dried parsley flakes
1   tablespoon salt
1   teaspoon dried basil
1/2 teaspoon ground black pepper
1/4 teaspoon dried thyme leaves
2   cups uncooked wide egg noodles
2   cups frozen peas (optional)

1. Wipe the chicken pieces with damp paper towels and discard the towels immediately to avoid cross-contamination. Trim off excess skin and fat. Set aside.

2. Put the onion, carrots, celery, parsley flakes, salt, basil, pepper, and thyme in a large slow cooker. Place the chicken pieces on top. Add water to cover. Place the lid on the slow cooker and cook on low heat 8 to 10 hours or on high heat 4 to 6 hours.

3. Thirty to 60 minutes before serving, remove the chicken pieces with tongs. When they are cool enough to handle, remove the skin and tear the meat from the bones and shred it. Return the meat to the pot. Add the noodles and cover and cook on high heat for 30 to 45 minutes.

4. Just before serving, stir in the peas, if desired, until heated through. Season to taste with additional salt and pepper.

Note: You may use a whole chicken, cut up, or all breasts or all legs as desired.

CONVERSATION STARTER:

Thanks, everybody, for going to Aaron's game yesterday. Wasn't it awesome? What was your favorite play, Aaron?

EVERYDAY **SALADS**

When going out to lunch, I like nothing better than one of the "new" salads of the 21st century. That's what I like to call them.

They are all about eating healthy. I love all the fruits and nuts mixed together with the many lettuces and other greens. I love warm steak salad that has the hot mixed with the cold. That to me is a real salad!

Everywhere we go we see new salad trends adorning the menus at darling little cafes popping up all over the world. My hat is off to the owners of all these wonderful places. Our good friend Bruno has opened his new little café in Brazil with lots of healthy salads and sandwiches.

I love that farmers' markets are opening in cities and towns across the country. When you're able to pick up fruits and vegetables grown close to home and harvested just hours before, the freshness, flavor, and nutritional value can't be beat...plus you're supporting the farmers in your community directly.

I know what kind of work it takes to create a new salad. It takes a lot of patience and good taste. I have been inspired to make my own version of some salads that I have eaten at restaurants and cafes. They are not exact, but pretty darn close!

My favorite way to serve a tossed salad is on separate salad plates or bowls, although that is not always practical or even desirable when serving the family. But if you're serving just a few people or hosting a dinner party, it's an elegant touch to create a mini work of art on each plate! Start with a pool of salad dressing, add a handful of greens, and then sprinkle on the other ingredients, such as fruit, nuts, or cheese. You can pass additional dressing for those who want more. But it's always better to start with too little dressing than too much.

Besides "21st century" salads, this chapter includes many classics and old favorites that I have tweaked to my family's liking over the years. There are many, many potato salads, chicken salads, and tuna mac salads out there, but my versions have been tried and tested and retried and retested over and over on my husband, my children, relatives, neighbors, and now my grand-children. So you're sure to like every one of them!

I am so excited about my salads. These are wonderful. Bon appetit!

Liz

EVERYDAY
SALADS

BLT SALAD WITH CHEESE AND ALMONDS

8 to 10 servings as a side dish; 4 to 5 servings as a main course

Whenever I take this salad to a shower or party, everyone asks for the recipe. I take all the ingredients in resealable plastic bags or containers so that I can put the salad together very fast just before serving. Do not make it ahead. This salad has to be eaten immediately.

DRESSING:
Juice of 1 lemon
2   garlic cloves, crushed
1   teaspoon salt
1/2 teaspoon ground
     black pepper
3/4 cup canola or olive oil

SALAD:
2   heads romaine lettuce
4   ounces bacon, cooked and diced
2   cups grape tomatoes
1   cup shredded Swiss cheese
2/3 cup sliced or slivered almonds
1/3 cup freshly grated Parmesan cheese
Salt and freshly ground black pepper
Homemade Croutons (p. 200),
     or packaged croutons

1. To make the dressing, whisk the lemon juice, garlic, salt, and pepper in a small bowl. Slowly add the oil in a steady steam and continue to whisk. Cover and let stand until ready to use.

2. Tear the lettuce into small pieces into a large salad bowl. Add the bacon, tomatoes, Swiss cheese, and almonds. Toss with the dressing and Parmesan cheese. Season to taste with salt and pepper and garnish with the croutons. Serve immediately.

Variation: substitute **Buttermilk Ranch Dressing** (p. 198) for the lemon dressing.

Can be made *Meatless*: Omit the bacon.

CONVERSATION STARTER:
There's some talk about eliminating physical education, art, and/or music in the schools. Do you think they're important? Why or why not?

PEAR GORGONZOLA SALAD

4 to 6 servings

8   cups spring mix
2   medium ripe pears (see Note)
1/2 cup crumbled Gorgonzola cheese
1/4 cup dried cranberries

Caramelized Walnuts (p. 201)
Balsamic Vinaigrette (p. 199)

1. Put the spring mix into a large bowl. (Spring mix is a combination of small-leafed lettuces, available at most supermarkets.)

2. Peel the pears. Cut in half, core, then cut into thin slices. Add the pears, cheese, cranberries, and walnuts to the greens.

3. Add just enough dressing to moisten the ingredients, and toss to coat and combine.

Note: The cut pear edges will oxidize and turn brown if cut up ahead of time so slice at the last minute before serving. Your pears should be just ripe and fragrant. If they are still hard they have no flavor, and if too ripe, they turn to mush. To check for ripeness, apply gentle pressure at the stem end of the pear with your thumb. If it yields to pressure, it's ready to eat.

After tasting this salad in many restaurants, I went home and created this recipe. I love the pears with the Gorgonzola and the caramelized walnuts. This salad is absolutely delicious—and so easy to put together just before you sit down to eat.

CONVERSATION STARTER:

Your cousin Mike just joined the Marines. What do you think about that?

SPINACH SALAD WITH FRUIT AND CHEESE

4 to 5 servings

This combination of spinach, fruits, and cheese is practically a complete meal in itself. My Poppy Seed Dressing ties everything together in the tastiest way!

4 to 5 cups spinach
1/3 cup shredded Swiss cheese
1/2 cup sliced fresh strawberries
1/3 cup mandarin oranges, drained

Easy Sugared Pecans (p. 201)
Poppy Seed Dressing (p. 199)

1. Tear spinach into pieces, if necessary, and put into a large salad bowl. Add the cheese, strawberries, mandarin oranges, and pecans.

2. Just before serving, add just enough dressing to moisten the ingredients, and toss to coat and combine.

Variation: Vary the fruits using red seedless grapes, blueberries, dried cranberries, or red apples.

CONVERSATION STARTER:
If you could trade lives with one person for a day, who would it be? Why? How would you spend your day?

NEW YORK STEAK SALAD WITH GORGONZOLA *5 main-course servings*

10 cups romaine lettuce pieces
2 cups **Homemade Croutons** (p. 200), or packaged croutons
2 medium tomatoes, cut into wedges
1/2 cup thinly sliced red onion
1 cup unpeeled sliced cucumbers

1 pound boneless New York steak
Olive oil
Seasoned salt, or salt and ground black pepper
1/2 cup Gorgonzola cheese crumbles
Honey Mustard Dressing (p. 200)

New York steak is a tender cut of beef equivalent to a porterhouse steak minus tenderloin and bone. Grill the steak instead of broiling if you like. The dressing really makes this salad.

1. Preheat the oven to low broil.

2. Mix the lettuce with the croutons, tomatoes, onion, and cucumbers in a large bowl.

3. Brush the steak lightly on both sides with the oil. Sprinkle with seasoned salt or salt and pepper. Broil 6 to 11 minutes per side for medium doneness, depending on thickness. (Meat will continue to cook when it is removed from the heat.) At the last minute, sprinkle on the cheese and continue to broil until the cheese is melted. Transfer the steak to a cutting board and let stand 5 minutes. Slice into 1/4-inch-thick strips.

4. Just before serving, add just enough dressing to moisten the salad ingredients, and toss to coat and combine. Arrange on individual plates.

5. Arrange steak slices on top of salad. Drizzle with salad dressing.

CONVERSATION STARTER:
What would you do if a teacher asked you to do something you felt was wrong?

FRUIT, NUT, AND CHEESE TOSS

4 to 6 servings

8 cups mixed salad greens	1/4 cup chopped pecans or walnuts
1 Fuji apple, diced	1/4 cup dried cranberries
1/3 cup shredded Swiss cheese	**Creamy Raspberry Vinaigrette (p. 198)**

1. Put the greens, apple, cheese, nuts, and dried cranberries into a large bowl.

2. Just before serving, add just enough dressing to moisten the ingredients, and toss to coat and combine.

Variation: Sugar the nuts (p. 201) before adding to the salad.

GARDEN SALAD WITH OLIVES

4 servings

2 cups spinach	1 (6-ounce) can pitted black olives, drained
2 cups green leaf or Boston leaf lettuce	1 tomato, cut into narrow wedges
2 cups red leaf lettuce	1 small can sliced beets (optional)
1/2 cup carrot slices (1/4 inch thick)	**Buttermilk Ranch Dressing (p. 198),**
1/2 cup cucumber chunks	**or bottled ranch dressing**

1. Tear the greens into bite-size pieces and place in a large bowl.

2. Add the carrots, cucumber, olives, tomato, and beets, if using.

3. Just before serving, add just enough dressing to moisten the ingredients, and toss to coat and combine.

REDS & GREENS SALAD

4 to 6 servings

4 cups romaine lettuce pieces
4 cups spring mix (see Note)
1 cup red seedless grapes, halved
2/3 cup crumbled feta cheese
1/2 cup sliced red onion
1/2 cup dried cranberries
1/2 cup pistachio nuts

Balsamic Vinaigrette (p. 199)
or **Creamy Raspberry
Vinaigrette** (p. 198)

Red grapes, red onion, and dried cranberries are great additions to a mix of salad greens in this wonderful salad. It has become a family favorite!

1. Toss the romaine pieces with the spring mix in a large bowl.

2. Add the grapes, cheese, onion, dried cranberries, and nuts.

3. Just before serving, add just enough dressing to moisten the ingredients, and toss to coat and combine.

Note: Spring mix is a mixture of small-leafed greens, available at most supermarkets.

CONVERSATION STARTER:
Let's make a list of the places we would most like to visit in the world. First category – places close enough to drive to...

MIXED GREENS AND MORE

4 to 6 servings

Salad can be as easy as lettuce tossed with your favorite dressing. If you have other fresh vegetables, add them too. Putting together a salad is a great way for kids to help with a meal.

8 cups salad greens
Optional fresh vegetables such as tomatoes, green onion, red peppers, cucumbers—whatever is fresh and appealing

Salad dressing of choice

1. Put the greens in a large bowl.

2. Add other vegetables of your choice.

3. Toss with your favorite dressing.

Variation: Add freshly grated Parmigiano-Reggiano cheese from Italy or crumbles of blue cheese for an extra flavor burst.

ELEGANT CHICKEN SALAD

8 servings

1   cup uncooked medium
     shell pasta
1/2 cup bottled coleslaw dressing
1/2 cup mayonnaise
2   cups (about 3/4 pound)
     shredded cooked chicken
1   (20-ounce) can pineapple
     chunks, drained
1   (8-ounce) can sliced water
     chestnuts, drained and diced

1/2 large red-skinned apple, diced
     (about 1 cup) (My favorite for
     this salad are Fuji or Cameo.)
1   cup green seedless grapes
3   celery ribs, diced (about 1 cup)
1/2 tablespoon grated onion
1   cup whole cashews
Salt and ground black pepper

1. Cook the pasta according to package directions. Drain and transfer to
   a large bowl.

2. Mix the coleslaw dressing and mayonnaise in a small bowl. Add to the
   pasta, tossing gently to combine. Refrigerate at least 2 hours.

3. Meanwhile, mix the chicken, pineapple, water chestnuts, apple,
   grapes, celery, and onion in a medium bowl. Refrigerate.

4. Just before serving, add the chicken mixture and cashews to the pasta,
   tossing gently until all the ingredients are combined. Season to taste
   with salt and pepper.

5. Spoon into a large serving bowl or spoon individual servings onto lettuce leaves on plates.

Variation: Use **Honey Mustard Dressing** (p. 200) instead of the bottled
coleslaw dressing.

*I often double this
main-dish salad to
serve at women's
luncheons, where it
is always a big hit.
Cook boneless, skin-
less chicken breasts
in advance or save
time by tearing
pieces off a ready-
to-eat rotisserie
chicken from the
deli. And after
Thanksgiving, you
can make this salad
with leftover turkey.*

DO AHEAD

Plan ahead to
refrigerate the
salad for at least
2 hours before
serving, or as
long as 2 days.

CONVERSATION STARTER:

*The library books we checked out
are due later this week. Have you
finished reading them? What was
your favorite part?*

PESTO-DRESSED PASTA SALAD WITH HAM AND CHEESE *8 servings*

SALAD:
1 pound uncooked radiatore pasta
12 ounces cooked ham, cut into long, thin strips
12 ounces Swiss cheese, cut into long strips
1/2 cup diced green onions

PESTO:
2 cups loosely packed fresh basil
1/2 cup pine nuts
1/2 cup freshly grated Parmesan cheese
3 garlic cloves
3/4 cup olive oil
1/2 cup white wine vinegar
1 tablespoon ground black pepper

1. Prepare the pasta according to package directions. Drain, cool, and place in a large bowl with the ham, Swiss cheese, and green onions.

2. In a food processor, mix the basil, pine nuts, Parmesan cheese, garlic, oil, vinegar, and pepper until smooth. Pour over the pasta mixture and mix well.

3. Serve the salad at room temperature.

Variation: Use prosciutto instead of ham. Can also be made *Meatless*.

TUNA MACARONI SALAD

8 servings

2 cups uncooked shell macaroni
2 cups frozen baby peas
1 to 2 (7-ounce) pouches albacore tuna in water, drained
2 cups finely diced celery
2 green onions, thinly sliced
1 cup mayonnaise
1 (2.25-ounce) can sliced black olives, drained
3 tablespoons evaporated milk, half-and-half, or heavy cream
Salt and ground black pepper

1. Cook the macaroni according to package directions. Rinse, drain, and put into a large bowl.

2. Thaw the peas quickly by running hot water over them in a strainer or colander; drain well. Add to the macaroni.

3. Add the tuna, celery, green onions, mayonnaise, olives, and evaporated milk to the macaroni. Mix well and season with salt and pepper to taste.

4. Refrigerate until ready to serve.

Variation: Substitute cooked cocktail shrimp for the tuna.

QUICK CAESAR-STYLE SALAD

4 to 5 servings

1   head romaine lettuce (or 6 to 8 cups packaged romaine pieces)
2   cups **Homemade Croutons** (p. 200), or packaged croutons
1/2 cup freshly grated Parmesan cheese
Bottled creamy Caesar salad dressing

1. Tear the romaine into bite-size pieces.

2. Add the croutons and cheese.

3. Just before serving, add just enough dressing to moisten the ingredients, and toss to coat and combine.

Variations:

◆ Top the Caesar with cooked chicken breast, salmon, shrimp, or sliced beef.

◆ Instead of the bottled Caesar dressing, use **Almost Caesar Dressing** (p. 198).

CONVERSATION STARTER:

I heard your friend Zach got pushed around by a bully in school today. Why do you think some kids feel the need to bully others? What would you do if a bully tried to pick on you?

Did you know that Caesar salad is more than 80 years old? Legend has it that it was first made in 1924 by Caesar Cardini at his restaurant in Tijuana, Mexico. It became popular with Hollywood movie people who visited Tijuana, and the recipe eventually made its way across the border into Los Angeles restaurants. It used to be an attraction all by itself at fancy "Continental" restaurants, where it would be tossed and served table-side. Now it is a popular salad every-where, without the theatrics. This is my version of a quick Caesar. It is both the easiest salad to make and the one that everyone will eat—there's nothing in it that anyone needs to pick out!

CLASSIC AMERICAN-STYLE POTATO SALAD

6 to 8 servings

This is my own creation, and everyone tells me it is just the right mix of flavors—not too sweet, not too much mayonnaise, just right. This recipe can be doubled or tripled easily for a crowd.

DO AHEAD

Plan ahead to refrigerate the salad for at least 2 hours and up to 2 days before serving.

SALAD:
5   medium russet potatoes (about 2 pounds)
6   eggs
2   celery ribs, finely chopped
1   small sweet pickle, finely chopped
1/3 cup chopped onion (optional)

DRESSING:
1   cup mayonnaise
2   teaspoons prepared mustard
1½   teaspoons sugar
1½   teaspoons sweet pickle juice
1   teaspoon cider vinegar
Salt and ground black pepper
Paprika

1. Scrub the potatoes and put them in a large pot with water to cover. Cover the pot and bring to a boil. Remove the lid and decrease the heat, keeping the water boiling. Cook about 30 minutes or until the potatoes fall apart when pricked with a fork. Drain and let stand until the potatoes are cool enough to handle.

2. Meanwhile, place the eggs in a saucepan with enough cold water to cover. Bring to a boil over high heat. Decrease the heat to just below simmering, cover, and cook 15 minutes. Immediately drain the eggs and run cold water over them to stop the cooking. Add ice cubes to cool the eggs quickly.

3. Peel the potatoes and dice them into a large bowl. Peel and chop the eggs and add to the potatoes. Add the celery, pickle, and onion, if using.

4. In a small bowl, mix the mayonnaise, mustard, sugar, pickle juice, and vinegar. Spoon into the potato mixture and combine. Season generously with the salt and pepper to taste. Lightly sprinkle on the paprika. Cover and refrigerate at least 2 hours before serving.

CONVERSATION STARTER:

Let's come up with a great birthday present to give to your grandmother!

(or grandfather, or a favorite friend)

ACINI DI PEPE FRUIT SALAD

16 to 20 servings

2   cups uncooked acini di pepe
    pasta
3   egg yolks, beaten
1 3/4 cups pineapple juice
1   cup sugar
3   tablespoons all-purpose flour
1/2 teaspoon salt
1   (8-ounce) container frozen
    whipped topping, thawed

1   (14-ounce) can crushed
    pineapple, drained
1   (20-ounce) can pineapple
    tidbits, drained
4 to 5 cups mini marshmallows
2   (11-ounce) cans mandarin
    oranges, drained

1. Cook the pasta according to package directions; do not overcook.

2. Meanwhile, whisk the egg yolks, pineapple juice, sugar, flour, and salt
    in a medium saucepan. Cook over medium heat, stirring constantly
    with a wooden spoon until thickened.

3. Drain the cooked pasta and put it in a medium bowl. Pour the egg
    mixture into the pasta and stir until well-mixed. Cover and refrigerate
    six to eight hours.

4. Fold in the whipped topping to loosen the chilled pasta mixture. Then fold in
    the pineapple and marshmallows. Gently fold in the oranges last to avoid
    breaking them up.

*Acini di pepe,
which is Italian for
"peppercorns," is
a form of pasta
that looks like tiny
beads. I got this
crowd-pleaser from
Phyllis, who called it
Frog's Eye Salad.*

DO AHEAD

Plan ahead to
refrigerate this
salad for several
hours or
overnight.

SIMPLE CABBAGE SALAD

4 servings

1/4 cup canola oil
2   tablespoons rice vinegar
    or white wine vinegar
1   teaspoon sugar

1/4 teaspoon salt
1/8 teaspoon ground black pepper

4   cups finely shredded green cabbage

1. Whisk the oil, vinegar, sugar, salt, and pepper in a small bowl.

2. Pour over the cabbage in a serving bowl. Toss to blend.

Variation: Use half cabbage and half shredded spinach. Add 1/4 cup finely sliced
green onions.

*This salad goes
together so easily!
And it's so nice and
crunchy. When you
add spinach, it's like
adding nutritious
green confetti.*

BUTTERMILK RANCH DRESSING

About 1½ cups

Here's a fresh homemade version of the old classic, with a little kick from the addition of lime juice and cilantro. Besides tossing it in green salads, I use this for my Taco Salad (p. 126) and as a sauce for my Fish Tacos (p. 95).

3/4 cup mayonnaise
1/2 cup buttermilk
1 tablespoon freshly squeezed lime juice
1 tablespoon minced fresh cilantro

1 teaspoon ground black pepper
1 teaspoon minced fresh garlic
3/4 teaspoon minced fresh oregano, or 1/4 teaspoon dried
1/2 teaspoon minced onion
1/4 teaspoon salt

1. Mix all the ingredients in a blender.

2. Use immediately or store in a tightly covered container and refrigerate up to 1 week. Shake well before using.

CREAMY RASPBERRY VINAIGRETTE

About 1 cup

Raspberry vinegar, available in most supermarkets, adds a special flavor to what would otherwise be a standard salad dressing.

1/2 cup mayonnaise
1 tablespoon raspberry vinegar
1/8 teaspoon salt

1/8 teaspoon ground black pepper
1/2 cup olive oil
1/8 teaspoon sugar (optional)

1. Whisk the mayonnaise with the vinegar in a small bowl. Add the salt and pepper.

2. Drizzle in the olive oil and continue to whisk. Adjust the seasonings to taste, adding the sugar if desired.

3. Use immediately or store in a tightly covered container and refrigerate up to 1 week. Shake well before using.

ALMOST CAESAR DRESSING

About 3/4 cup

This simple dressing gives Caesar-salad flavor without the raw egg or anchovies...though you could always add a few.

1/4 cup plain yogurt
1 tablespoon lemon juice
1/2 teaspoon Worcestershire sauce
1 garlic clove, minced

1/8 teaspoon salt
1/8 teaspoon ground black pepper
1/4 cup olive oil

1. Whisk the yogurt with the lemon juice, Worcestershire sauce, garlic, salt, and pepper in a small bowl.

2. Drizzle in the olive oil and continue to whisk. Use immediately.

SWEET RED WINE VINAIGRETTE

About 1¼ cups

1/2 cup sugar	1 teaspoon dry mustard
1/4 cup red wine vinegar	3/4 teaspoon salt
1 tablespoon grated red onion	1/2 cup canola or olive oil

1. Blend the sugar, vinegar, onion, dry mustard, and salt in a blender.

2. With the blender on low speed, drizzle in the oil until thoroughly mixed.

3. Use immediately or store in a tightly covered container and refrigerate up to 2 weeks. Shake well before using.

If you prefer a mellower, sweeter taste in your salads, this is the dressing for you.

BALSAMIC VINAIGRETTE

About 3/4 cup

1/2 cup olive oil
Juice of 1 lemon
2   tablespoons balsamic vinegar
2   teaspoons Dijon mustard

1. In a small bowl, whisk the oil, lemon juice, vinegar, and mustard. (Or mix the ingredients in a blender.)

2. Use immediately or store in a tightly covered container in the refrigerator for up to 2 weeks. Shake well before using.

Balsamic vinegar is both tangy and a little sweet, and so good.

POPPY SEED DRESSING

About 1½ cups

3/4 cup olive oil	3/4 teaspoon salt
1/3 cup sugar	1/2 teaspoon minced onion
1/3 cup red wine vinegar	1/2 teaspoon Dijon mustard
1 teaspoon poppy seeds	

1. Whisk all ingredients in a small bowl or mix in a blender.

2. Use immediately or store in a tightly covered container in the refrigerator for up to 2 weeks. Shake well before using.

This dressing is an old favorite for salads that combine greens and fruit, such as my Spinach Salad (p. 188).

HONEY MUSTARD DRESSING

About 1½ cups

I'm always drawn to
honey like, well, like
a bee is drawn to
honey! I love this
dressing on my New
York Steak Salad,
and it's wonderful
for a change on
spinach salad and
my Elegant Chicken
Salad (p. 193).

1   cup mayonnaise
1½ tablespoons red wine vinegar
1½ tablespoons white vinegar
1   teaspoon Dijon mustard
1/2 cup honey
1   teaspoon sugar

1   teaspoon minced white onion
Dash dried parsley flakes
1/2 cup canola oil
Salt and ground black pepper

1.   In a blender, mix the mayonnaise, red wine vinegar, white vinegar, and
     mustard until smooth. Blend in the honey, sugar, onion, and parsley.

2.   Slowly add the oil while the blender is running and mix until well-blended.
     Season with salt and pepper to taste.

3.   Use immediately or store in a tightly covered container and refrigerate up to
     1 week. Shake well before using.

HOMEMADE CROUTONS

Croutons are a
welcome addition to
many green salads,
as much for their
crunchy texture as
for their flavor.
They're easy to
make at home and a
great way to use up
leftover bread.
French bread is
ideal, but any crusty
bread can be used
for these delights.

Dense French bread
Butter
Garlic salt
Ground black pepper (optional)

1.   Slice the French bread about 1 inch thick. Spread with butter and sprinkle
     with garlic salt and pepper, if desired.

2.   Lay the slices on a cookie sheet and broil until lightly browned. For crisper
     croutons, broil the bread on both sides.

3.   Cut into 1/2-inch cubes.

CARAMELIZED NUTS

About 2/3 cup

1   tablespoon butter
1   tablespoon honey
1/2 cup walnut or pecan halves or pieces
1/4 teaspoon sugar

1. Preheat the oven to 350 degrees.

2. Melt the butter in a small saucepan over medium heat. Add the honey and stir until bubbly and a bit foamy. Add the nuts and continue to stir about 1 minute. Sprinkle with the sugar and continue stirring until most of the foamy mixture is soaked into the nuts, about 1 minute. Remove from the heat.

3. Transfer the nuts to a small baking pan, and bake for 4 minutes. Spread on aluminum foil to cool.

4. Break apart and store refrigerated in resealable plastic bags for several days or frozen for several months.

Both caramelized and sugared nuts add a crunchy "sweet spot" and a touch of sophistication to a variety of salads. Sugared nuts are easier to prepare, while caramelized nuts are a little more complex. With a harder coating that you have to break apart, they are almost like peanut brittle. Try both and see which you prefer!

EASY SUGARED NUTS

About 3/4 cup

2/3 cup walnut halves or pecans
1/4 cup sugar

1. Mix nuts and sugar in a small skillet over medium heat until the sugar is melted. Stir well to coat.

2. Spread on aluminum foil and let cool.

3. Break apart and store refrigerated in resealable plastic bags for several days or frozen for months.

EVERYDAY
SIDE DISHES

Here are the side dishes that will complement your theme nights. Most of the recipes I have gathered through the years from wonderful friends and then tweaked them for my family's tastes or my own convenience.

I have been in many homes now as the Food Nanny, and I am surprised how many are not serving

vegetables. Some people don't have even a single can of vegetables in their cupboard.

Vegetables are such an important part of any meal. When I go to a restaurant that serves me vegetables, I think I am really getting my money's worth! For just about any meal, you can heat up a can of corn or green beans, or cook frozen vegetables in the microwave if you don't have fresh. Canned butter beans are fabulous! And sautéed mushrooms are a real treat with a piece of meat. Nowadays fresh vegetables are more available than ever, especially in the many farmers' markets springing up all over.

Vegetables are a must with almost any meal except breakfast. Think about serving more than one vegetable and going lighter on the meat and carbs (whether potatoes, pasta, rice, or bread). This is a great way to introduce vegetables to your kids. Serve a couple of vegetables with the meal and have your kids try them. They don't have to eat every piece; just taste them. This is how we acquire a taste for new foods—by trying them a little at a time.

I serve these vegetables and all of the side dishes in this chapter many times during the year. I know they will be a big help to you in your meal planning.

Liz

EVERYDAY SIDE DISHES

One of my favorite things to serve with fish, meat, or lasagna is a beautiful platter of steamed or sautéed vegetables. You can choose from any of these vegetables; at least three vegetables make an appealing presentation:

- *Asparagus roasted in olive oil*

- *Zucchini slices, sautéed in light olive oil*

- *Butter beans, heated through*

- *Carrot slices, steamed and lightly seasoned*

- *Artichokes, steamed, lightly seasoned with lemon and garlic*

- *Red and yellow bell peppers, sliced and sautéed in olive oil*

- *Spinach, steamed and lightly seasoned*

- *Fresh green beans, steamed and lightly seasoned*

- *Fresh corn, steamed*

- *Fresh cut broccoli spears, steamed and lightly seasoned*

- *Fresh peas, steamed*

- *Edamame (young soy beans), steamed*

- *Baby white, red, or golden potatoes, steamed (one per person)*

- *Potato chunks sautéed in a little olive oil*

- *Baked yams*

- *plus explore your local farmers' market or greengrocer for new things to try*

PARMESAN-TOPPED CREAMED CORN

6 servings

Everyone loves this corn that the girls and I perfected over the years. But you'll want to eat just a small serving; it is very rich.

1	(16-ounce) bag frozen corn, thawed	2	tablespoons milk
1	tablespoon butter	1	tablespoon sugar
1	tablespoon all-purpose flour	1/2	teaspoon salt
1/2	cup heavy cream or half-and-half	1/8	teaspoon ground white pepper
		1/4	cup grated Parmesan cheese

1. Cook the corn according to package directions and set aside.

2. Melt the butter in a medium saucepan over medium heat. Stir in the flour and cook until bubbly, about 1 minute. Gradually whisk in the cream and milk. Cook, stirring constantly, until the sauce thickens and bubbles. Decrease the heat to low and add the sugar, salt, and pepper. Mix in the corn.

3. Preheat the broiler to low. Pour the corn mixture into a small greased casserole or baking dish that can go under the broiler. Top with the cheese. Broil until hot and bubbly.

SWISS GREEN BEAN BAKE

6 to 8 servings

About 15 years ago on a flight to Mexico, I met an interesting woman who was one of the first flight attendants hired by Western Airlines. Lois and I had the most delightful visit and shared recipes. This is one of hers, and it's become a must at every Thanksgiving ever since. Lois made it with canned green beans, but we have since switched to fresh.

2	pounds fresh green beans, trimmed and cut in half, or 2 (14.5-ounce) cans	1/2	teaspoon sugar
		1/2	teaspoon salt
		1/8	teaspoon ground black pepper
1	cup cornflakes cereal	1	tablespoon grated onion
2	tablespoons butter, divided	1/2	cup sour cream
1	tablespoon all-purpose flour	1	cup shredded Swiss cheese
1/4	cup milk		

1. Preheat the oven to 400 degrees and grease a 1½-quart casserole.

2. Steam the beans 10 to 15 minutes, until tender.

3. Meanwhile, put the cornflakes in a resealable plastic bag and crush coarsely with a rolling pin. Melt 1 tablespoon butter in a small bowl in the microwave and stir in the crumbs. Set aside.

4. Melt the remaining 1 tablespoon butter in a medium saucepan over medium heat. Whisk in the flour, and cook and stir until the mixture is bubbly. Whisk in the milk. Remove from the heat and stir in the sugar, salt, pepper, onion, and sour cream until well-blended. Stir in the cheese. (The cheese need not melt.)

5. Drain the beans if necessary and combine them with the cheese sauce. Spoon the mixture into the prepared casserole. Sprinkle the crumbs over all. Bake for 20 minutes.

BAKED BUTTERED CARROTS

4 servings

2 to 3 large carrots (about 1 pound)
1   tablespoon butter, softened
1/4 teaspoon sugar
Coarse salt and ground black pepper

1. Preheat the oven to 400 degrees.

2. Peel the carrots and cut them in half crosswise and then again lengthwise. Place them in a square baking pan and cover the carrots with water. Cover with aluminum foil and bake for 1 hour.

3. To serve, drain the carrots well and place them on a platter. Dot them with the butter and sprinkle with the sugar and salt and pepper to taste.

Here's an easy way to prepare cooked carrots. Just put them in the oven and set the timer! Buy individual carrots for better taste. The bagged carrots are less fresh and more likely to have a bitter taste.

STIR-FRIED GREEN BEANS

6 to 8 servings

3   tablespoons olive oil
1   pound fresh whole green beans, trimmed

3 to 4 garlic cloves, minced
Coarse salt and ground black pepper

1. Heat the oil in a large skillet or wok over medium-high heat. Add the beans and garlic. Stir-fry, using tongs, until the beans turn a bright green color, 5 to 6 minutes. Decrease the heat to low and continue to stir until the beans are almost done. Cover and remove the pan from the heat and let the beans steam a few more minutes.

2. Season with salt and pepper to taste.

CHEESY BROCCOLI RICE BAKE

8 servings

This casserole has been a part of our Thanksgiving dinner for almost 30 years. It is delicious with any cut of meat.

1   tablespoon butter
2 to 4 tablespoons minced onion
1   pound fresh broccoli, cut into 1-inch pieces, or frozen chopped broccoli
1   (10.75-ounce) can condensed cream of mushroom soup

1/2 cup milk
1   (8-ounce) jar processed cheese sauce
1   cup cooked white rice (regular or instant)

1.   Preheat the oven to 350 degrees.

2.   Melt the butter in a small saucepan or skillet over medium heat and cook and stir the onion until it is soft. Set aside.

3.   In a large saucepan, cook fresh broccoli, covered, in salted boiling water for 2 to 4 minutes. (Or cook frozen broccoli according to package directions.) Drain into a colander and set aside.

4.   In the same saucepan, combine the soup, milk, and cheese sauce and cook over medium heat until smooth. Remove from the heat.

5.   Stir the rice, onions, and broccoli into the cheese mixture. Spoon into a square baking dish and bake for 20 minutes, or until hot and bubbly.

CHEESE SAUCE FOR VEGETABLES

About 1½ cups

If you can't get your children to eat broccoli or cauliflower, try serving this cheese sauce on the side. It's also a real treat over baked potatoes.

2   tablespoons butter
2   tablespoons all-purpose flour
1/4 teaspoon salt
1/8 teaspoon ground white pepper

1   cup milk
1   cup shredded medium Cheddar cheese

1.   Melt the butter in a small saucepan over medium heat. Blend in the flour, salt, and pepper. When the mixture is bubbly, quickly add the milk. Cook, stirring constantly, until the mixture thickens and bubbles.

2.   Remove from the heat and add the cheese, stirring until smooth.

Serve over baked potatoes, broccoli, or cauliflower.

Variation: Cheese-Sauced Potatoes: Peel and slice five russet potatoes, place in a greased square baking dish, and cover with the sauce. Bake at 350 degrees for 1 hour.

TWICE-BAKED POTATOES

9 to 12 servings

6	medium russet potatoes	1	teaspoon minced green onions (optional)
1/2	cup (1 stick) butter	2	cups shredded Cheddar cheese, divided
1/4	cup sour cream		Salt and ground black pepper
1/4	cup mayonnaise		
1	egg		

1. Preheat the oven to 400 degrees.

2. Scrub, dry, and cut the tips off the potatoes, to allow air to escape during baking. Set on an oven rack or a baking sheet (do not wrap in aluminum foil) and bake for 1 hour. Allow to cool. Cut in half lengthwise so each half is boat-shaped. Reduce the oven temperature to 350 degrees.

3. Scrape out the insides into a medium bowl. Set the skins on a sheet pan or cookie sheet.

4. Add the butter, sour cream, mayonnaise, egg, green onions, and 1 cup of the cheese. Mix with an electric mixer until smooth. Season with salt and pepper.

5. Spoon the mixture into the potato skins. (You will probably end up with more skins than mixture.) Sprinkle the remaining cheese evenly over the potatoes. Bake about 30 minutes or until the potatoes are heated through and light brown on top.

Our neighbor Rebecca, who was only 15 at the time, brought these to a dinner party we once had with Lizi's friends. They were so good, we asked for the recipe and have been making them ever since. For a leaner version, decrease the amounts of butter and cheese and use low-fat sour cream and mayonnaise.

CAN DO AHEAD

Bake potatoes 1-2 days before completing the recipe.

CONVERSATION STARTER:

Let's talk about safety in our home so we can all be prepared to be safe in case of a natural disaster. What kinds of things might happen and what are some of the things we would need to do?

CHEDDAR HASHBROWN CASSEROLE

6 to 8 servings

My sister Jan is the best at finding easy, tasty recipes, and this is one of them. For a leaner version, use low-fat soup and low-fat sour cream.

1	(24-ounce) package frozen hashbrown potatoes, thawed	1/4 to 1/2	teaspoon garlic salt
1	cup sour cream	3/4	cup shredded Cheddar cheese
1	(10.75-ounce) can condensed cream of chicken soup	1	cup corn flakes
		1	tablespoon butter, melted

1. Preheat the oven to 350 degrees and lightly grease a square baking pan.

2. Spread the thawed hashbrowns on paper towels to soak up excess moisture, then transfer to a large bowl. Combine with the sour cream, soup, garlic salt, and cheese. Mix thoroughly and spoon into the prepared dish.

3. Put the corn flakes into a resealable plastic bag and crush them coarsely with a rolling pin. Transfer to a small bowl and mix in the butter. Sprinkle on the casserole.

4. Bake until hot and bubbly, about 35 minutes.

BAKED BEANS WITH MAPLE AND COCOA

6 to 8 servings

You've probably heard of maple baked beans, but have you ever added cocoa? It may sound odd, but it contributes a subtle richness that makes these baked beans extra-special.

2	(15-ounce) cans baked beans	1/4	cup pure maple syrup
1/4	cup packed brown sugar	1	tablespoon unsweetened Dutch-process cocoa powder
1	tablespoon dry mustard		
1/4	cup ketchup	1/4	cup water

CAN DO AHEAD

This dish may be made ahead of time. Reheat to serve.

1. Preheat the oven to 300 degrees. Grease a square baking pan or small casserole dish.

2. Mix all the ingredients in a large bowl and pour the mixture into the pan. (Or simply mix the ingredients in the baking dish.)

3. Bake uncovered 50 to 60 minutes or to desired consistency.

Variation: Baked Beans for a Crowd Double the recipe and mix all the ingredients in a slow cooker. Cook on low at least 2½ hours or to desired consistency.

Meatless if made with vegetarian baked beans

CLASSIC MASHED POTATOES

6 to 8 servings

6   medium (about 2 pounds) russet or Yukon Gold potatoes
Coarse salt
6   tablespoons milk or cream
2 to 4 tablespoons butter
Salt and ground black pepper

1. Peel and cut the potatoes into 2-inch chunks. Put them in a large saucepan with salted cold water to cover by 1 inch. Bring to a boil, cover slightly, and cook until they are tender when pierced with a fork, 15 to 20 minutes. Drain completely and cover to keep hot.

2. Heat the milk and butter in a small pan or in a measuring cup in the microwave.

3. With the hot potatoes in the same pan or in a large bowl, mix with an electric mixer on moderate speed or by hand with a potato masher. Add the milk and butter. Season with salt and pepper to taste. Serve immediately.

Variations:

◆ **Tangy Mashed Potatoes:** Substitute 3/4 to 1 cup of yogurt, sour cream, or buttermilk for the milk.

◆ **Cheese-Topped Oven Mashers:** Preheat the oven to 350 degrees and cover a sheet pan with aluminum foil. Spoon mashed potatoes into six mounds on the foil. Sprinkle shredded Cheddar cheese on top. Bake just until the cheese melts and the potatoes are hot. To serve, lift the potatoes with a spatula onto each plate.

◆ **Garlic Mashed Potatoes:** Ahead of preparing the mashed potatoes, roast a whole garlic bulb. Preheat the oven to 350 degrees. Cut the tops off the cloves. Drizzle the bulb with olive oil, sprinkle with coarse salt, and wrap in foil. Place in a baking dish and bake 20 to 30 minutes. When cool enough to handle, squeeze out all the pulp (it will have the consistency of jam); discard the skins. Stir the pulp into the mashed potatoes and mix well. Alternatively, cook garlic cloves along with the potatoes and mash them all together.

We love mashed potatoes! Add gravy and they're one of my most beloved foods. I'm glad I am the cook so I can make mashed potatoes whenever I am hungry for them! The best mashed potatoes I ever ate were at my friend Candice's country home. She used Yukon gold potatoes, seasoned with sea salt, and mashed with generous amounts of butter and cream. Then when my friend Cathy came to visit and help me with some cooking for this book, she made sure I included her Garlic Mashed Potatoes as a variation, below right.

SIMPLE PARMESAN RISOTTO
6 to 8 servings

Risotto may sound intimidating, but really it's very simple. The key is to use a high-starch, short-grain rice. Arborio is the most popular. As you stir the rice as it cooks, the starches are released and you will get the beautiful creamy risotto. This is my newest recipe because it comes from my colleague at Sur la Table in Salt Lake City, Chef Scot Rice. I have learned so much since I started working with him.

5 cups chicken broth
4 tablespoons (1/2 stick) butter, divided
1½ cups finely chopped onion
1½ cups arborio rice

1 cup grated Parmesan cheese
Salt and ground black pepper
2 tablespoons chopped fresh Italian parsley
Shaved Parmesan cheese

1. Bring the broth to boiling in a medium saucepan. Decrease the heat to low and cover the pan.

2. Melt 2 tablespoons of the butter in a heavy large saucepan over medium-low heat. Add the onion; cook and stir until very tender but not brown, about 10 minutes. Increase the heat to medium. Add the rice and stir 1 minute.

3. Add 1½ cups of the hot broth. Boil gently until the broth is absorbed, stirring frequently. Add another 1 cup broth; stir until broth is absorbed. Add the remaining 2½ cups broth, 1/2 cup at a time, allowing the broth to be absorbed before adding more. Stir frequently until the rice is tender and the mixture is creamy, about 20 minutes.

4. Stir in the remaining 2 tablespoons butter and the grated Parmesan. Season with salt and pepper to taste. Transfer to a serving bowl. Sprinkle with the parsley and shaved Parmesan.

Can be made *Meatless*: Use vegetable broth or mushroom broth in place of the chicken broth.

CONVERSATION STARTER:

This meal we're sharing is great food for our bodies. Now, what can we do as a family to "feed" our brains?

RICE PILAF

6 servings

2	tablespoons unsalted butter	1	teaspoon salt
1/2	small yellow onion, finely chopped	1	teaspoon ground white pepper
3 to 4	medium garlic cloves, minced	1¼	cups long-grain white rice
		2½	cups chicken broth

1. Melt the butter in a medium saucepan over medium heat. Add the onion, garlic, salt, and pepper. Stir until the onion is soft but not brown. Stir in the rice until it is well-coated. Add the broth and bring to a boil.

2. Cover, decrease the heat, and simmer until the rice is tender and the liquid is absorbed, 15 to 20 minutes.

Can be made *Meatless*: Use vegetable broth or mushroom broth in place of the chicken broth.

Variations:

◆ Add mushrooms and/or peas after adding the broth.

◆ Use basmati rice instead of long-grain white rice for a nuttier flavor.

◆ For extra texture, substitute precooked wild rice for 1/4 to 1/2 cup of the white rice and add it to the pilaf at the last minute. (Wild rice, which is actually not a rice, but a marsh grass, takes up to 1 hour to cook, although there is quick-cooking wild rice on the market.)

The first time we ate this rice pilaf was more than 35 years ago. It was a cold and snowy night when my friend Ann made this to go with salmon and served it to us in her 300-year-old kitchen with the fire raging in the old brick fireplace.

CONVERSATION STARTER:

The average rice consumption per person per year in the world is more than 175 pounds! We don't eat anywhere near that much, but for some people, that's all they have to eat. What foods that we eat are you most grateful for?

TRADITIONAL BREAD STUFFING

8 to 10 cups; enough for stuffing a 14- to 17-pound turkey

Making stuffing for the first time was a bit scary for me. I wanted to make it like my mother's, but she did not have any measurements for her recipe. She just said to add a little bit of this and a little bit of that. How much bread? How much onion? How much sage? It took me awhile to come up with my own recipe. Now I've been making this for over 25 years. Double or triple the recipe for a family Thanksgiving with plenty of leftovers, which your family will love you for!

1 regular-size loaf white or wheat bread	1 small onion, diced (optional)
1 teaspoon ground sage	3/4 cup diced celery
1/2 teaspoon salt	1 egg, beaten
1/4 teaspoon ground black pepper	1 cup chicken broth
1/3 cup butter	Butter, for dotting the top (optional)

1. Tear the bread into bite-size pieces and lay it out in a single layer on a sheet pan to dry out. Cover with paper towels and stir occasionally over two or three days.

2. Put the torn bread into a large bowl and sprinkle with the sage, salt, and pepper.

3. Melt the butter in a large saucepan over low heat. Add the onion and celery and cook and stir about 15 minutes, until the onion is soft. Pour the mixture over the bread.

4. Stir in the beaten egg. Add just enough chicken broth to hold everything together without becoming soggy, up to 1 cup. Remember that if you will be baking the stuffing in a roasting bird, the stuffing will absorb meat juices from the bird.

5. To bake stuffing in a bird, heat the mixture just before spooning it—lightly—into the bird. To bake the stuffing outside the bird, moisten it with additional broth and turn it into a large, shallow greased baking dish. Dot the top with butter as desired. Cover with aluminum foil and bake in a preheated 350-degree oven, stirring occasionally, until the stuffing is heated through, 30 to 45 minutes.

Variations:

◆ Add 1/2 to 3/4 cup whole-berry cranberry sauce or dried cranberries (or both!).

◆ Add 8 ounces fully cooked country bulk sausage.

(Use one variation or the other; don't add both cranberries and sausage.)

Can be made *Meatless*: Substitute vegetable broth for the chicken broth.

DO AHEAD

Start this stuffing by putting the bread out to dry (Step 1) two to three days ahead.

CORN BREAD STUFFING

About 8 cups

Buttermilk Corn Bread (p. 241)
2   slices bread, toasted medium brown
3   ribs celery, chopped
2   small yellow onions, chopped
2   cups chicken broth
1/2 teaspoon salt, divided

1½ teaspoons minced fresh sage or 1/2 teaspoon dried
1/4 teaspoon ground black pepper
2   eggs, beaten
1   teaspoon chicken bouillon granules (optional)

1. Three to four days in advance of stuffing the bird, prepare the corn bread and make the toast. Crumble the corn bread and tear the toast into pieces into a very large bowl. Let the bowl sit uncovered so the mixture dries out. Stir it occasionally so it will dry thoroughly.

2. In a medium saucepan, combine the celery, onions, broth, and 1/4 teaspoon of the salt. Bring to a boil, cover, and reduce the heat to medium-low and cook until the vegetables are fork-tender, about 5 minutes.

3. Add the vegetable mixture to the bread and mix thoroughly. Add the remaining 1/4 teaspoon of salt, the sage, and the pepper. Blend thoroughly and adjust the seasonings. Gradually stir in the eggs and mix well. If the mixture seems to require more moisture, remember that if you will be baking the stuffing in a roasting bird, it will absorb meat juices from the bird. If you will be baking the stuffing in a separate dish and it needs more moisture, dissolve the chicken bouillon in 1 cup of hot water and add this broth a little at a time until the stuffing is the desired moistness.

4. To bake stuffing in a bird, reheat the mixture just before lightly spooning it into the bird. To bake the stuffing outside the bird, turn it into a large, shallow greased baking dish. Bake uncovered in a 350-degree oven until the top has formed a crust and the stuffing is heated through, 25 to 40 minutes.

Can be made *Meatless*: Use vegetable broth or mushroom broth in place of the chicken broth and chicken bouillon granules.

My friend Julie in Granbury, Texas, gave me this old family recipe of hers when we lived in the same town. The first time I took a bite of it I knew I had to have the recipe! It is a labor of love to create it, but worth every bite for those of us who love Southern corn bread stuffing. You can use my Buttermilk Corn Bread (p. 241), or any corn bread. The addition of toast keeps the stuffing from being gummy. All the ingredients are necessary to meet everyone's taste: the moist, the dry, and the crusty!

DO AHEAD

Start this stuffing by putting the bread out to dry (Step 1) three to four days ahead.

CARAMELIZED SWEET POTATOES OR YAMS

6 to 8 servings

Years ago, we had just moved to Chicago. A distant cousin I'd never met invited us to her beautiful home. The dinner table was set perfectly. (By contrast, Steve and I at that time had just a card table in our tiny apartment.) My cousin fixed this dish and we have been making it ever since. The caramel that forms on top is divine!

4 large sweet potatoes or yams	1/4 cup milk
1/4 cup (1/2 stick) butter	2 cups powdered sugar
1/4 cup packed brown sugar	Walnut halves

1. Preheat the oven to 350 degrees.

2. Scrub the sweet potatoes and cut off the tips. Bake for 1 hour or until soft in the center when poked with a fork. When cool enough to handle, peel the potatoes and cut in half lengthwise and then into 1/2-inch-thick slices. Lay the slices in an oblong baking dish, overlapping slightly as needed.

3. Melt the butter in a medium saucepan over medium heat. Add the brown sugar and milk and bring to a boil, stirring constantly. Let the mixture thicken slightly. Remove the pan from the heat and add the powdered sugar; whisk until smooth.

4. Spread the sugar mixture over the sweet potatoes. Place a walnut half on each slice. Bake until bubbly and slightly browned, about 20 minutes.

Variation: For color interest, use both sweet potatoes and yams (two of each) and place them alternately in the oblong pan. The mix of yellow sweet potato slices and orange yam slices, each topped with a walnut half, makes a beautiful dish that is so appropriate for autumn!

SWEET POTATO

YAM

BREADS WE CAN'T LIVE WITHOUT

BREADS WE CAN'T LIVE WITHOUT

My mother and grandmothers baked bread all their lives. Fresh-baked bread was delicious to look at and more delicious to bite into, spread with butter and honey or jam. There was nothing in the cooking arena that I did not want to just dive right into, so I began my longtime love affair with bread making.

I really can't remember the very first time I ever made bread, but it was sometime soon after we were married. In the first eight years of my bread baking, I kneaded all the dough by

hand. Looking back, that was my workout for that day. I was making four to six loaves at a time, even then.

I do remember the first time I made homemade rolls. It was also right after we were married and we had our friends the Porters over for Sunday dinner. The rolls were a hit with my husband and our guests, so that gave me great confidence. I continued to experiment with any recipe that someone told me was wonderful. I have made hundreds of recipes of each—every kind of bread and every kind of roll.

The recipes that I have in this chapter are the ones that I just keep going back to. I have some quick breads that are simply wonderful. The white and wheat bread recipes are the easiest yeast recipes I have for you to start baking for the first time. They are very good breads. I am thrilled to be able to share them all with you.

My homemade crescent rolls are my signature bread. I have been making them for almost 30 years. I try all kinds of new recipes, but always come back to these. I take them to every dinner and every party we are invited to.

As the Food Nanny, I find that one thing all cooks have in common is that they want me to teach them how to make French bread. Now you can learn too. Happy bread baking! Let me know how you're doing.

Liz

TRIED AND TRUE TRICKS
FOR YEAST BREADS

Making yeast breads is an art, a gift, a labor of love. If you have the desire, you can make any kind of bread you want to. It's very rewarding and the results taste so good. Try your hand at it and before you know it, you will have the confidence to try any recipe.

There are many variables in bread making, beginning with the flour! Flours can vary greatly from brand to brand, and even the same brand of flour may be different in different regions because of where the wheat was grown. Bread flour has more protein than all-purpose, so it gives yeast breads more structure and chewiness. You may substitute it in my yeast bread recipes, but its higher protein content will overpower other baked goods. Flour is also affected by how it is stored. It may have more moisture in it if it is stored at room temperature in a humid climate, or it may be really dry if it is stored in the freezer. Flour variances can make a difference in all baked goods and especially in bread making. That's why bread recipes generally give a range for how much flour to add. It depends. The more experienced you become with bread making, the more you will get a "feel" for how the dough should be.

Here are tips and techniques for achieving success with any yeast dough.

Equipment

Obviously you do not need a heavy-duty stand mixer or food processor to make yeast bread or rolls—our grandmothers or great-grandmothers did fine mixing everything with a big wooden spoon. But if you have the space and can afford to add a food processor or stand mixer (with a dough hook) to your kitchen, mixing and kneading bread dough will go more quickly and easily—and you won't hesitate to make bread more often. Even if you have only a hand-held electric mixer, you can save time and effort by mixing in about half the flour before you have to switch to a wooden spoon to stir in the rest.

Heavy-duty stand mixers knead perfectly with a lot less effort than hand kneading. Some large food processors can knead bread dough, but they can handle only relatively small batches of dough. Read the manual that came with your machine for guidelines and recommendations.

Working with Yeast

Please note that my recipes call for measuring the yeast. This is because I buy my yeast in a larger quantity, rather than individual packets. Each packet contains 2¼ teaspoons of yeast, so two packets is the equivalent of 1½ tablespoons.

Before mixing the dough ingredients, active dry yeast must be dissolved in warm liquid, usually water, that is at a temperature of 105 to 115 degrees. Use your candy thermometer to test water temperature at first, to get a sense of how warm to the touch this temperature is. After awhile, you will be able to sense it yourself without a thermometer.

A rule of thumb is that it should feel slightly warmer than body temperature. If you were to drop a drop of warm water on the inside of your wrist, you would feel it as "warm." If the water were only your body temperature (nearly 100 degrees), you would not feel that warm sensation. Water that is 105 to 115 degrees should feel warm, but not hot.

Instant yeast, also called bread yeast, can be substituted for active dry yeast in any of these recipes. Simply mix the yeast with the other dry ingredients rather than dissolving it in liquid. Heat the liquids and fat to 120 to 130 degrees before combining with the flour/yeast mixture.

The No. 1 tip for good results in yeast breads and rolls is to work in a warm kitchen without drafts. The dough needs to be kept warm if the yeast is to do its job of raising the dough. A temperature of 70 to 85 degrees is best. This is warmer than many of us keep our houses in these days of energy conservation. For bread-baking days, you may want to raise your thermostat to 70 or 72, or turn on the oven at a low heat to warm up your kitchen a bit.

One time when my publisher, designer, and editor were staying at our home, I made my cinnamon rolls for them. I had mixed the dough very early in the morning and left it covered to rise on the kitchen counter as I crept back into bed for a few more winks. When I went back to my dough, it had hardly risen. I was aghast! And then I discovered windows open and realized the kitchen was too cool. My cinnamon rolls finally did rise and they were delicious in the end, but not without waiting far too long for them to rise. Lesson: Close the windows and doors if there is even a slight cool breeze.

Also bring all ingredients, including eggs and butter, to room temperature before bread making.

Kneading

When kneading by hand, grease or flour your hands to prevent sticking. Turn the dough onto a lightly floured surface and ball it up into a mass with your hands. Start kneading by folding the dough over and pushing

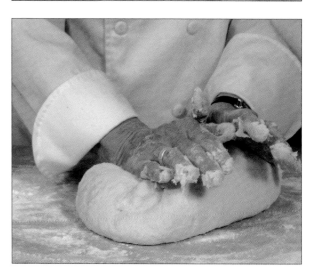

it down against the work surface in a rolling motion with the heels of your hands, curving your fingers over the dough. Give the dough a quarter turn, then fold it over and push down again. Give the dough another quarter turn and repeat this process until the dough is smooth and elastic. If the dough becomes too sticky, sprinkle the board under the dough with a small amount of flour and rub your hands with the flour again. When finished, most doughs should be tacky rather than sticky. If you add too much flour, you risk making the bread texture too dry.

If you own a heavy-duty stand mixer with a dough hook attachment, prepare the recipe as usual, but use the dough hook for kneading. Make sure the mixer bowl is large enough to hold the dough with room left over. Knead just a few minutes and the dough will come away from the sides of the bowl and will be smooth and elastic.

Successful kneading in a food processor requires a large bowl and a heavy base for stability. The appliance won't really knead dough fully, but it mixes the dry and liquid ingredients very well to form the dough. Breads that require a stiffer dough (most unsweet breads) will have to be kneaded by hand on the counter after processing, but this kneading time should be just a few minutes.

Rising

When the dough has been kneaded, by hand or machine, cover the bowl of dough to keep it warm and and to keep the surface of the dough from drying out. Cover with plastic wrap that has been sprayed on one side with oil or cooking spray, and/or with a clean dish towel.

To create a warm place for your dough to rise, place a pan of warm water in an unheated oven and then place the bowl of dough on a rack over it. Or turn your oven on to the minimum setting until it is just warmed (up to 85 degrees, not hot) and then turn it off. Place the bowl of dough in the oven and let it rise there. Do not allow the bread to rise in an over-warm place; this will result in inferior bread.

To test whether the dough has risen enough, insert your finger into the dough. If the impression remains, the dough is ready for forming into rolls or loaves. Test risen rolls and loaves in a similar way: Press down slightly with your finger at one corner; if the dough does not spring back up, it is ready to bake.

Baking

When loaves or rolls in pans have doubled in size, they are ready for the oven. Most baking is done on the middle rack, although I have found that for my crescent dinner rolls it's best to bake them for the first half of the baking time on the bottom rack to ensure that the bottoms of the rolls are adequately browned. Then I switch them to the center rack for the remainder of the baking time. Ovens vary greatly, so see how your oven responds when you make my dinner roll recipe and make adjustments accordingly. You may find that they bake perfectly fine on the middle rack for the entire baking time.

Another aspect you may want to experiment with is adding humidity to your oven to make a crisp crust. As *Joy of Cooking* notes in its Yeast Breads chapter, "Professional ovens have special steam injectors that fill the oven with steam during the first few minutes of cooking, but at home we need to improvise." I have achieved good results by spraying water in the oven with a spray bottle just before baking and again a few times during baking. (Be sure to avoid spraying the oven light bulb, which could cause it to crack.) Another option is placing a shallow pan of water in the bottom of the oven during baking. This is what I do when baking French baguettes. You might want to try the bread recipes with and without applying these techniques and compare the results.

To reheat bread to serve it hot at mealtime, cut it into thin slices, spread with softened butter, and put the slices back into a loaf shape. Place the "loaf" on a long sheet of aluminum foil, draw up the sides, leaving the top exposed, and place in a 350-degree oven up to 30 minutes before serving.

The recipe for this Italian bread is on the next page.

ITALIAN BREAD

2 large loaves

I remember the first time I ate Italian bread in Italy. It was so good and was served with olive oil and balsamic vinegar, which was a real novelty to me at the time. In Italy butter is not served with bread unless you ask for it. My friend Becky shared this fast and easy recipe with me many years ago, and it's just like the wonderful breads I've had in Italy— soft in the middle and crisp on the outside. It's delicious as is and also for sandwiches and French toast.

3 cups warm (105–115 degrees) water
1½ tablespoons (2 packets) active dry yeast
2 tablespoons plus 1/2 teaspoon sugar, divided
1 tablespoon salt

1/4 cup (1/2 stick) butter, melted
7 to 9 cups all-purpose flour, divided

Butter
1 egg white
Sesame seeds (optional)

1. In a small bowl combine the water, yeast, and 1/2 teaspoon of the sugar. Stir just until the yeast is dissolved. Cover with a small plate or paper towel and let stand until the mixture is bubbly or foamy, 5 to 10 minutes.

2. In a large mixing bowl or in the bowl of a heavy-duty mixer, mix the salt, the remaining 2 tablespoons of sugar, butter, the yeast mixture, and 3½ cups of the flour. Keep adding flour, 1/2 cup at a time, up to 3½ cups, for a total of 7 cups. The dough should be firm and completely away from the sides of the bowl. If the dough is still sticky, add more flour 1/4 cup at a time, up to the remaining 2 cups.

3. Knead by hand on a lightly floured surface, or with the dough hook on low to medium speed, about 10 minutes. Transfer the dough to a large, lightly greased bowl and turn it once to coat. Cover with a dish towel and let the dough rise in a warm place, away from drafts, until doubled in bulk, 20 to 40 minutes. Grease a baking sheet or sheet pan and set aside.

4. Punch down the dough and divide in half. On a lightly floured surface, form each half into a thick baguette shape, about 10 inches long. Place the loaves on the prepared pan. With a sharp knife, make three angled 1/2-inch-deep slashes on the top of each loaf. Beat the egg white with a fork and brush it over the loaves (see photo on p. 222). Sprinkle with the sesame seeds if desired. Let the loaves rise uncovered until doubled in bulk, 20 to 40 minutes.

5. Meanwhile, preheat the oven to 350 degrees. When the dough has doubled, bake for 30 minutes. For a crisper crust, spray water in the oven with a spray bottle just before baking and again a few times during baking. (See p. 223.)

6. Turn the loaves out onto a cooling rack. Serve the bread hot if desired or allow to cool. Pass olive oil and balsamic vinegar in a dish as an alternative to butter: Pour olive oil into a shallow dish, pour in balsamic vinegar, and then dip!

Variation: To make rolls, pinch off about 1½-inch balls of dough for each roll and place side by side on a greased sheet pan. Let rise until doubled in bulk, 30 to 45 minutes. Bake at 350 degrees until the rolls are lightly browned, 10 to 13 minutes.

FRENCH BAGUETTES

2 baguettes

1½ **cups warm (105–115 degrees) water, divided**
1½ **tablespoons (2 packets) active dry yeast**
2 **teaspoons sugar, divided**

3¼ **cups all-purpose unbleached flour**
2 **teaspoons salt**
Melted butter, for brushing on loaves (optional)

1. In a small bowl, combine 1/2 cup of the water, the yeast, and 1 teaspoon of the sugar. Stir just to combine and cover with plastic wrap or a plate. Let the mixture stand about 5 minutes or until bubbly or foamy.

2. In a large mixing bowl or the bowl of a heavy-duty mixer or food processor, blend the flour, salt, the remaining 1 teaspoon of sugar, and the yeast mixture. Gradually add water, up to the remaining 1 cup, and mix until the dough forms a smooth ball that is not too sticky to handle. (If the dough ends up too sticky, add a little more flour.) Turn the dough onto a floured surface and knead briefly, until the dough is smooth and elastic.

3. Cut the dough in half and shape the halves into baguettes. Grease a baguette pan (available at kitchen stores) and place the loaves in the pan. Score the loaves down the middle (make a shallow cut—see the photo on p. 217), cover with a dish towel, and let rise in a warm place about 30 minutes, or until doubled in bulk.

4. Meanwhile, preheat the oven to 450 degrees and place a shallow pan of water in the bottom of the oven to create steam (see the beginning of the chapter). Bake the baguettes for 15 minutes or until they have a hollow sound when tapped with a knife. If desired, brush the tops of the loaves with butter halfway through baking. For a softer crust, brush with butter when they have finished baking.

I will not forget the first time we bought a baguette in France. We all savored every bite. Denser than Italian bread, it is wonderful plain or with butter, and also makes excellent garlic bread and bruschetta. When the kids were young, I would make an extra loaf for French toast the next morning. It makes cute little rounds and tastes so good!

GARLIC BREAD
1 loaf

1   **French Baguette (p. 225 or Italian Bread (p. 224)**
2   **whole garlic cloves**
Olive oil, for drizzling

Basil, dried or fresh, chopped, for sprinkling
Grated Parmesan cheese, for topping (optional)

1. Preheat the broiler and adjust the oven rack to the middle position. (Broiling on a higher rack will broil the bread too fast.)

2. Slice the loaf in half lengthwise. Place the halves on a cookie sheet cut side up. Run under the broiler until barely light brown.

3. Rub one garlic clove over the cut side of each half. Drizzle oil over the bread and sprinkle on the basil. Top with the cheese, if desired, and broil just until the cheese is melted. Cut into slices and serve.

Note: If you purchase the French bread, choose a dense baguette, not a soft loaf.

CONVERSATION STARTER:
If you could have some weird pet, what animal would you choose?

HEARTH BREAD

2 loaves and one 8-inch square of focaccia

In the old days in Europe, women would mix up a little flour, yeast, and water before going to bed at night and then in the morning form the dough into a loaf. It was called hearth bread because the yeast mixture stayed warm by the hearth all night. As I've mentioned before, one of the most important rules in making bread is having a warm kitchen. I like to use a baking stone (see p. 145) for this bread because it seems more "Old World." As you make this bread, you might picture yourself out in the French countryside where Monet worked his magic or on the Champs-Élysées in Paris. Wherever your imagination takes you, you will have great joy in baking hearth bread for your family.

5 to 6 cups all-purpose flour, divided
2   teaspoons active dry yeast, divided
2   cups warm (105–115 degrees) water, divided
1   teaspoon coarse salt
1/4 cup olive oil (or half olive oil and half canola)

Cornmeal, for sprinkling on the baking stone, if using

OPTIONAL FOCACCIA INGREDIENTS:
Fresh herbs, minced
Sun-dried tomatoes, chopped
Garlic cloves, minced

1. Before you go to bed at night, mix 1 cup of the flour, 1 teaspoon of the yeast, and 1 cup of the water in a large bowl. Cover with plastic wrap (oiled on one side) and then again with a towel. Place a pan of hot water on the bottom of an unheated oven (to warm the oven) and place the bowl of dough on a center rack in the oven.

2. In the morning add to this mixture 1 cup of the flour, the remaining 1 teaspoon of yeast and 1 cup of water, the salt, and the oil. Mix well. Add 3 more cups of the flour and stir with wooden spoon. (Alternatively, you may mix the dough with a heavy-duty mixer.)

3. Turn the dough onto a floured surface. Gradually add more flour as you knead the dough to form a soft, smooth dough that does not stick to the floured surface, about 5 minutes. (If using a mixer, knead with a dough hook for 5 minutes.) Return the dough to the bowl (or let it rise in the mixer bowl) and re-cover it with plastic wrap (oiled on one side) and a towel. Set in a warm place to rise, about 1 hour.

4. Punch the dough down and knead briefly to remove the air bubbles. Divide the dough in half. From each half, pinch off a piece of dough about the size of a golf ball and set aside for the focaccia. If you'll be using a baking stone, start preheating the oven to 425 degrees, with the stone on a lower rack; it takes about 30 minutes for the stone to get hot.

5. With the two dough halves, form two small loaves or rounds and place them side by side on a greased baking sheet. Or, if you're using a baking stone, place the loaves on a baker's peel covered with flour. Cover the loaves with oiled plastic wrap and then again with a towel, and allow to rise while you make the focaccia square.

6. **TO MAKE THE FOCACCIA:** Knead the two golf-ball pieces of dough together a few times into one mass. If desired, knead in up to 1/4 cup fresh minced herbs, chopped sun-dried tomatoes, or 1 to 2 fresh garlic cloves, minced. Pick up the dough and rotate and stretch it in your hands like a pizza crust, to about the size of an 8 x 8-inch baking pan. Grease the pan and place the dough in it, stretching it a little more with your fingers as necessary. (It need not completely fill the pan.) Or place the square on another baker's peel. Use the handle end of a wooden spoon to dimple the dough very close together. Cover with plastic wrap (oiled on one side) and a dish towel and allow to rise 10 to 15 minutes.

7. If using a baking stone, sprinkle the stone with cornmeal just before sliding the loaves from the baker's peel onto the stone. (Feel free to give the loaves a little "boost" as needed.) Sprinkle the focaccia with coarse salt if desired and place it on a higher rack in the oven. Spray the sides of the oven with water and close the oven door. Spray a couple of times again as the bread is baking and spray directly onto the loaves as well. Bake 20 to 25 minutes or until the loaves are light brown on the top and bottom and the focaccia is golden. Turn loaves onto a cooling rack. Serve breads hot or allow to cool.

Note: Any bread can be baked on a baking stone instead of in a standard pan, as described above. Don't let a lack of bread pans keep you from baking bread!

TIP: Because the first rising of the Hearth Bread dough is overnight in the oven, it's a good idea to put a sign on the oven door so no one accidentally turns the oven on.

Bread
is
Rising!

BREADSTICKS

About 12 large or 24 small breadsticks

FAVORITE
YEAST BREADS

Basic Pizza Dough (p. 135)
1/3 cup butter, melted
1/4 to 1/2 teaspoon garlic salt or garlic powder

1. Make the pizza dough. Grease a sheet pan.

2. Pinch off balls of dough to equal about 2 tablespoons and roll between your hands to form small breadsticks. (If you have a small kitchen scale, it's fun to weigh each ball of dough so the breadsticks turn out uniform.) Lay them on the prepared pan.

3. Mix the butter and garlic in a small bowl. Brush onto the breadsticks, reserving some for later. Let the breadsticks rise until doubled in bulk, 15 to 20 minutes. Preheat the oven to 425 degrees.

4. After the breadsticks have risen, bake about 10 minutes or until they are golden brown. Brush on additional garlic butter halfway through baking and again after the breadsticks come out of the oven.

Serve the breadsticks as you would dinner rolls or with **Alfredo Sauce** (p. 71), **Marinara Sauce** (p. 140), or **pizza sauce** (p. 137) for dipping.

Variation: For Parmesan breadsticks, brush with melted butter; sprinkle lightly with garlic salt and heavily with grated Parmesan cheese.

These breadsticks make a tasty alternative to dinner rolls and add an interesting shape variation to a meal. I started making these when my kids were growing up, when it was a big treat to go to the Olive Garden for hot breadsticks with Alfredo sauce. Now they're grown up and they still love my bread-sticks, as do my grandchildren.

CONVERSATION STARTER:

Have a read-aloud night while you're still at the table after dinner. Each person picks a 5–10 minute piece to read. Discuss afterward what you liked about each piece.

LIZ'S CRESCENT DINNER ROLLS

About 24 rolls

My friend Sid gave me this recipe many years ago, and now it has become my signature. I have made these for everyone in our town for over 25 years. I have made 200-plus rolls, or about nine times this recipe, for many occasions.

2   tablespoons active dry yeast
1/4 cup plus 1 tablespoon warm
    (105–115 degrees) water
1   cup milk
3   eggs
1/2 cup sugar
1/2 cup canola oil
About 5½ cups all-purpose flour, divided
2   teaspoons salt
Butter

1. In a small bowl combine the yeast and water. Cover and let the mixture stand about 10 minutes.

2. Meanwhile, heat the milk in the microwave until just warm, not scalding.

3. In a large bowl, beat the eggs, sugar, and oil with a whisk. Stir in the milk and yeast mixture. With a wooden spoon stir in 5 cups of the flour and salt until combined. Turn the dough onto a lightly floured surface and knead to form a moderately soft dough, still slightly sticky.

4. Cover with plastic wrap sprayed with oil or cooking spray and allow the dough to rise in a warm place until it is sticky, 2 to 3 hours.

5. Lightly grease a 12 x 18-inch sheet pan and set aside.

6. Punch the dough down and turn it onto a lightly floured surface. Pat it with additional flour if necessary for handling, and keep your hands floured.

7. Divide the dough into thirds. Roll one section into a circle about the size of a dinner plate. With a pizza cutter, cut once down the middle, then across, then diagonally (the same way a pizza is cut) to make eight wedges. Roll up each wedge from the wide end toward the point. Place the rolls point side down on the prepared pan. Repeat with the remaining sections. (All rolls should fit on one sheet pan.)

8. Cover with a clean dish towel and let rise until doubled in bulk, about 15 minutes.

9. Meanwhile, preheat the oven to 400 degrees. Bake 5 minutes on the bottom rack; move to the middle rack and bake 5 minutes or until the rolls are light brown. Remove the rolls from the oven and brush the tops with butter.

CINNAMON ROLLS

20 large rolls

My friend Barbara shared this recipe with us and we have made it our own over 25 years. These are a grand treat to have right out of the oven. And I love to eat them with my chili (p. 49).

DOUGH:
1/4 cup warm (105–115 degrees) water
1 tablespoon active dry yeast
1 cup warm (105–115 degrees) milk
1/2 cup canola oil
1/2 cup sugar
1 teaspoon salt
5 to 5½ cups all-purpose flour, divided
2 eggs

FILLING:
6 tablespoons softened butter
1/2 cup granulated sugar, divided
1/2 cup brown sugar
2 teaspoons ground cinnamon

Walnuts, raisins, dates, for filling (optional)

Cream Cheese Frosting (recipe follows)

1. Measure the water into a glass measuring cup and add the yeast. Stir to dissolve and let it stand 5 minutes.

2. Heat the milk in the microwave and pour it into a large mixer bowl. Add the oil, sugar, and salt. Mix in 1 cup of the flour. Add the eggs and beat again. Stir in the yeast mixture. Adding 1 cup at a time, stir in 4 more cups of flour. Add enough remaining flour to make a soft dough.

3. Turn the dough onto a floured surface and knead gently until the dough is smooth and elastic. Cover and let rest while you wash the mixing bowl.

4. Lightly grease the mixing bowl and put the dough in the bowl, turning once. Spray plastic wrap with cooking spray and cover the bowl. Let rise in a warm place until the dough is doubled in bulk, 1 to 1½ hours. Grease a 12 x 18-inch sheet pan and set aside.

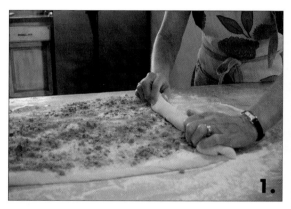

Use heavy-duty thread or dental floss to cut dough.

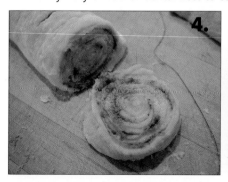

5. Punch down the dough. Roll out the dough on a floured surface into a large rectangle, about 20 x 14 inches or larger. Spread generously with the butter. Mix the granulated and brown sugar and the cinnamon in a small bowl and sprinkle the mixture over the dough. If desired, sprinkle the dough with chopped walnuts, raisins, or dates. Starting on one long side, roll up the dough into a tightly rolled log.

6. Mark the center of the roll with a knife mark and then make nine evenly spaced marks on each side of center, marking off a total of 20 rolls. Slice with a strand of heavy-duty thread or dental floss: place the thread under the dough, crisscross it over the dough, and pull quickly to make a clean cut for each roll. (See photos, previous page.) Place the rolls in the prepared pans.

7. Cover the filled pans with dish towels and let rise again until nearly double, about 30 minutes. Meanwhile, preheat the oven to 400 degrees. When the rolls have risen, bake 10 to 15 minutes, until just lightly browned.

8. Make the frosting and frost the rolls in the pan while still warm. Serve right away. Freeze cooled rolls in resealable plastic freezer bags.

Variation: For orange rolls, omit the brown sugar and cinnamon in Step 5. Mix 1/2 cup softened butter, 1/2 cup sugar, and grated peel of a large orange. Spread the mixture on the dough before rolling up. Then in the cream cheese frosting below, substitute orange juice for the lemon juice.

CREAM CHEESE FROSTING

4   ounces cream cheese, softened
2   tablespoons butter, softened
1   cup powdered sugar, sifted
1   teaspoon milk
1/2 teaspoon vanilla extract
1   teaspoon fresh lemon juice
    (or orange juice for the orange
    rolls variation)

Combine all the ingredients with an electric mixer until smooth.

SIX-WEEK BRAN MUFFINS

About 40 muffins

My youngest daughter, Lizi, and her friend Jamie started making this family favorite with whole wheat flour as a healthful variation. As the name implies, the batter keeps in the refrigerator for up to six weeks, so you can bake only the amount you want each day and always have freshly baked muffins.

5	cups whole wheat flour		3	cups sugar
5	teaspoons baking soda		4	eggs
2	teaspoons salt		1	cup canola oil
2	teaspoons ground cinnamon		1	quart buttermilk
6	cups raisin bran or bran flakes cereal		2	teaspoons vanilla extract

1. Combine the flour, baking soda, salt, and cinnamon in a very large bowl. Add the cereal and sugar, and mix.

2. Beat the eggs in a large bowl. Blend in the oil, buttermilk, and vanilla. Pour the egg mixture into the cereal mixture and stir well.

3. Transfer the batter to a large plastic container with a tight-fitting lid and refrigerate until ready to use. The batter will keep for 6 weeks.

4. When ready to bake, preheat the oven to 375 degrees and generously grease muffin cups or use cupcake liners. Do not stir the batter before filling the cups about 2/3 full. Bake until the tops spring back when touched, about 20 minutes.

THEME NIGHTS GO TO COLLEGE

When my daughter Lizi, far right, went off to college, she began cooking in her apartment, using my theme nights. Her roommates loved it! It made their apartment seem like home and took the stress out of deciding what to fix for dinner. They prepared healthy meals, and didn't gain the "freshman 15."

They ended up feeding friends, and the young men came by to ask if they were fixing a certain dish. It was a lot of fun for them. When Lizi looks back over her first year of college, she sees how rewarding it was to have my theme nights. It kept her going and gave her direction for making dinner. There is enough variety for everyone to have sufficient motivation to "get cooking."

So many of my meals are so quick and easy. Anyone can prepare them with little fuss or stress. This can be a great help to college kids and other young adults.

I'm proud that I've been able to pass on my love of cooking to Lizi. She plans to go on to culinary school and increase her knowledge in the kitchen. She hopes to help other young adults as they strive to figure out how to eat healthy!

Liz

OLD-FASHIONED BISCUITS

About 10 biscuits

*Most biscuit recipes
call for baking them
on a baking sheet,
but I've always
made mine in a
square pan and
have found that
the biscuits fluff up
more as a result.
Give it a try!*

2   cups all-purpose flour
1   tablespoon baking powder
1/2 teaspoon salt
1/2 teaspoon sugar

1/4 cup (1/2 stick) butter
      or shortening
3/4 cup milk

1.   Preheat the oven to 450 degrees.

2.   Sift (or whisk) the flour, baking powder, salt, and sugar in a medium bowl. With a pastry blender or fork, cut the butter into the flour mixture until the mixture resembles coarse crumbs. Pour in the milk all at once. Stir quickly with a fork just until the dough clings together; do not overmix.

3.   Turn the dough onto a lightly floured surface and knead gently 10 or 12 times. Excess handling makes biscuits tough. Just be sure all the ingredients are well-distributed throughout the dough. Gently roll or pat the dough to about 1/2 inch thick. Press a floured 2-inch biscuit cutter into the dough and swivel once or twice to make sure it has cut through. Dip the cutter into flour between cuts. Gather up the dough scraps into a ball and pat out again to cut one or two more biscuits.

4.   Place the biscuits close together in a square baking pan and bake until light brown, about 12 minutes. Serve warm, right out of the oven.

Buttermilk Biscuit Variation: Add 1/4 teaspoon baking soda to the flour mixture. Increase the butter or shortening to 1/3 cup and use 1 cup buttermilk in place of the milk.

HONEY BUTTER

About 1 cup

*Make this for your
family for a real
treat on biscuits,
corn bread, dinner
rolls, and scones.*

1/2 cup (1 stick) butter, softened
1/2 cup honey
1/2 teaspoon vanilla extract

1.   Combine all the ingredients. Beat with an electric mixer about 2 minutes.

2.   Store in a covered container in the refrigerator for three to four weeks.

Maple Butter Variation: This is even easier. Just combine 1 teaspoon maple syrup with 1/4 cup (1/2 stick) softened butter.

BUTTERMILK CORN BREAD

9 servings

1 cup all-purpose flour	1/2 teaspoon salt
1 cup yellow cornmeal	1 cup buttermilk
2/3 cup sugar	1/2 cup (1 stick) butter, melted
1/2 teaspoon baking soda	2 eggs, beaten

1. Preheat the oven to 350 degrees. Grease an 8 x 8-inch baking pan or generously grease a 9-inch cast-iron skillet.

2. Combine the flour, cornmeal, sugar, baking soda, and salt in a large bowl.

3. Combine the buttermilk, butter, and eggs in a medium bowl and mix well. Add to the flour mixture and stir just until blended. Do not overmix.

4. Scrape the batter into the prepared pan and bake for 25 to 30 minutes, or until the top is golden brown and the center feels firm when pressed.

Serve with honey butter or maple butter.

When we lived in Atlanta, I discovered that corn bread is so quick to prepare. And to Southerners, it's not corn bread without buttermilk!

NORTHERN-STYLE CORN BREAD

9 servings

1½ cups plus 2 tablespoons all-purpose flour	1¼ cups milk
2/3 cup sugar	2 eggs
1/2 cup white cornmeal	1/3 cup canola oil
1 tablespoon baking powder	3½ tablespoons butter, melted
1/2 teaspoon salt	
	Butter and honey

1. Preheat the oven to 350 degrees and grease an 8 x 8-inch baking pan.

2. Combine the flour, sugar, cornmeal, baking powder, and salt in a medium bowl.

3. In a small bowl, combine the milk, eggs, oil, and butter and mix well. Add to the flour mixture and stir just until blended. Do not overmix.

4. Pour the batter into the prepared pan and bake for 35 minutes. The corn bread is done when the edges are lightly browned and a toothpick inserted in the center comes out clean.

Serve with honey butter or maple butter (previous page).

This recipe is sweeter and "cakier" than Buttermilk Corn Bread— and amazingly good, especially when served with butter and honey!

BANANA BREAD

1 loaf

My daughter-in-law Kim gave us this recipe, which was a tradition in her family. It has become our all-time favorite banana bread.

3   bananas, cut up
1   cup sugar
1/2 cup (1 stick) butter (at room temperature)
2   eggs
1   teaspoon vanilla extract

2   cups all-purpose flour
1   teaspoon baking powder
1/2 teaspoon baking soda
1/8 teaspoon salt
1/2 cup coarsely chopped walnuts or pecans (optional)

1. Preheat the oven to 300 degrees and grease a 9 x 5 x 3-inch loaf pan.

2. In a large bowl, mash the bananas. Add the sugar and butter and mix with an electric mixer until smooth. Add the eggs and vanilla and mix on low about 1 minute.

3. Sift the flour, baking powder, baking soda, and salt onto a square of wax paper (or mix in a bowl). Add to the banana mixture all at once. Stir with a wooden spoon just until combined. Fold in the nuts, if using.

4. Scrape the batter into the prepared pan and bake 60 to 70 minutes, until a toothpick inserted in the center comes out clean, but not dry. Let cool in pan 10 minutes, then turn out onto a wire rack.

Chocolate Lover's Variation: Fold in 1/2 cup chocolate chips as a last step before turning the batter into the pan.

PUMPKIN CHOCOLATE CHIP BREAD

1 loaf

This bread is a family favorite, especially from October to Christmas, but we make it all year long to keep the great taste (and aroma!) of pumpkin around. Keep an extra can of pumpkin in your pantry because this bread is a great last-minute dessert. It makes a wonderful gift bread too.

1   cup canned pumpkin
2   eggs
1½   cups sugar
1/2   cup canola oil
1²⁄₃ cups all-purpose flour
1   teaspoon baking soda
3/4   teaspoon salt

1/2   teaspoon ground cinnamon
1/2   teaspoon ground cloves
1/2   teaspoon ground nutmeg
1/4   teaspoon baking powder
1/2   cup semisweet chocolate chips

See assembly instructions, opposite.

ZUCCHINI BREAD

2 large or 4 mini-loaves

2	cups peeled and grated zucchini (about 2 medium)
3	cups all-purpose flour
1	teaspoon salt
1	teaspoon baking soda
1/4	teaspoon baking powder
4	teaspoons ground cinnamon
1	cup chopped walnuts
2¼	cups sugar
3	eggs, slightly beaten
1	cup canola oil
1	teaspoon vanilla extract

My mother, my sisters, and I have been making this family recipe for over 50 years. Now my girls are making it for their families.

1. Spread out the grated zucchini on paper towels to soak up excess moisture.

2. Preheat the oven to 325 degrees and generously grease two 9 x 5 x 3-inch loaf pans or four mini-loaf pans.

3. Sift (or whisk) the flour, salt, baking soda, baking powder, and cinnamon into a large bowl. Stir in the nuts, if using. Set aside.

4. Mix the sugar, eggs, oil, vanilla, and zucchini in a large bowl. Stir in the dry ingredients with a wooden spoon.

5. Scrape the batter evenly into the prepared pans and bake the large loaves about 1 hour and 15 minutes, the mini-loaves 25 to 30 minutes, until a toothpick inserted in the center comes out clean, but not dry. Do not overbake; the breads should be moist.

Pumpkin Chocolate Chip Bread instructions:

1. Preheat the oven to 350 degrees. Generously grease and lightly flour a 9 x 5 x 3-inch loaf pan.

2. In a large bowl, whisk together the pumpkin, eggs, sugar, and oil.

3. Sift the flour, baking soda, salt, cinnamon, cloves, nutmeg, and baking powder onto a square of wax paper (or mix in a bowl). Stir into the pumpkin mixture and combine, but do not overmix. Stir in the chocolate chips.

4. Scrape the batter into the prepared pan and bake 55 to 65 minutes, until a toothpick inserted in the center comes out clean, but not dry. Do not overbake; the bread should be moist. Cool in the pan on a rack for 10 minutes. Turn out onto the rack to cool completely.

Nut Lover's Variation: Substitute chopped nuts for the chocolate chips.

COCONUT TEA BREAD

1 loaf

After I tasted this luscious tea bread the first time, I drove straight home and prepared it for my family. It's lovely as a snack with a cup of herbal tea or a glass of milk, or for a simple dessert in place of cookies.

2   eggs
1   cup sugar
1/2   cup canola oil
1/2   cup buttermilk
1   teaspoon coconut extract
1¼   cups all-purpose flour
1/4   teaspoon baking soda
1/4   teaspoon baking powder
1/4   teaspoon salt
1/2   cup coconut

GLAZE:
1/4   cup sugar
1/4   cup water
1   tablespoon butter

1. Preheat the oven to 350 degrees. Generously grease and flour a 9 x 5-inch loaf pan. (I prefer glass.)

2. Whisk the eggs, sugar, and oil in a large bowl until well-blended. Whisk in the buttermilk and coconut extract.

3. Sift the flour, baking soda, baking powder, and salt onto a square of wax paper (or stir in a bowl). Add to the egg-sugar mixture and stir just until blended; do not overmix. Stir in the coconut.

4. Pour the mixture into the prepared pan and bake for 45 to 60 minutes, or until a toothpick inserted in the center comes out clean. Remove from the oven and place on a cooling rack.

5. Meanwhile, make the glaze: Stir the sugar, water, and butter in a small saucepan and bring to a boil. Simmer for 5 minutes.

6. Pour the glaze over the bread while still warm in the pan. The bread will absorb the glaze and may sink as it cools. Slice the bread in the pan and serve.

DESSERTS
WE LOVE

THE FOOD NANNY RESCUES DINNER

DESSERTS WE LOVE

Other than birthdays, I had dessert only on Monday nights. The kids could count on dessert that night—mainly because we were all bummed that it was Monday! It marked the beginning of another hard week of school, cooking, laundry, taking care of kids, homework, ball practice, and the list goes on and on. We deserved a dessert on Monday night.

True, on other nights of the week, one of the kids might sneak in and make our favorite chocolate malt (p. 274). We always had vanilla ice cream on hand and Hershey's chocolate syrup, which the kids would put into the blender with milk and malt mix. We would pour this into little paper cups, so no one had a big glass of malt! Just a couple of gulps was enough. We also had home-made cookies after school many days, but dessert every night is not a habit your family needs to get in to.

Take it from the Food Nanny: A bite of something sweet will do most of the time. Do not keep candy bars lying around or

chocolate treats in dishes all over the house. Have candy for special occasions only. If you order dessert in a restaurant, share with some-one else. If your entire family is out to dinner, order just a couple of desserts and share them. Really, all any of us needs or even wants is a couple of bites.

I always worked to make Monday a special night at our home. What could be better than comfort food followed by a favorite dessert? I might make a cake or pie, apple crisp, Rice Krispies Treats, an ice cream dessert—anything I was hungry for.

Through the years I think I have made practically every cake and pie known to man! I love dessert. Cake is my weakness. Of course we had so many birthdays in the family that I got pretty good at making even cake-mix cakes amazing!

One of our favorites is still German chocolate cake, using the recipe right off the Baker's German's Sweet Chocolate package. I recently found out this cake didn't really come from Germany. The sweet chocolate used in the recipe was developed by a man named Samuel German. How about that?!

These are the recipes that I used most when I was raising my family. They are still the recipes I reach for when I am hungry for a dessert.

Liz

ALL-AMERICAN APPLE PIE

One 9-inch pie; 8 servings

The first time I tasted this pie from my friend Sherrie, I knew it was a keeper. Make your own pie pastry from this recipe, or save time with a packaged refrigerated pie crust. Many people think that making pie crust is intimidating, but it goes together quickly. When you use your own homemade crust, it makes eating and sharing the pie all that much more enjoyable.

PASTRY for a double-crust pie:
2½ cups flour
1   teaspoon salt
3/4 cup shortening
1/4 cup (1/2 stick) chilled butter, cut in small pieces
4 to 6 tablespoons ice-cold water

FILLING:
4 or 5 medium-large Granny Smith apples
3/4 cup sugar
3   tablespoons flour
3/4 teaspoon ground cinnamon
1/4 teaspoon allspice

1. To make the pie crust, stir the flour and salt in a large bowl. Cut in the shortening and butter with a pastry blender or two knives until the mixture resembles coarse crumbs (see Note). Sprinkle with the ice water, a tablespoon at a time, and stir with a fork to moisten all the dough. Gather the dough into a ball with your hands. Divide the dough in half. Roll out one half on a lightly floured surface and fit it into a 9-inch pie plate. Roll out the other half and set aside.

2. Preheat the oven to 375 degrees.

3. Peel and core the apples and cut them into thin slices into a large bowl. Combine the sugar, flour, cinnamon, and allspice in a small bowl and toss with the apples. Spoon the filling into the pastry-lined pie plate. Dot with butter.

4. Position the top crust over the pie and seal the edges. Cut steam vents in the top crust in a design of your choice. Trim and flute the edges.

5. Beat one egg with a fork, brush it over the crust, and sprinkle lightly with sugar. Cover edges with aluminum foil or a pie crust shield. Bake for 25 minutes; remove the foil. Bake an additional 25 to 30 minutes until the crust is golden brown and the filling is bubbly.

Variation: Add 1/4 cup raisins to the filling.

Note: See "Ingredients for a Flaky Pie Crust" on page 250.

PUMPKIN PIE

One 9-inch pie; 8 servings

PASTRY for single-crust pie:
1¼ cups flour
1/2 teaspoon salt
1/4 cup plus 2 tablespoons shortening
2 tablespoons chilled butter, cut in small pieces
2 to 3 tablespoons ice-cold water

FILLING:
2¼ cups canned pumpkin puree
1 cup firmly packed brown sugar
1¾ cups evaporated milk

2 eggs, beaten
2 tablespoons butter, melted
1¼ teaspoons ground cinnamon
3/4 teaspoon salt
1/4 teaspoon ground nutmeg
1/4 teaspoon ground ginger
1/4 teaspoon ground cloves

SWEETENED WHIPPED CREAM (optional):
1/2 pint heavy cream
2 teaspoons granulated sugar
1/4 teaspoon vanilla extract

My cousin Veldron sent me this recipe over 30 years ago. Since then, I have never had Thanksgiving dinner without this pie!

1. To make the pie crust, stir the flour and salt in a medium bowl. Cut in the shortening and butter with a pastry blender or two knives until the mixture resembles coarse crumbs (see Note). Sprinkle with the ice water, a tablespoon at a time, and stir with a fork to moisten all the dough. Gather the dough into a ball with your hands. Roll out the dough on a lightly floured surface and fit it into a 9-inch pie plate. Trim and flute the edge. Set aside.

2. Preheat the oven to 375 degrees. Put a small bowl into the freezer to chill for whipping the cream later.

3. In a large bowl of an electric mixer, combine the pumpkin, brown sugar, evaporated milk, eggs, butter, cinnamon, salt, nutmeg, ginger, and cloves. Beat on low just until combined. Do not overmix.

4. Pour into the pie shell. Cover the edges with aluminum foil or a pie crust shield and carefully place the pie into the oven. Bake for 25 minutes, remove the shield, and bake for 25 more minutes, or until a knife inserted near the center comes out clean.

5. To whip the (optional) cream, pour the cream into the chilled bowl. Beat with a handheld electric mixer until the cream just starts to thicken. Add the sugar and vanilla. Continue beating and add sugar to taste. Beat to desired consistency. Be careful not to make butter!

Note: See "Ingredients for a Flaky Pie Crust" on page 250.

INGREDIENTS FOR A FLAKY PIE CRUST

Vegetable shortening gives a pie crust the most flakiness, and butter provides a rich taste, so a combination of the two is the best of both worlds. The exception is savory dishes, like quiche and potpie (p. 37). Then my favorite fat to use in the crust is lard.

Whichever fat you use, make sure it is chilled. As you cut the cold fat into the flour with a pastry blender, you are aiming to leave it in firm, separate pieces. Some of the dough should be like coarse crumbs and some like small peas. During baking, these chunks of fat melt, leaving gaps in the dough that fill up with steam and expand, giving the crust layers of flakiness.

As you start to mix the ingredients, they will cling to the pastry blender, so just scrape them off with a knife and then keep working the mixture. When you have reached the "small peas" stage, then add the chilled water a tablespoon at a time, mixing with a fork, until the dough begins to form small balls. If the mixture gathers into a mass on its own, without pressure, it is too wet. This makes pie crust tough and soggy.

So many people tell me they would never attempt a pie crust. But have you heard the saying "easy as pie"? It really is!

More Tips for a Perfect Pie Crust:

Top left: Roll from the center out, using even pressure. Carefully turn the dough frequently a quarter turn to keep the shape round.
Left: Gently roll the dough up over the rolling pin to transfer it to the pie plate.
Bottom left: Use your thumbs and forefingers to "flute" (pinch) the edges together.
Bottom center: An egg glaze adds a beautiful sheen.
Bottom right: Foil strips around the edges keep the crust from getting too dark.

JAM ROLL-UPS

leftover pie crust
jam

1. Roll out the leftover pie pastry and spread with your favorite jam. (Or sprinkle with sugar and cinnamon instead.)

2. Roll up as you would cinnamon rolls.

3. Cut little rounds with a sharp knife and place them in a pan lined with aluminum foil.

4. Bake in the oven with the pie (same temperature) until the rolls are lightly browned, about 15 minutes. Remove from the oven and place the rolls on a plate.

There is always a little pastry left when you've made a pie. From this leftover dough, you can make my tiny jam rolls-ups with your kids. They are so easy and delicious. Then let your kids make them all by themselves.

My mother taught me how to make these when I was but 3 years old. I still make them every time I make a pie. Everyone looks forward to them as much as the pie!

CHOCOLATE SOUR CREAM SHEET CAKE WITH HALF & HALF FROSTING *16 servings*

My dear friend Nancy gave me this recipe many years ago. It's great for kids because some like chocolate frosting and some like white—and this way everyone can have what they want. Whenever I make this cake, I think fondly of Nancy. She kept inspiring me to write my book and never gave up on me.

2	cups sugar
2	cups all-purpose flour
1	teaspoon baking soda
1/2	teaspoon salt
2	eggs
1/2	cup sour cream

1	cup (2 sticks) butter
1/4	cup unsweetened cocoa powder
1	cup water

Half & Half Frosting (recipe follows)

1. Preheat the oven to 350 degrees. Grease a 12 x 17-inch jelly roll pan.

2. Stir the sugar, flour, baking soda, and salt in a large bowl of an electric mixer. Add the eggs and sour cream and beat on low speed until well-blended.

3. Melt the butter in a medium saucepan over medium heat. Add the cocoa and water, increase the heat, and bring to a boil. Remove from the heat and gradually add the hot mixture to the batter in the bowl, mixing on low speed to combine thoroughly; do not overmix.

4. Pour the batter into the prepared pan. Bake for 20 minutes, or until a toothpick inserted in the center comes out clean. Meanwhile, make the frosting. Remove the cake from the oven and cool in the pan for 10 minutes. Frost the cake. Serve warm or allow the cake to cool completely.

HALF & HALF FROSTING

1/2	cup (1 stick) butter
1/4	cup plus 2 tablespoons milk
1	teaspoon vanilla extract
6	cups powdered sugar, sifted
2	tablespoons unsweetened cocoa powder
	Chopped walnuts or pecans (optional)

1. Melt the butter in a medium saucepan over medium heat. Add the milk and bring the mixture to a boil. Remove from the heat. Add the vanilla and powdered sugar. Beat with a wooden spoon until smooth. Add milk if necessary for desired spreading consistency.

2. Spread half of the frosting on half of the cake.

3. Add the cocoa to the remaining frosting. Spread this on the other half of the cake. Sprinkle nuts on top if desired.

MEXICAN COCOA CAKE WITH BITTERSWEET CHOCOLATE ICING *10 to 12 servings*

1/2 cup milk
1½ teaspoons cider vinegar
1 cup (2 sticks) unsalted butter
1/2 cup unsweetened Dutch-process cocoa powder
3/4 cup water
2 cups sugar
2 eggs

2 tablespoons vanilla extract
2 cups all-purpose flour
1 teaspoon baking soda
1/2 teaspoon ground cinnamon
1/4 teaspoon salt

Bittersweet Chocolate Icing (recipe follows)

1. Preheat the oven to 350 degrees with a rack in the middle position. Very generously grease a 9-inch nonstick tube pan or 12-cup nonstick Bundt pan and dust with flour, shaking out the excess.

2. Combine the milk and vinegar in a glass measuring cup or small bowl. Set aside to allow milk to curdle.

3. Melt the butter in a 3-quart heavy saucepan over medium-low heat. Whisk in the cocoa. Add the water and whisk until smooth. Remove from the heat and allow to cool slightly.

4. Whisk the sugar, eggs, vanilla, and the milk mixture into the cocoa mixture.

5. Sift the flour, baking soda, cinnamon, and salt onto a square of wax paper (or mix in a bowl). Stir into the cocoa mixture just until combined. The batter will be lumpy.

6. Scrape the batter into the prepared pan and bake 35 to 45 minutes, until a toothpick inserted in the center comes out with just a few crumbs adhering. Cool in the pan on a rack for 10 minutes. Meanwhile, make the icing.

7. Loosen the edges of the cake with a plastic knife and invert onto a cake plate. Drizzle the icing over the top and sides of the still-warm cake.

BITTERSWEET CHOCOLATE ICING

1/4 cup (1/2 stick) butter
4 ounces fine-quality unsweetened chocolate (I use Ghirardelli.)
1 (5-ounce) can evaporated milk

1/2 cup plus 2 tablespoons sifted powdered sugar
1/8 teaspoon salt
1/4 teaspoon vanilla extract
1 to 2 cups chopped pecans

1. Melt the butter and chocolate in a 2-quart heavy saucepan over low heat. Stir in the milk, powdered sugar, and salt and cook until slightly thickened, 1 to 2 minutes.

2. Remove from the heat and stir in the vanilla and pecans.

My friend Ann made me this cake, and after I swooned, she handed me the recipe. If you like dark, bittersweet chocolate, you are going to love this cake. It is so decadent, and is as delicious served cold from the refrigerator as it is warm or at room temperature. I love the Dutch-process cocoa, which has a darker color and mellower flavor than regular baking cocoa. Look for it in the supermarket baking section. I also love pecans in my frosting, although my kids do not. Consider them optional.

CARROT CAKE

16 servings

I have tried just about every carrot cake recipe. This is my favorite by far and now I am famous for this cake. No pineapple, no nuts inside the cake. It is so moist it will melt in your mouth. You need only a small slice because it is so rich.

2 cups all-purpose flour
2 teaspoons cinnamon
1¼ teaspoons baking powder
1 teaspoon baking soda
1 teaspoon salt
2 cups sugar
1¼ cups canola oil
4 eggs

4 cups peeled and grated carrots (4 or 5 large carrots)
1 cup coconut
Almond-Scented Cream Cheese Frosting (recipe on next page)
Coconut, for sprinkling on the cake (optional)
Chopped walnuts, for sprinkling on the cake (optional)

1. Preheat the oven to 350 degrees and grease two 9-inch-round cake pans. Cut two 9-inch-diameter circles out of parchment paper or wax paper and place in the bottom of each pan. Spray again and dust with flour. Shake out the excess.

2. Sift the flour, cinnamon, baking powder, baking soda, and salt onto a square of wax paper (or mix in a bowl) and set aside.

3. In a large bowl of an electric mixer, beat the sugar, oil, and eggs on low speed until well-blended. Mix in the dry ingredients just until blended. Fold in the carrots and coconut. The batter will be thick. Divide the batter evenly into the prepared pans. Bake 35 to 45 minutes, until a toothpick inserted in the center comes out clean.

4. Cool in the pans on a wire rack for 10 minutes. Loosen the layers around the edges with a knife. Carefully invert each layer by placing another rack directly over the layer and turning all upside down. Tap on the pan to loosen the layer. Carefully peel off the paper. Cool completely on the racks. Meanwhile, make the **frosting**, opposite.

5. To frost the cake, place one layer top side down on a cake plate. Spread with half the frosting. Place the second layer top side up on the frosting. Spread the remainder of the frosting on top of the cake. (No need to frost the side of the cake.) Sprinkle with coconut and walnuts, if desired.

Variation: Bake mini-cupcakes in mini-muffin tins and then frost the minis—fabulous! Bake minis about 15 minutes.

OATMEAL CAKE WITH CARAMEL COCONUT GLAZE _12 to 15 servings_

1½ cups water
1 cup quick-cooking or old-fashioned rolled oats
1½ cups flour
1 teaspoon baking soda
1 teaspoon salt
3/4 teaspoon ground cinnamon
1/4 teaspoon ground nutmeg

1/2 cup (1 stick) butter, softened
1 cup granulated sugar
1 cup firmly packed brown sugar
1 teaspoon vanilla extract
2 eggs

Caramel Coconut Glaze
(recipe follows)

1. Boil the water in a small saucepan. Stir in the oats. Cover and let stand for 20 minutes.

2. Preheat the oven to 350 degrees. Grease a 9 x 13-inch baking pan.

3. Sift the flour, baking soda, salt, cinnamon, and nutmeg onto a square of wax paper (or mix in a bowl). Set aside.

4. Beat the butter, sugar, and brown sugar in a large bowl. Add vanilla and eggs and beat well. Stir in the oats mixture. Stir in the dry ingredients and mix well.

5. Scrape the batter into the prepared pan and bake 45 to 55 minutes, until a toothpick inserted in the center comes out clean.

6. Mix the glaze and spread it on the warm cake.

CARAMEL COCONUT GLAZE

1/4 cup (1/2 stick) butter
1/2 cup firmly packed brown sugar
2 tablespoons milk

3/4 cup coconut
3/4 cup chopped pecans or walnuts (optional)

Melt the butter in a medium saucepan. Add the brown sugar and milk. Bring to a boil; boil for 1 minute. Remove from the heat and add the coconut and nuts, if using.

ALMOND-SCENTED CREAM CHEESE FROSTING

3 cups powdered sugar
1 (8-ounce) package cream cheese, at room temperature

5 tablespoons butter, at room temperature
1 teaspoon vanilla extract
1 teaspoon almond extract

1. Sift the powdered sugar into a small bowl of an electric mixer. Add the cream cheese, butter, vanilla, and almond.

2. Beat until well-blended and smooth enough to spread. Avoid overbeating, which may make the frosting too soft.

My neighbor Maxine was the first to make this recipe. Kids love it! I love the taste of the caramel and coconut together. It is so moist, and the oats means it's a tasty way to add fiber to the diet.

Note: The 350 degree oven temperature is for a metal pan. If using a glass pan, bake the cake at 325 degrees.

Some people think of a lemony cream cheese frosting when they think of carrot cake, but this almond-scented version is our favorite.

SOUR CREAM DEVIL'S FOOD CAKE WITH FUDGE FROSTING *12 servings*

Our oldest son, David, always requests this cake for his birthday. It is our family's favorite cake. The fudge frosting was my grandma's recipe from long ago, so everyone in the family has been making it for 100-plus years. She used only Hershey's cocoa, which came out in 1894. She started putting the frosting on cake-mix cakes when they came on the market in the 1940s. Mixes made it so fast and easy to bake a wonderful cake, and then all Grandma had to do was top it with her fabulous frosting. This fudge frosting is very good spooned over ice cream as well.

1   (18-ounce) package Devil's Food cake mix
1/2 cup sour cream

Fudge Frosting (recipe follows)

1. Preheat the oven to the temperature stated on the cake mix package. Grease and lightly flour a 9 x 13-inch baking pan.

2. Prepare the cake according to package directions and add the sour cream to the batter. Pour the batter into the pan and bake according to package directions.

3. Meanwhile, prepare the frosting and keep warm.

4. Remove the cake from the oven and allow it to cool slightly. While the cake is still warm, poke a few holes in the top with a fork. Pour the warm frosting over the cake. Serve immediately or allow the cake to cool.

Variation: Substitute a yellow cake mix for the devil's food, as these sisters are enjoying, opposite.

FUDGE FROSTING

1/2 cup (1 stick) butter
1   cup sugar
1/2 cup evaporated milk
1/4 cup unsweetened cocoa powder

1   teaspoon vanilla extract
1/8 teaspoon salt
Chopped walnuts (optional)

1. Melt the butter in a medium saucepan over medium heat. Add the sugar, milk, and cocoa. Stir and bring to a boil. Boil for 3 minutes. Remove from the heat and allow to cool slightly.

2. Stir in the vanilla and salt. Beat the mixture with a wooden spoon for a few minutes, let the mixture rest a couple of minutes, and beat again for a couple of minutes until the mixture is thickened but still pourable.

3. Add chopped walnuts, if desired, or sprinkle the nuts over the frosted cake.

DREAMY CREAM CHEESE PIE

1 9-inch pie; 10 servings

My childhood neighbor and friend Ann gave us this recipe when we were but teenagers. My sisters and I have been making it ever since.

DO AHEAD

The pie should be refrigerated at least 5 hours before serving, so plan ahead.

CRUST:
- 9   whole graham crackers (1 package)
- 1/4 cup (1/2 stick) butter, melted

TOPPING:
- 1   cup sour cream
- 3½ tablespoons sugar
- 1   teaspoon vanilla extract
- Ground cinnamon

FILLING:
- 12 ounces cream cheese, at room temperature
- 2 eggs, beaten
- 3/4 cup sugar
- 2 teaspoons vanilla extract
- 1 teaspoon grated lemon peel
- 1 teaspoon fresh lemon juice

1. Preheat the oven to 350 degrees. Position a rack in the center of the oven.

2. Break the crackers into a blender or food processor and pulse to make 1⅓ cups fine crumbs. Thoroughly combine the crumbs and butter. Pat the mixture into a 9-inch pie pan, going up the sides as far as possible.

3. In a medium bowl of an electric mixer, make the filling by combining the cream cheese, eggs, sugar, vanilla, lemon peel and juice. Beat until the mixture is light and frothy, about 2 minutes. Pour into the crust and bake for 30 minutes.

4. Meanwhile, to make the topping, combine the sour cream, sugar, and vanilla.

5. Remove the pie from the oven and let it cool for 5 minutes. Pour the sour cream mixture over the pie and spread evenly. Sprinkle lightly with cinnamon, return to the oven, and bake for 10 minutes. Cool on a rack for 20 minutes, then refrigerate at least 5 hours before serving. The pie keeps, refrigerated, for up to 5 days.

SURPRISE FRUIT COBBLER

6 servings

1/2 cup (1 stick) butter, cut up
1 cup all-purpose flour
1 cup granulated sugar
2 teaspoons baking powder
3/4 cup milk
3½ cups fresh or canned fruit, drained (see Variations)

3/4 cup firmly packed brown sugar
Ground cinnamon

Ice cream or whipped cream (optional)

This recipe comes from my longtime neighbor Sid, who always has something wonderful for me to try. Celebrating life through food is her way of spreading happiness. This recipe is one of her delicate surprises. The "surprise" is the way the dough starts on the bottom and then travels to the top during baking to form a cake-like "crust."

1. Preheat the oven to 350 degrees.

2. Melt the butter in a square baking pan in the oven. Remove the pan from the oven.

3. Stir the flour, granulated sugar, and baking powder in a medium bowl. Stir in the milk. Gently pour the mixture into the melted butter in the baking pan. Do not stir.

4. Place fruit of your choice evenly over the batter, top with the brown sugar, and sprinkle with cinnamon. Bake until the cobbler is well-browned and the fruit is cooked (if using raw fruit). The baking time will vary depending on the fruit. Start checking for doneness at 40 minutes.

Serve right out of the oven, plain or with ice cream or whipped cream, or my favorite way—with milk poured over it.

Variations: Use sliced peaches or blueberries (or a combination), sliced apples, sliced pears, or red cherries.

APPLE CRISP

6 servings

This recipe is a
Halloween tradition
for my sister Jill and
her husband Evan.
Many years ago,
Evan made this
apple crisp for us.
Never again did we
try another apple
crisp recipe! This
one is gooey and
crunchy at the same
time. If you're used
to having cinnamon
with apples, feel
free to add it, but
we like it better
without.

4	medium apples in the variety of your choice or a mix of varieties (such as Granny Smith with Fuji, Gala, or Jonagold)
3/4	cup all-purpose flour

3/4 to 1 cup sugar	
1/4	teaspoon cinnamon (optional)
1/2	cup (1 stick) chilled butter, cut into small pieces

1. Preheat the oven to 400 degrees and grease an 8 x 8-inch baking dish.

2. Peel and core the apples and cut them into thin slices. Spread the slices in the prepared baking dish.

3. Combine the flour, sugar, and cinnamon, if using, in a medium bowl. Cut in the butter with a pastry blender or fork until the mixture is crumbly. Spread evenly over the apples.

4. Bake uncovered until golden brown, 40 to 45 minutes.

To double this recipe, bake it in a 13 x 9-inch pan for 50 to 60 minutes.

BEST-EVER BROWNIES

16 brownies

My editor Ann and
I came up with this
recipe, and I think
you'll find these
brownies to be
plenty chocolatey
as they are. But if
your family is a fan
of frosted brownies,
as mine is, then
go ahead and
be decadent by
frosting them
with your favorite
chocolate frosting.

3	(1-ounce) squares unsweetened chocolate
1/2	cup (1 stick) butter
3/4	cup flour
1/2	teaspoon baking powder

1/4	teaspoon salt
1½	cups sugar
3	eggs
1	teaspoon vanilla extract
3/4	cup chopped nuts (optional)

1. Preheat the oven to 350 degrees (325 degrees for a glass pan). Grease an 8 x 8-inch baking pan.

2. Melt the chocolate and butter in a medium saucepan over very low heat. Remove from the heat and allow to cool slightly.

3. Meanwhile, sift the flour, baking powder, and salt onto a square of wax paper (or mix in a bowl). Set aside.

4. Add the sugar, eggs, and vanilla to the chocolate mixture. Beat vigorously by hand until smooth. Stir in the flour mixture and nuts, if desired.

5. Scrape the batter into the prepared pan. Bake 35 to 40 minutes until a toothpick inserted halfway between the center and the side comes out clean. Do not overbake. Let cool completely. Cut into bars.

CHOCOLATE CHIP COOKIES

About 5 dozen cookies

1	cup (2 sticks) butter, at room temperature
1	cup granulated sugar
1	cup firmly packed brown sugar
1	teaspoon vanilla extract

2	eggs
3	cups all-purpose flour
1	teaspoon baking soda
1	teaspoon salt
1½	cups semisweet chocolate chips

1. Preheat the oven to 350 degrees.

2. In a large bowl of an electric mixer, beat the butter, sugar, and brown sugar until light and fluffy. Add the vanilla and eggs. Beat about 1 minute.

3. Sift the flour, baking soda, and salt onto a square of wax paper (or mix in a bowl). Add to the butter mixture and mix until all ingredients are well-combined. Stir in the chocolate chips.

4. Drop tablespoons of dough onto ungreased cookies sheets and flatten slightly with the palm of your hand. Bake 8 to 10 minutes. Remove to a cooling rack. These cookies freeze well; store in resealable plastic bags and take out as many at a time as needed.

Variation: Add a handful of coconut and walnut or pecan pieces to the dough along with the chocolate chips.

Cookies are my one exception to my "desserts only on Mondays and birthdays" rule. If I was home in the afternoon, some days I would have warm cookies ready as an after-school treat. Plus my cookie recipes are so easy, your kids can make them themselves.

PEANUT BUTTER COOKIES WITH KISSES

About 40 cookies

1/2 cup granulated sugar
1/2 cup firmly packed brown sugar
1/2 cup (1 stick) butter
1/2 cup creamy peanut butter
1   egg
2   tablespoons milk
2   teaspoons vanilla extract

1³/₄ cups all-purpose flour
1   teaspoon baking soda
1/2   teaspoon salt

Granulated sugar

40   chocolate kisses

We discovered these wonderful peanut butter cookies thanks to our friend Paula, who brought them to us one Christmas many years ago. They are sure to become one of your favorite cookies— with or without the kisses!

1. Preheat the oven to 350 degrees.

2. In a large bowl of an electric mixer, cream the granulated sugar, brown sugar, butter, and peanut butter on low speed. Beat in the egg, milk, and vanilla.

3. Sift the flour, baking soda, and salt on a square of wax paper (or mix in a bowl). Stir into the sugar mixture and mix thoroughly.

4. Shape into 40 walnut-size balls. Roll in granulated sugar in a small bowl. Place on an ungreased cookie sheet and bake for 8 minutes.

5. Remove from the oven and immediately press a chocolate kiss into each. Transfer the cookies to a wire rack to cool.

Variation: Omit the chocolate kisses; flatten the sugared balls on the cookie sheet with a fork dipped in water. Press down in one direction and then across. Bake as directed.

OATMEAL COCONUT CHOCOLATE CHIPPERS

About 3 dozen cookies

Anna Dean gave us this recipe over 25 years ago. She grew up in a small, rural town and was one of the top cooks in the county. These cookies became a family favorite of ours for after-school snacks. We store the cookies in the freezer in resealable plastic bags so they never go stale. They stay chewy and they thaw as you eat them! Try this. You will never keep your cookies in a cookie jar again.

1 cup (2 sticks) butter	1/2 teaspoon salt
1 cup granulated sugar	3 cups old-fashioned or quick-cooking rolled oats
1 cup firmly packed brown sugar	1 teaspoon vanilla extract
2 eggs	1/2 cup coconut
1½ cups all-purpose flour	1½ cups semisweet chocolate chips
1 teaspoon baking soda	

1. Preheat the oven to 350 degrees and lightly grease a cookie sheet.

2. Beat the butter, sugar, brown sugar, and eggs in a large bowl of an electric mixer until blended. Beat for 1 minute.

3. Sift the flour, baking soda, and salt onto a square of wax paper (or mix in a bowl). Add to the butter mixture and blend well. Stir in the oats and vanilla. Stir in the coconut and chocolate chips with a wooden spoon.

4. Drop by teaspoonfuls onto the prepared cookie sheet and bake until lightly browned and almost firm when lightly pressed on the top, about 10 minutes. Remove to a rack to cool.

Variations:

◆ Omit the coconut.

◆ Add 1½ cups raisins in place of the chocolate chips.

◆ Add 1 cup chopped pecans.

GRANDMA'S SUGAR-COOKIE CUTOUTS
WITH ICING *About 2 dozen cookies*

COOKIES:
1   cup granulated sugar
1/2 cup (1 stick) butter
1   egg
1   teaspoon lemon extract
2   cups all-purpose flour
1   teaspoon baking powder
1/2 teaspoon salt
1/4 cup milk

ICING:
1/4 cup (1/2 stick) butter,
    at room temperature
1   (1-pound) box powdered sugar
    (about 4 cups), sifted
1   teaspoon vanilla extract
1   (5-ounce) can evaporated milk
Food coloring (optional)

1. In an electric mixer bowl, blend the sugar, butter, and egg. Add the lemon extract and beat for 1 minute.

2. Sift the flour, baking powder, and salt onto a square of wax paper (or mix in a bowl).

3. Add the dry ingredients alternately with the milk to the butter mixture, mixing well after each addition. Divide the dough in half, wrap in plastic, and refrigerate until firm, at least 1 hour.

4. Preheat the oven to 400 degrees.

5. On a lightly floured surface, roll half the dough to 1/4 inch thick. Dip a cookie cutter into flour, cut into the dough, and place the cookies on an ungreased cookie sheet. Repeat with the other half of the dough. Scrape the dough scraps together, add flour to the rolling surface as needed, roll out again, and cut out additional cookies. Bake 7 to 10 minutes and cool on racks.

6. To make the icing, combine the butter, powdered sugar, and vanilla in a mixer bowl. Beat with an electric mixer until blended. Add the evaporated milk 1 tablespoon at a time and continue to beat to desired spreading consistency. If desired, divide the icing into separate bowls and tint each one a different color, starting with just a drop of food coloring.

7. Spread the icing on the cooled cookies.

Grandma Edmunds gave us this recipe before she passed away over 30 years ago. She made these cookies for her family often. My husband always asks for them around Christmastime. I know how much he misses his mom when he recalls her in the kitchen making these cookies. We have never found a sugar cookie that we like better than this one.

CARROT COOKIES WITH ORANGE ICING

About 2 dozen cookies

4 or 5 medium carrots, peeled and sliced
3/4 cup (1½ sticks) butter
1 cup granulated sugar
1 egg

2 cups all-purpose flour
1 teaspoon baking powder
1/2 teaspoon salt
1 teaspoon vanilla extract

Orange Icing (recipe follows)

1. Put the carrots in a medium saucepan with water to cover and bring to a boil. Decrease the heat and simmer until they are soft, about 15 minutes. Drain and mash the carrots with a fork to make 1 cup mash. Set aside.

2. Preheat the oven to 325 degrees. Lightly grease a cookie sheet.

3. Mix the butter, sugar, and egg in a medium bowl of an electric mixer. Beat until light, about 1 minute.

4. Sift the flour, baking powder, and salt onto a square of wax paper (or mix in a bowl). Add to the creamed mixture and combine. Mix in the vanilla and carrots.

5. Drop the dough by teaspoonfuls onto the prepared cookie sheet. Bake for 10 minutes, taking care not to overbake.

6. Meanwhile, quickly make the icing. Place the cookies on aluminum foil and ice them while they are still hot.

ORANGE ICING

4 cups powdered sugar
1 teaspoon butter
Juice of 1 to 2 oranges
Pinch salt

1. Sift the powdered sugar into an electric mixer bowl.

2. Add the butter, juice of 1 orange, and salt. Mix until smooth, adding more orange juice as needed for spreading consistency.

HELLO DOLLY BARS

16 bars

1/2 cup (1 stick) butter
1¼ cups finely crushed graham crackers (about 7 whole crackers)
1 cup chopped walnuts or pecans
1 cup semisweet chocolate chips
1⅓ cups coconut
1 (14-ounce) can sweetened condensed milk

1. Preheat the oven to 350 degrees and melt the butter in a square baking pan in the oven.

2. Layer, in order, the graham cracker crumbs, nuts, chocolate chips, and coconut over the butter. Pour the milk slowly and evenly over the top.

3. Bake for 30 minutes, cool, and cut into bars.

Variation: Add a layer of 1 cup butterscotch chips after the chocolate chips.

I have been baking these bars since my kids were very small. We all crave them from time to time and we always eat way too many! But everyone deserves a splurge once in a while!

COCONUTTY CEREAL TREATS

About 8 cups; 16 servings

3 cups Corn Chex cereal
3 cups Golden Grahams cereal
1/2 cup slivered almonds
1/2 cup coconut
1/2 cup (1 stick) butter
1/2 cup corn syrup
1/2 cup sugar

1. Combine the Corn Chex, Golden Grahams, almonds, and coconut in a large bowl.

2. Melt the butter in a small saucepan over medium heat. Stir in the corn syrup and sugar. Bring to a boil and boil for 4 minutes. Pour over the cereal mixture. Mix all ingredients well with a wooden spoon and serve.

3. Store in an airtight container or cover with plastic wrap.

This recipe came from my daughter-in-law Shana. She brings this treat to all of our family gatherings. Once you take a bite of it, you won't be able to put it down. Fix it for your next party and you will have everyone asking you for the recipe.

FRESH FRUIT...
THE DAILY DESSERT

While many desserts should be only a once-a-week treat, fresh fruit can be a sweet finale to any dinner. Here are some suggestions. You'll probably come up with lots of ideas of your own, too!

◆ A wedge of cantaloupe with a squeeze of lime juice. Try it with blueberries or raspberries on top.

◆ Strawberries or mixed berries with just a dusting of sugar (or try a few sprinkles of balsamic vinegar).

◆ Blueberries and yogurt with a sprinkling of cinnamon sugar on top.

◆ In-season peaches or nectarines with a scoop of frozen yogurt.

◆ A ripe pear, peeled and sliced and topped with a few crumbles of blue cheese.

◆ Sliced bananas topped with plain or vanilla yogurt or nonfat sour cream and a sprinkle of brown sugar. Assemble this in individual bowls before you sit down to dinner to let the sugar melt to a caramel-like consistency.

◆ Chilled orange slices with just a drizzle of chocolate sauce.

◆ Stewed rhubarb (cook 2 cups chopped rhubarb with 1/2 cup sugar over low heat for 10 minutes or so until sauce is formed, stirring occasionally; for a variation, mix in chopped strawberries).

◆ A pile of fresh plums in a bowl to eat out of hand.

◆ A bowl of sweet cherries.

◆ Green or red grapes.

◆ Sliced kiwis.

◆ Wedges of watermelon.

◆ Papaya or pineapple or a combination.

◆ or any combination that sounds good to you!

AFTER-
SCHOOL
SNACKS

AFTER-SCHOOL SNACKS

Kids often arrive home famished! They need a little something to tide them over until dinner is ready. My idea of a snack is a couple of homemade cookies and a glass of milk. A few graham crackers. Hot chocolate. Some popcorn. A piece of fruit and a slice of cheese. Cheese and crackers. A slice of bread with peanut butter.

Candy bars are not a good snack. Neither are most chips like tortilla or potato chips. I used to cringe when my boys would take out the entire package of chips and just start eating. I would say, "Put those back; they are for lunches." A few chips with a sandwich is fine—a few.

As the Food Nanny, I've noticed that kids nowadays are snacking on granola bars, fruit bites in individual plastic bags, fruit leather, dried fruit with raisins and nuts, and seemingly every combination of fruit mix. Some of these can add up to way more calories than you think, and they can be addicting. Once you take a bite, you can't stop, just like most varieties of chips. Plus, these snacks can be costly when all the kids in the neighborhood help themselves.

That's why more healthful snacks like the ones listed below and on the next pages are the best deal. They taste so good and last a lot longer.

Liz

- a slice of whole wheat bread spread with peanut butter, or peanut butter with jam, jelly or honey
- apple slices with peanut butter
- a banana
- orange segments, put in freezer for 15 minutes so they're frosty
- celery stuffed with light cream cheese or peanut butter
- broccoli florets, carrots, and/or cubes of turkey ham with ranch dressing
- yogurt
- tuna salad on crackers
- nuts—almonds, cashews, or peanuts
- popcorn
- hot chocolate
- cheese and crackers
- milk and cookies— making them is a great after-school project. See pages 260-267 for cookie recipes.

DEVILED EGGS

6 servings

When my son Joey
is around, there are
never enough of
these deviled eggs.
They are sure to be
a hit at your next
family gathering,
and they're a great
after-school snack
that kids can make
themselves.

6 eggs	1/8 teaspoon butter
1/4 to 1/3 cup mayonnaise	1/8 teaspoon salt
1 teaspoon cider vinegar	Pinch ground black pepper
1 teaspoon prepared mustard	Paprika

1. Place the eggs in a medium saucepan. Cover with cold water by at least 1 inch and bring to a boil over high heat. Decrease the heat to just below simmering. Cover the pan and cook for 15 minutes. Immediately run cold water over the eggs; to quickly cool, add ice cubes. Let stand 2 minutes. Drain. Crack them on the countertop and slide the shells off.

2. Halve the eggs lengthwise. Remove the yolks to a small bowl; place the whites on a platter. If you are not filling the eggs immediately, cover and refrigerate until ready to prepare.

3. Mash the yolks with a fork. Add the mayonnaise, vinegar, mustard, butter, salt, and pepper. Mix well. Fill the whites evenly with the yolk mixture. Sprinkle with paprika. Cover and refrigerate until ready to serve.

DILL DIP

About 2 cups

Simple to make and
delicious to serve
with assorted raw
vegetables or
focaccia!

1 cup sour cream
1 cup mayonnaise
1 tablespoon Bon Appetit seasoning salt
  or Beau Monde seasoning
1 tablespoon dried minced onion
1 tablespoon dried dill weed

Mix all the ingredients in a small bowl. Refrigerate. Keep covered in the refrigerator for up to one week.

MARSHMALLOW CREAM CHEESE FRUIT DIP

About 4 cups

1   (8-ounce) package cream cheese
1   (7-ounce) jar marshmallow cream

Mix the ingredients with an electric mixer until the mixture is smooth.

Serve with fresh fruit such as strawberries, grapes, bananas, green or red apples, watermelon, and cantaloupe.

Leaner Variation: Use low-fat cream cheese (Neufchatel) and a favorite fruit-flavored yogurt instead of the marshmallow cream.

Fresh fruit is such an easy after-school snack. Add a fruit dip to make it even better.

CITRUSY CREAM CHEESE FRUIT DIP

About 1 cup

3   tablespoons honey
1   (8-ounce) package cream cheese or low-fat cream cheese, softened
1/4 cup orange juice
1   teaspoon sugar
1/4 teaspoon ground cinnamon

Assorted fruits, including grapes and sliced bananas

1. Stir the honey into the cream cheese. Add the orange juice and stir to combine. Turn out into a serving dish.

2. Combine the sugar and cinnamon. Sprinkle over the top of the cream cheese mixture.

3. Serve with fruits.

Variations:

◆ Add orange zest (grated orange peel) for more orange flavor.

◆ Stir in small bits of candied ginger.

LEMONADE SLUSH TO DIE FOR *6 servings*

Friends in California pick Meyer lemons from the prolifically bearing tree in their yard. The lemons are so fragrantly sweet you almost don't need to add any sugar to this icy lemonade slush. Grow a Meyer lemon tree indoors for your own supply!

6	Meyer lemons
2	cups ice cubes
1	cup sugar
3	cups water
6	sprigs of fresh mint (optional)

1. Squeeze the lemons. Strain the juice to remove any seeds.

2. Put the ice into the blender and add the lemon juice, sugar, and water. Blend to make the slush.

Pour into glasses and serve each with a sprig of mint.

Variations: Use regular lemons or a combination of 5 lemons and 1 lime and increase the sugar to 1½ cups.

CHOCOLATE MALTS

2 to 3 servings

My dad would often make strawberry malts that were better than any we could buy. This tradition has carried over into our family as well—except chocolate is our favorite. When you don't want to bake, but want something sweet, fix malts. No one needs to drink a full glass; just a taste is good. We often use our smallest glasses!

4	scoops vanilla ice cream	1/2 to 3/4 cup milk	
2	tablespoons malted milk powder	2	tablespoons chocolate-flavored syrup

1. Put the ice cream in a blender. Add the malted milk powder and pour in the milk and chocolate syrup. Blend well. If you like a thinner malt, add more milk.

2. Divide between two (or more) glasses.

Variations:

◆ For strawberry malts, use strawberry jam in place of the chocolate syrup.

◆ Omit the malted milk powder and the malt becomes a milkshake.

GROCERY SHOPPING AND MENU PLANNING TIPS

If there is a place you can cut back on your household budget, it is with food. If you don't have any idea how much money you spend on food in a month, you need to find out. Keep all your receipts for a month, and then add up how much you spent on groceries and eating out. You may be shocked. This is where my cookbook comes in. You can save a lot of money by cooking at home and by buying *ingredients*, rather than prepared, packaged foods. All it takes is desire—and planning.

Take the time to sit down and make a budget. Then stick to it. Sticking to a food budget can be fun as well as rewarding. Plan meals within your budget. It is so rewarding to take your grocery list to the store and then come in under budget when you check out. Here are some tips to make it happen:

- Use my plan to map out two weeks at a time. The less time you spend in the stores, the less you end up buying. When I was raising my family I bought only what I had on my list and then left. The meats that I wasn't going to be using in the next couple of days, I wrapped and put in the freezer. I returned to the store only once a week to buy more milk and fresh fruits and vegetables.

- Watch for what is on sale at your favorite market. Buying on sale will save you hundreds of dollars a year.

- Consider when specific fruits and vegetables are in season. In-season produce is not only likely to be on sale, but it's also likely to be better flavor and better for you, since it's not spending days traveling from somewhere far away. So when it's asparagus season, feast on asparagus!

- Take advantage of quantity buying and sales, such as buying chicken breasts in a family pack and then dividing them into smaller packages to put in your freezer. Watch the ads for grocery stores near you so you can buy canned goods and meats on sale. Or buy them in bulk.

- Don't grocery-shop when you're starving. You have heard this many times. You will buy

everything that looks good! And you will leave with way too many goodies and items that you don't need.

- Shop when you have the time to look for expiration dates on cheeses and meats. Otherwise, you might not realize that the loaf of bread you just bought will be out of date the next day. Get your money's worth and buy products that are baked or prepared fresh that day. Don't rush your grocery shopping experience.

- Consider online shopping. More and more local grocery stores are adding this service for a small additional cost.

Meal Planning

As you plan your weekly or biweekly menus, think of all the meals for the day and the week. Any one meal need not be nutritionally balanced all by itself. What matters are the foods your family is eating over the course of a whole day or a whole week. Some days, like Comfort Food Night, your meals are likely to be heavier in fat and calories. That is okay as long as you balance them out with leaner meals on other days. Moderation overall is the key to healthful eating. Here's how to get started:

1. Think of the theme for the day you're planning. If it's for Monday, then simply turn to the comfort food chapter and choose a main dish.

2. Add a side dish to complement the main dish. For example, if the main dish is creamy or saucy, then you will want to choose a simpler side dish with a different consistency, perhaps something crunchy or crispy. Likewise, a simple main dish can be accompanied by a creamy or saucy side dish.

3. Choose a hot or cold vegetable or fruit or a salad of fruits and/or vegetables. These are so important for rounding out the nutrition in any meal, yet they're often neglected. And a good

way to make your meals leaner is to increase the portion size on the fruits and vegetables and reduce the size of the other dishes. Think of the dinner plate divided into thirds, with one-third main dish, one-third side dish, and one-third fruits and/or vegetables.

Make Meals Appetizing

As you're planning your meals, try to include a variety of colors, flavors, shapes, textures, and temperatures. I've already mentioned balancing soft foods with crunchy foods. But there are other ways to add interest to your meals:

- Plan for color variety. A meal of chicken breasts, mashed potatoes, and creamed corn would look drab, especially if served on white plates! Dress up plain foods with colorful garnishes and accompany them, for example, with leafy salads or other colorful vegetables. Mimic some of the presentation ideas you see in restaurants.

- Vary the size and shapes of the foods you serve. A meal of meatballs, round dinner rolls, and Brussels sprouts might be colorful, but a plate of all round foods would look a little funny. Instead, serve the meatballs with pasta strands and carrot sticks. Leave some foods whole and serve others sliced, cubed, mashed, or cut into strips.

- Balance mild foods with not-so-mild flavors. For example, serve Sweet & Sour Baked Chicken with rice and serve chili with corn bread.

- Plan a balance of hot and cold foods. This is why soup and sandwich is such a popular combination.

Finally, pay attention to the meals that your family especially likes and use them again and again. You'll enjoy cooking more when your spouse and children enjoy what's being served. This book is full of tried-and-true favorites from my family, and they are sure to become favorites of your family's too. Follow my theme nights and your meal planning will become easier and faster as you go along.

Measurement Conversions

Liquid Measures

1 cup	1/2 pint	8 fluid ounces	237 ml
2 cups	1 pint	16 fluid ounces	474 ml
4 cups	1 quart	32 fluid ounces	946 ml

Dry Measures

3 teaspoons	1 tablespoon	1/2 ounce	14.3 grams	
2 tablespoons	1/8 cup	1 ounce	28.3 grams	
4 tablespoons	1/4 cup	2 ounces	56.7 grams	
5 1/3 tablespoons	1/3 cup	2.6 ounces	75.6 grams	
8 tablespoons	1/2 cup	4 ounces	113.4 grams	
12 tablespoons	3/4 cup	6 ounces	170 grams	
32 tablespoons	2 cups	16 ounces	453.6 grams	1 pound
64 tablespoons	4 cups	32 ounces	907 grams	2 pounds

Measurement conversion calculators are also available on the Web.

THE WELL-STOCKED KITCHEN

Even if you diligently plan a week's worth of menus every week and buy everything you need for those meals, you will still want to have grocery items on hand for spontaneous, quick, easy, healthy, and creative cooking. Many items are basic to almost any cooking. Others you can add as you go along, depending on the recipes you make and the storage space you have available. When you make a dish that calls for an ingredient you don't have, say, onion salt, you can buy that ingredient and add it to your cupboard at that point. The following are grocery items in various categories that I like to have on hand, but if you are on a tight budget, start small and add gradually. You may choose to delete some of these and add others. Let your favorite recipes be your guide.

BAKING
Almond extract
Baking cocoa
Baking powder
Baking soda
Cake mixes, assorted
Canola oil
Chocolate chips
Cooking spray
Cornmeal
Cornstarch
Flour—all-purpose
  and whole wheat
Food coloring
Honey
Lemon extract
Nuts, assorted
Raisins
Rolled oats—
  quick or old-fashioned
Salt
Shortening
  (non-hydrogenated
  now available)
Sugar—granulated,
  brown, powdered
Vanilla extract
Yeast (packets or jar)

SEASONINGS
Allspice
Basil leaves, dried
Bay leaves
Chili powder
Cinnamon
Cayenne pepper
Chili powder
Cinnamon, ground
Cloves, ground
Crushed red pepper
Cumin, ground
Dry mustard
Garlic cloves (or
  bottled minced or
  chopped garlic)
Garlic powder
Garlic salt
Ginger, ground
Kitchen Bouquet
  browning sauce
Lemon pepper
Nutmeg, ground
Onion, dried minced
Oregano, dried
Paprika
Pepper, ground black
Rosemary, dried
Seasoned salt
Tarragon, dried
Thyme, dried
White pepper

CONDIMENTS
Horseradish sauce
Ketchup
Lemon juice
Mayonnaise
Mustard—regular
  and Dijon
Olive oil
Pickles of choice
Salsa
Soy sauce
Tabasco sauce
Vinegar—balsamic, cider,
  red wine, white wine
Worcestershire sauce

STAPLES
Beans, dried—assorted
Bouillon granules—
  beef, chicken, fish
Bread crumbs
Broth—low-fat beef,
  chicken, vegetable
  (carton or can)
Cornflakes
Crackers—saltine,
  graham
Jams and jellies
Maple syrup
Pasta: spaghetti, elbow
  macaroni, egg noodles,
  lasagna
Peanut butter
Rice—white, brown,
  instant

CANNED GOODS
Evaporated milk
Olives—black, green
Soups, condensed—
  assorted
Sweetened condensed
  milk
Tomato paste
Tomato sauce
Tomatoes—diced
  and whole
Tuna
Vegetables, assorted

DAIRY
Butter
Cheddar cheese (or your
  favorite cheese)
Cream cheese
Eggs
Milk
Parmesan cheese
Sour cream

FRESH FOODS
Fruits, assorted
Lettuce or packaged
  salads
Onions
Potatoes
Vegetables, assorted

FROZEN FOODS
Orange juice
  concentrate
Vegetables of choice

KITCHEN SUPPLIES

Wander through any kitchen store or even the kitchen department of a discount store, and you can be overwhelmed by the number of pots and pans and bowls and gadgets and small electric appliances. Just how many are really essential? The answer is not that many. Our grandmothers cooked plenty with a lot fewer items and got along just fine. That doesn't mean that "minimal" should be your goal. Think about adding pieces over the years or decades as needed and as your budget and cabinet space allow.

MUST-HAVES

Chef's knife
Paring knife
Cutting board
Large (12-inch) skillet with lid
Small (8-inch) skillet
Saucepan (3 quarts is a good
    standard) with lid
Dutch oven or stockpot with lid
    (4 to 6 quarts or larger)
"Jellyroll" or half-sheet baking pan
    (18 x 12 x 1 inch)
12-cup muffin pan
9-inch (1 1/4 inches deep) pie pan
9x5x3-inch loaf pan
9x13-inch baking dish or pan
8-inch square baking dish or pan
9-inch round cake pans (2)
Wire cooling racks
Set of graduated mixing bowls
Set of measuring cups
Clear glass or plastic measuring cup
    with spout for liquids
Wooden spoons in various sizes
Rubber spatulas in two sizes
Flexible spatulas in metal and
    silicone (for nonstick pans)
Can opener, bottle opener
Grater/shredder
Strainers in two sizes
Meat thermometer
Handheld electric mixer
Wire whisks in two sizes
Potholders
Food scale

HANDY TO HAVE

Roasting pan or roaster
Pizza pan and pizza cutter
Saucepans in additional sizes
Skillets in additional sizes
Griddle
Cookie sheets
Baking pans or dishes in duplicate
    or additional sizes
Tube pan (for angel food cake)
Serrated knife
Carving knife
Meat mallet
Basting brush
Kitchen shears
Cutting boards in additional sizes
Slotted spoon
Tongs
Sifter
Pastry blender
Rolling pin
Additional measuring cups and spoons
Soup ladle
Wire whisks in additional sizes, shapes
Metal or plastic colander
Vegetable peeler
Potato masher
Oil/candy thermometer
Steamer basket to fit in large saucepan
Pastry brushes in various sizes
Citrus press or juicer (manual)
Garlic press
Pastry scraper
Pasta fork or spoon
Slow cooker

NICE TO HAVE... EVENTUALLY

Food processor
Stand mixer
Baking stone(s)
Pizza peel
Blender
Immersion blender
Pasta machine
Potato ricer
Rice cooker
Waffle maker
Wok
Bundt pan

THE RECIPES

INDEX

THE FOOD NANNY'S FAMILY HAVE THEIR SAY...

This book is an incredible "tool" that can be used by anyone to change and enrich their own and their family's lives. It is a simple, yet revolutionary, idea. This tool can be used to eliminate frustration at dinnertime and to strengthen families all the way around.

What I see as the real benefit of this book is to help young mothers get organized and excited about being modern-day homemakers. In most cases, society has stripped them of the tools that they need to succeed. Many do not have a role model they can emulate. I see this book as the missing "tool" that can be used by these mothers, who have the desire but don't know how to begin. It will help them get organized and inspired until they catch the vision of modern homemaking. As their confidence grows, they can then adjust and modify it to fit their own family's needs. — **Stephen Edmunds**

My mother seemed to intuitively understand that her homemade delights could alter her children's consciousness. The most profound of her concoctions was her bread. I don't know what was better—the smell of her bread as it permeated throughout the house, or the anticipation of tasting it. I never ate a sandwich with store-bought bread; my friends were jealous beyond belief. To this day, I coerce my wife into making homemade bread, to capture feelings of warmth.

My mother's homemade delights stimulated conversations about future dreams and aspirations. I know my mother's cooking influenced our family in a deeply profound way. Any mother has the capability of creating such an environment for her children; all that is required is the desire. — **David A. Edmunds**

My memory of my mom calling us to dinner and everyone running for the table comes back to me vividly. Now I have two small children and I want to do it all—just like my mom! My menus are planned two weeks in advance. So I get my shopping done and don't stress every day about dinner. I have been writing on my calendar (which hangs on my kitchen wall) each day's meal. My husband refers to it often and looks forward to coming home for tacos or fried chicken or whatever night it happens to be.

My mom's program works! I couldn't imagine doing it any other way. It has made my little family's life so great. My baby even eats what we're having for dinner each night. I use a baby food grinder and she loves all the new flavors from each meal!
— **Katie Edmunds Bunker**

When I think back on my childhood, I could mention many things my parents did to help me learn and grow. One of the first things I would talk about is dinnertime. As a parent now myself, I look back with a new perspective, and I can see how important that time was for me as a kid.

Consistency: I knew every evening when I got home there was going to be a good meal. I never wondered if there was enough food, or whether I needed to fend for myself. I was so certain about this that I never hesitated to invite a friend, and I could usually give my friends a "warning" about what the menu was, because my mom followed the theme nights.

Health: As a kid I never cared how healthy the food I ate was, so I am so grateful my mom did. Every night we had a variety of foods that included some kind of vegetable and of course we had to drink our milk. My mom was by no means a "health nut," but the meals we ate at home were a lot better than any fast-food diet.

Conversation: I don't think enough could ever be said about the time we spent as a family eating dinner and doing the dishes. Around the table we learned how to talk as a family, which is probably the single best thing a family can learn to do. And by doing the dishes we learned, through lots of fighting and crying, that you have to do some work and help each other too. — **Stephen "Brent" Edmunds**

The best memories of my childhood are sitting in the kitchen watching my mom cook. Even though there were some meals that I looked forward to more than others, I think dinner every night made me feel secure. It made me warm from the inside.

I really think sitting down to the table every night together as a family and talking about the day or week's events with everyone, even when I was mad at a sibling, kept our family close. Dinner is still what keeps our family gathering at my parents' house as often as we can. My husband loves when I take the time to make dinner, and I have no doubt that I want to do the same as my family grows. — **Emaly Edmunds Brand**

When I was growing up, nothing was better than to be around my family every night. I was so lucky to know that there was going to be a home-cooked meal on the table. I took it for granted. Kids love schedules and they love food even more! When I was in high school all of my friends would beg to come over for dinner because they said their mothers didn't make meals for them. Now that I am a father, I can see how important it is to have home-cooked meals for your kids because they need them, and also it is a great time to talk to your kids and actually be a part of their lives. — **Joey Edmunds**

I have such happy memories of dinnertime. It made my day, when I was feeling tired or hungry at school, to think about what night it was. With my mom's theme nights we most likely knew what we were going to eat that night. I don't know how my mom did it day in and day out. She said it was her theme nights that kept her going.

I remember how lucky I felt to be at the dinner table with all of my siblings. Our dad was gone a lot, but he made up for the time he was gone when he was with us. Dad always made dinnertime such a happy time when he was home. And the one thing I loved about my mom was that she usually saved our best or most "expensive" meals for when my dad was home.

I am now using the theme nights, and my husband is so appreciative of my home cooking and the way I am sticking to our food budget. He loves knowing that each night after a hard day's work he will have something good and hot waiting for him. He didn't have that when he grew up so it means a lot to him now. I have two kids now and I am happy to be able to keep the dinners coming on a consistent basis with my mom's meal plan.
— **Aimee Edmunds Heiner**

In my family, dinnertime was the time of day that all of us would get to hang out and have fun. We would sit at the dinner table and talk about our days. My parents would go around asking all of us what happened that day. It was always such a fun quality time that I would cherish, because I loved being around my siblings. And I would always look forward to the dinners. Without fail my mother had an amazing meal. I now know the meals were not "amazing," but they were good. My mom did everything for us and still found time every night to make sure we had a hot meal on the table. My friends always loved coming to my house because they would always say, "Your mom is such an amazing cook."

Dinnertime is a special time that families need to bond together. I'm so thankful that I had a mom and dad that taught how important home-cooked meals are. I know that dinnertime is what keeps families close. — **Lizi Edmunds Heaps**

ACKNOWLEDGMENTS

It is not every day that you run into a wonderful person who instantly hears and feels what your passion for life is. I don't know how in this big world I got so lucky. I now have a new friend for life who took a chance on me. I am in my second career, really. I raised seven children and lived and breathed everything that goes along with that from day to day for 33 years—and then I met Pati Palmer. She called me and announced that she would like to publish my book. After I fainted and came back to life again, she was still there and it was real. Pati had a vision for me. She helped me develop the other person that I was for all those years while being a wife and mother: I was also The Food Nanny. Consistent dinnertime at home around your own table with good food is my passion in life. This is what I know. I know that if you have consistent dinnertime in your homes, you will have peace and contentment in your homes. This is what my publisher also knew and she and I came together on this project and hopefully we will help to change many families' lives forever with my plan. Thank you, Pati, for taking a chance on me!

I would also like to thank my editor, Ann Gosch. What a wonderful human being. She not only edited my recipes but she tested them, as did others, but Ann was my rock. She and Norm gave me much confidence along the way that my recipes were as wonderful as I thought they were. If I had a question, Ann always knew where to find the answer. She also encouraged me and I again found another friend for life. Thank you, Ann!

I would also like to thank Linda Wisner, my designer. She always came through for me. She listened to me, wanted to kill me at times, and still she always came through for me. No one's happy, agreeable smile could mean more to me, and just watching her work her magic on the computer is real! I love how she just knew instantly how to design something that I was struggling with. She is so great! Again I have found another friend for life. Thank you, Linda!

I also thank these wonderful people, some of whom have helped me throughout my life and others who were there for me at the right time when I needed them. I will be forever grateful to:

Shauna Bradley, Drake Busath, Sid Crnich, Debbi Fields, Dave Labrum, Cathy Latta, Ann Luther, Nancy Maynes, Kristina McDonnell, Scot Rice, Dian Thomas

Thank you, too, to the families who opened their homes to us for photography — in Utah: the Rick Alden family, Rick and Nancy Maynes, and Rand and Deb Clark; in Portland, Ore: Pati and Paul, Linda, Melissa Watson, Dave and Joanne DiBenedetto Burdick, and Molly, Dan, Gyllian and Ellie Mullen; in Stockton, Calif: Dave, Robin and Hannah Wisner, and Lori Wilson.

Many thanks, also, to the additional people who graciously agreed to be photographed for this book: Michele Blackerby with her daughers Katy and Jenny, her neice Sara Schouten, and her parents, Florence and Benny DiBenedetto; Kiah L. Cornelious; Norm Gosch; Leanne Litttrell and her son Johnny DiLorenzo; Zulma, Max and Diego Magana; Joely Ramirez; Jessica Stray; Jeff, Marilyn, Linnea and Lauren Watson; and of course my own children and their families—David and Shana Edmunds and family; Colin and Katie Bunker and family; Brent and Kim Edmunds and family; Rich and Emaly Brand; Joey and Lisa Edmunds and family; Aaron and Aimee Heiner and family; and Chris and Lizi Heaps.

I also thank Pati Palmer's generous husband, Paul Tucker, who was my on-call grocery shopper during photo shoots in Portland and who provided other welcome support throughout.

As this cookbook was coming together, Liz Edmunds' passion for the importance of family dinnertime led a kitchen-store manager to dub her "the food nanny." The moniker stuck! Today Liz serves as part teacher, part counselor, part coach for families in need of organizational help and cooking instruction so they can implement a weekly dinner plan in their own homes. She also teaches cooking classes at Sur La Table in Salt Lake City and travels around the country as a guest chef.

Liz's interest in family dinners began at a very early age, with her beautiful mother delivering a delicious feast to her family every night of the week. Liz recalls:

All six of us gathered in our cramped little kitchen to sit at our big table for a celebration at the end of the day. The meal was so delicious it seemed to make our hurts and disappointments disappear for just that hour. We were together as a family, and that's all that mattered in the whole world. We had something going on very special in our home and that something very special was dinnertime.

Growing up in La Mirada, California, Liz would envision the kind of home life she wanted when she grew up: a house full of laughter, happiness, loyalty, love, homemade bread, and dinner on the table every night. Liz wanted a house where the excitement level was high because there was not enough time in the day to accomplish everything. At the same time, she would set clear boundaries for her family and strive for order in the household.

When Liz and her husband, Stephen Edmunds, started having children, Liz set a goal to create a consistent dinnertime with the family, despite her husband's extensive travels as a pilot, first for the U.S. Air Force and then for Delta Airlines. She began implementing her "theme nights" more than 30 years ago and has been developing and refining her recipes ever since.

Over the years Liz has shared her theme-night plan with people all over the country, and many have encouraged her to write this book. Some of Liz's four daughters used the plan in college to cook for their roommates and friends; and now that the daughters are married, they are following the plan with their own families.

Steve and Liz are the parents of seven children and grandparents of 14. When Liz is not in her own or others' kitchens, she enjoys bicycling and in-line skating. She and Steve, now retired from flying, continue to travel extensively throughout the world. They have lived in their mountain home outside Park City, Utah, for 20 years.

See you at dinner...